# GETTING THE BEST OUT OF
# Yourself

# GETTING THE BEST OUT OF
# Yourself:

Body, Mind, and Soul

DON WILLINGHAM, JR

TATE PUBLISHING
AND ENTERPRISES, LLC

*Getting the Best Out of Yourself: Body, Mind, and Soul*
Copyright © 2013 by Don Willingham, Jr. All rights reserved.

No part of this publication may be reproduced, stored in a retrieval system or transmitted in any way by any means, electronic, mechanical, photocopy, recording or otherwise without the prior permission of the author except as provided by USA copyright law.

Scripture quotations, unless otherwise indicated, are taken from the Holy Bible, King James Version, Cambridge, 1769. Used by permission. All rights reserved.

Scripture quotations marked (NIV) are taken from the Holy Bible, New International Version®, NIV®. Copyright © 1973, 1978, 1984 by Biblica, Inc.™ Used by permission of Zondervan. All rights reserved worldwide. www.zondervan.com

The opinions expressed by the author are not necessarily those of Tate Publishing, LLC.

Published by Tate Publishing & Enterprises, LLC
127 E. Trade Center Terrace | Mustang, Oklahoma 73064 USA
1.888.361.9473 | www.tatepublishing.com

Tate Publishing is committed to excellence in the publishing industry. The company reflects the philosophy established by the founders, based on Psalm 68:11, *"The Lord gave the word and great was the company of those who published it."*

Book design copyright © 2013 by Tate Publishing, LLC. All rights reserved.
*Cover design by Jan Sunday Quilaquil*
*Interior design by Jomel Pepito*

Published in the United States of America

ISBN: 978-1-62510-414-4
1. Religion / Christian Life / Personal Growth
2. Self-Help / Motivational & Inspirational
13.06.21

# Dedication

I would like to dedicate this work foremost to my sweet and loving wife, Corrina. You have been my rock and my haven of solitude through many storms. You have often been the only one that truly believed in me, and you have always been my biggest fan. You also have a *special* connection with God that has greatly inspired me and has been evident on many occasions. Thank you for all the great years we've spent together. You are truly a Godsend. I love you so much! I pray daily for your health, strength, and endurance. You're the most amazing woman I've ever known!

I would also like to dedicate this book to my three beautiful daughters: Kara, Lindsey, and Christian. You have each brought many years of happiness, laughter, and priceless memories to my life. I love you all equally, with all my heart, and I am extremely proud that you are mine!

Finally, I must dedicate this compilation of efforts to my dearly departed father and mother, Don and Betty Willingham. Thank you both for the rich Christian childhood you gave me, full of laughter, encouragement, and constant refuge from the world in the form of a loving home. It is because of the two of you that I came to know Christ at an early age, and now that I am growing older, He's still at the center of my heart and life. From your "little preacher boy." I'll be there one day soon to join you. What a glorious reunion we're going to have! I love and miss you both!

# Contents

Preface ................................................................................... 9

Chapter One    Defining the Concrete Elements............. 13

Chapter Two    The Soul ................................................... 33

Chapter Three    The Mind ................................................. 75

Chapter Four    The Body ................................................ 111

Chapter Five    Improving Your Self-Image ................... 147

Chapter Six    Staying In Control

    (Don't Let Go of the Wheel!) ............... 187

Chapter Seven    Bringing It Home ................................. 221

Chapter Eight    Teaching an Old Dog New Tricks!

    Diet and Exercise for the

    Body, Mind, and Soul ........................... 277

End Notes ........................................................................... 329

# Preface

For many years now, I have believed that God not only wants man to manage his soul but his mind and body as well, creating the *total human experience*. This is what God fully intended when he first created man and "breathed into his nostrils the breath of life!"

Christians are under attack by the largest margin in modern times. Adultery, fornication, homosexuality, and abortion are just a few of the open and blatant sins that are completely acceptable, condoned not only in the world but becoming more often ignored by the Church as well.

The liberal media, along with left-wing political groups, are having a heyday tearing down the moral stands of well-meaning Christians. You can dance a jig on the football field, use the f-word on television, and even give someone the finger. But don't dare kneel to God so the world can see your faith openly!

Literally everything that Christians attempt is blasted with criticism and/or threats of violence. The agenda of the immoral is to justify their actions by finding some kind, any kind, of fault in those who proclaim that they are attempting to live a godly life. They seem to believe that they can make anything and everything acceptable, as long as no one is perfect.

These signs should appear before us as giant strobe lights, blatantly indicating a world out of control! The reason this has happened is that man has wondered further and further away from God, completely losing control of the three concrete elements of life: *body*, *mind*, and *soul*. When we lose control of ourselves, then we naturally lose control of everything around us as well.

It doesn't take a very thorough look to discover the stark reality of our overwhelming lack of discipline. Whether it is physical, mental, or spiritual discipline, few people seem to possess the will or know-how to *get in the driver's seat* in their life.

No matter what you hear on the news, or how many politicians try to twist the statistics, this is still a *mostly conservative* nation! The vast majority believes it's not simply because Christians have grown complacent and silent for too many years! We don't agree with them; we've simply failed to do anything about it.

But the midterm election of 2011 brought to light exactly how many of *us* there really were out there! When we rise up, *nothing* can stop us as we move this great country of ours back to the center by the power, and might, of the almighty God of heaven!

But in order for us to get control of this country, we first have to get control of ourselves! *Getting the Best Out of Yourself: Body, Mind, and Soul* is a book for every single person, Christian or not, that believes they have lost control of his or her life.

No matter what area of life you are struggling in, this book will bring new hope to you and, if properly applied, move you onward and upward toward your greatest dreams, goals, and aspirations in life.

You are never too old, never too young, and never too unintelligent to accomplish whatever you set your heart on. And it's never too late to start...save the day you take your last breath!

Stop saying "I can't!" Stop wallowing in self-pity! Stop focusing on your past mistakes! You know what it feels like to fail. So what? Now that you know for certain what *not to do*, you can get on with doing what you *should do*! This book will teach you how to get out of your current rut, and get back into the "driver's seat" of your vehicle!

Go after your dreams! I dare *you* to turn the page and begin now, once and for all, to get the best out of yourself!

—Don Willingham, Jr.

## Chapter One

# Defining the Concrete Elements

Life is a series of *choices*. That's it! If you are looking for an overall synopsis of this book, then that pretty much sums it up. You could close it right now and just be done with it because everything else I'm going to say from here on out revolves around the fact that what *you* choose to do has *everything* to do with where you are currently and, more importantly, where you will ultimately wind up.

But the purpose of this exposé put to pen is not to insult your intelligence by presuming you've never known that life is about choices but rather which particular choices one should make in order to get the best out of yourself!

Not unlike every other person on earth, we all believe deep inside that we are capable of much more than the surface exuberates, and secretly, we long to tap into or *unleash* the full God-given potential currently lying dormant way down and deep within us.

Even if we consider all the incidentals in life (i.e., the mishaps, the accidents, the unexpected, and perhaps even the unavoidable), it still remains true that life is 10 percent what happens to you and 90 percent how you react to it. In fact, *how* one reacts to daily happenings and situations makes all the difference in the world as to the outcome. It might even mean the contrast between living or dying, walking or being confined to a wheelchair (I personally know a man that has lived this harsh reality), being rich or living in poverty, and so on. In that moment of truth, when the entire weight of your future rests on a single decision, what choice will you make? Will it be the right one, or will you live in regret like so many do, always looking back to that one moment when a *single bad decision* altered your path forever in a negative direction?

Take heart, my friend! Even if you made a choice years ago that's been haunting you, pounding you relentlessly at every turn, there is a way to get past it and move on! My wife and I know all too well the cold, hard reality of how past actions tend to come back and bite you over and over. It really is difficult to escape the past! Many people receive a label or a title after making a mistake, and therefore, they feel they are never given the opportunity to prove themselves of value again. They're simply forced by others to live in the shadow of their mistakes for the rest of their life.

Not only is that not fair, but it's not reality! The truth is that *any* person at *any* time can change the direction of his or her life and even permanently erase past labels.

But in order to alter one's path to this degree, it is imperative that they gain total control over the three concrete elements of the human existence. Those three elements are the same today as they've always been, and every single human has had to cope with them and live within their parameters since man first stepped foot on this planet. And the kicker is, they can either make or break your life, depending first, on how you recognize them and secondly, how you ultimately control them. The three basic elements of our human existence are these: body, mind, and soul.

That's it! Every aspect of the human aura of existence falls under one of these three categories.

Think about it for a moment. Every one of us has a body, right? You're in it right now! It's helping you hold this book you are reading, and it is sustaining life here on earth for the *real you* deep inside. But the truth is that it's nothing more than a shell... the *transportation*, if you will, for the Jim, Jack, or Jill way down somewhere inside.

If you could step outside your body for just a moment, you would discover that in reality, it's nothing but a machine of sorts, no doubt, "fearfully and wonderfully made" (Psalms 139:14, NIV), a mechanism by which the living entity inside functions in this world. Even science acknowledges this fact.

It has long been the dream of science to develop a process by which the human brain can be kept alive outside the body. In essence, the minds of geniuses, the greater minds of our time could be preserved until implanted again into another shell or body.

Although on the surface this procedure might appear to achieve limitless possibilities toward continuing the cumulative combined genius of the ages, the obvious inanimate state in which the mind would inevitably lie for an undeterminable time might indeed drive a person to insanity before the entire process could be completed. I don't believe any reality could be more horrifying than for one to be fully conscious, locked in a sort of black hole... in a state of darkness, deafness, and immobility.

I have more than once contemplated the terrible state of helplessness during such an *out-of-the-body* process. The powerless reality of being fully alive, without the ability to act out life, could only be described by those who have suffered severe spinal injuries yet continue to live on. It takes a very strong-willed person to overcome such a debilitating reality, and one could only applaud the extreme courage of those who are faced with such a future.

Individuals such as Stephen Hawking and Christopher Reeve are just a couple of the numerous people who have succeeded in carrying on in life even when the body is fully incapacitated. These inspiring individuals stand as monuments that deny the majority any right to use an uncooperative body as an excuse for failure.

However, one might observe that if indeed we had been created as nothing more than piles of brain matter, then we obviously would have no need of the physical body. Perhaps we would simply sit around in one place every day, communicating telepathically with other piles of brain matter, and eventually, *our* pile would grow old and die. That would be a drab and meaningless existence indeed.

Instead, God created the *inner man* with an *outer shell* so that we not only could move around, but we might also improve our lives by improving our surroundings, reaching out to boldly go where no man has gone before! So we have this fascinating transportation we dwell in daily known as the *body*.

Second, we all have a *mind* (although I might be able to rustle up a couple of people that would contradict that statement). Many people mistakenly believe that the *mind* is who we really are. They believe that because the mind reasons and controls all of the functions of the body, then the *real you* is completely within your mind. Over time, our physical and mental faculties evolved to its current state because we evidentially were not created with the necessary equipment to survive and thrive on this planet from the get-go.

As far-fetched as this may sound, we have science to thank for this elaborate hoax. I doubt we could find any other scientific theory that has been elevated to such grandeur without having first established a shred of evidence to support it.

Through the work of counterfeit geniuses like Darwin, society has come to believe largely that we are all nothing more than evolutionary products of our environment. We are who we are simply because we have adapted to what we needed to be.

I would not deny that man is capable of adapting to his environs. In reality, he is likely the most capable of all creations in the expertise of survival, regardless of his surroundings. But to *adapt* to one's setting is an entirely different idea than that of *evolving*. *Adapting* simply implies that we adjust to the circumstances at hand, sort of like someone that has survived a plane crash high up in the mountains. At that moment, they are faced with the reality of adapting or better yet *acclimatizing* to the environment and situation at hand or face certain death.

However, to *evolve* in that same situation would insinuate that if they stayed in that environment for an extended period of time, they would begin to grow longer hair, thicker skin, and possibly webbed feet in order to survive the cold and walk around more efficiently. (I feel sorry for our poor friends in Alaska!) Most of us would chortle at the mere insinuation that such a transformation is even remotely possible. But if you think about it, that's exactly what Mr. Darwin expected us to believe.

Since we *evolved* beyond the confines of gills and a tail after stepping out of the sea muck eons ago (although I'm not sure why we wouldn't want a tail anymore… it's kind of nice!), we simply *willed them* away, and—*poof!*—they eventually disappeared! Amazing!

Oh, and don't forget that before we were actually able to step out of the sea muck, we needed lungs. So I suppose we simply swam around near the shore for millions and millions of years, generation after generation of these fishy things, longing for lungs? Eventually, our longings paid off because one day, out of nowhere, a little fishy thing was born with them! Hallelujah! All because a little fishy thing *willed it*, we now have lungs!

I've always wondered why that little fishy thing didn't just stay in the water. Why move if he was fully adapted to his environment and had all the necessary gear for daily life? Oh yeah, maybe the water was drying up? But how did he know that? How did he grow lungs in time before all the water was gone? (Frankly, I believe there was a plethora of water at the time.)

Evolutionists would retort that nature *selected* this little amoeba for change. Well, then, *who* or *from whom* is this power you call *nature*? Perhaps, it's the elements? Maybe it's the wind or some other invisible force? If that's the case, then how is it that this *nature* knows what's best, and with what power does it set into action this evolutionary force? Once something is created, would it not likely adapt to its surroundings rather than evolve? Evolutionists want us to believe that because a plant or mammal *wills it*, it will eventually come to pass. It's more or less like a certain specie's wishes for something, sits back for a couple of million years, wishing over and over, "I think I can. I think I can. I think I can" until one astonishing day, it eventually sort of magically happens!

I admit that this theory concerns me. Not only does it insult our intelligence, but it makes us consider also the implications. If indeed all the sea creatures really want to walk on dry land, I'm not sure why they wouldn't. Then I presume that when I see the dolphins at Sea World dancing near the edge of the tank or when Shamoo slides up on the deck and waves his tail to the audience, in reality, they're just *willing* themselves for future generations of dolphins and whales to grow legs? The handful of lucky patrons that see that show will definitely get their money's worth! I can see the billing now: "Killer Whale Walks Out of Park at Sea World" and "Jogging Dolphins Are Suspect in Escape!" (Hey, it's no more ridiculous than the stuff they're peddling!)

Darwin himself admitted that the proof for his theory would be discovered in the next one hundred years. Well, where's the beef? If indeed we are all continually evolving, then why aren't there still people with tails or people that aren't quite through the last evolutionary change?

Are they suggesting that if we continue to explore the seas and live underwater as many scientist are doing, one day, all of the sudden, one of their offspring will be born with gills? And wouldn't that sort of be going backward since supposedly, that's where we came from in the first place?

And if we continue to explore space, will we then one day have babies that are born with the ability to live without the need of oxygen? If not, then I ask, "Why not?" Come on, guys, let's be consistent!

All I can say is, if man truly came from apes, I sure feel sorry for all the monkeys that, for some reason or another, never got to complete the evolutionary progression. They undoubtedly got the short end of Darwin's stick! I get to lie in a comfy bed at night, snacking on goodies I picked up from the market down the street, surfing channels on my fifty-two-inch plasma! Oh well, thanks, Mother Nature, better them than me!

Disclaimer: Yes, I understand that the theory of evolution is more complex than the sarcastic bit I have outlined. If you just can't live without the full story, you may do the research yourself. I suggest instead that your time would be better spent reading the word of God, the Bible, starting with page one, Genesis 1:1. You don't need a PhD to understand it, and it makes a lot more sense. No gaps, no holes, no unexplainable leaps in sequence.

I suppose you've surmised by now that I'm not at all a supporter of the *theory* of evolution. That's right, theory, a hypothesis (i.e., an *educated guess*!). Personally, I choose to put my faith in *intelligent* design, not in a guess!

You see, once we understand not only *who* we are but also *how* we got here and *why* we are here, it becomes much easier to gain control of our lives. Rather than thinking that we are nothing more than a random accident with no particular purpose, we embody the revelation that indeed we are all created in our present form, with a purpose. And when that revelation finally sinks in, it then changes our perspective from the lackadaisical (don't really care, doesn't-really-matter attitude most people personify) to that of specific direction and accomplishment. Knowing your life counts for something changes everything!

That set of beliefs then leads us to another interesting twist regarding this mortal life we are living. If there truly is a God, then that means there must be a heaven that, in turn, proposes that there is also likely a hell!

I surmise that the main reason evolutionists refuse to admit the flimsiness of their theory (guess) is that they are very much afraid of the reality that comes with admitting there is a Creator or God. In essence, men and women are now accountable to a higher power. That doesn't change one iota the undeniable fact that man is a free agent here on this earth. He or she is still free to live out life in any fashion they desire. You can be moral or immoral, hero or bully, educated or uneducated, athletic or sedentary. You are uninhibited in every facet, limited only by the law of the land. Actually, you may even live outside the law, if you so desire. So in reality, there's nothing stopping you but law enforcement and your guts!

Sadly, most people live and die without the belief that there's anything after this life and they can therefore live life any way they choose as though they will never have to give an account for their actions.

Transversely, I believe that if men and women realized that they would be held accountable after this life for their actions here on earth, it would make a significant difference in their response to the life they've been given.

The seven-hundred-pound evolutionary gorilla in the room should be obvious! Science has made a gargantuan mistake in the study of the human psyche to assume that the *mind* is the center of a man, and that the mind, and the mind alone, is responsible for our personality, our actions, and our accomplishments.

Now, I know what my critics will say. "What qualifications does this man have to make such accusations?" "What plaque hangs on his wall?" "What experience and expertise does he exhibit in order to make such claims?"

Frankly, none! At least not in the sense men would recognize. Truth of the matter is, I don't have a degree. I'm not a psychologist (I had to look up the spelling on that one!). However, I am a *thinker*! And being a thinker allows me to search for answers outside the norm. Unlike some doctors, psychologists, and evolutionists, I am not obligated to invent a theory and then reach hither and thither to reel in all the loose ends so as to somehow substantiate my claims. Hence, I am impregnable to the never-ending chain of literature that is crammed down one generational throat after another!

Conversely, a student that enters the educational system, from preschool through university, is given the same foundational information as the class before. It rarely changes. It is passed rhetorically from generation to generation, like robots being programmed at a factory. The same beliefs are implanted year after year till eventually we have a world full of androids, where no one questions the validity of what they've been forced to learn. It is naively accepted as fact since no objector exudes the wherewithal to renounce it.

Also, keep in mind that the federal government determines much of what is taught, and what *they* want us to believe. It is apparent from recent administration's lack of defense against ousting God from our schools, sporting events, money, and even the sacred Pledge of Allegiance, that giving credit to God for anything in this country is dejected and unwelcome.

While we must admit that many of the standards taught in math and science are inarguably truth, the fact still remains that when it comes to the construction of the universe, as well as the study of man's place in it, much of what our children are subjected to is merely opinion and hypothesis. Yet it appears that there is absolutely no room for debate.

On the other hand, a few scientists now admit that intelligent design is a more plausible explanation. Yes, they now believe we might have been planted here by some alien race eons ago. Way to go, guys! From one foolhardy theory to another! The ignorance of man never ceases to amaze! Seems once again that God didn't make the cut when it comes to probable intelligent sources of creation. Whatever happened to Genesis 1:1 (KJV): "In the beginning God created…" Our forefathers are turning over in their graves!

Competent man (in all his wisdom) has enlightened the masses on a topic so finitely complicated, that only an omnipotent God could possibly understand. Hence, students are educated in the accepted *theories* and facts based on what the great minds of time have pieced together from their findings and are mentally manipulated to never repudiate what the grand thinkers have construed. But is the latter statement completely true?

A more honest conclusion personifies that the textbooks today are not just scientific fact in nature but, in reality, a combination of fact, theory, and the personal beliefs of the authors. And if these matriarch are allowed to sway our children and, in turn, our society toward their own individual beliefs, then why may I not profess my personal convictions as well?

It might surprise you what the average Joe is capable of discovering! Whether by blind luck, stumbling onto something, or just down-home logic, there are millions of *average* people that are quite capable of figuring out the proverbial question of how we got on this big ball, as well as our purpose here, without any help from big brother.

In fact, I believe I have an advantage. I am free to start from scratch, logically processing life on earth as I see it. And there are great benefits when starting from a clean slate. I am not heavily influenced by the beliefs of my predecessors. Yes, I hear and read what they have to say. The difference is that a *free thinker* is not bound to the belief that everything the good doctor has to say is set in stone. I'm not pursuing a degree or certificate to frame. I'm not tested daily on what some other guy has to say about this life.

And don't think for a moment that I am the only one to have ever approached the realm of discovery in this manner. In fact, every scientist that has ever ventured into virgin territory did so by first walking blindly into the unknown, with no previous perception of what he might find. Blind studies are designed by science to do exactly that—start from a clean slate, with no idea which group is which, so as not to be biased in any fashion by previous knowledge.[1]

Men like Nikola Tesla, Albert Einstein, and Sir Isaac Newton all dove headfirst into new sciences, using little, if any hypothesis from previous studies. Had they believed what others might have concluded about what was possible, and what was not, they would have never moved forward to make the great discoveries that they are now famous for, and that ultimately changed life as we know it.

Look at it this way. If great athletes became fixated on what the guy or gal before them believed was possible, then records would never be broken. For instance, Marc White of Cambridge University set the original pole vault record on June 8, 1912. He cleared the bar at 4.02 meters, or a little over thirteen feet.

As the years went by, the pole cropped up remarkably higher till in July of 1994, Sergey Bubka of Ukraine cleared an amazing 6.14 meters, which calculates to over twenty feet![2]

One might ask, "Why didn't Mr. White simply jump twenty feet to begin with?" Well, one likely factor might be equipment. Pole vaulting poles have come a long way over the years. The poles used today are much more flexible than those in the early days of the sport. They are often made of fiberglass, rather than the ash wood or bamboo poles of the early days. But there's more to it than that.

Simply put, Marc White didn't need to clear twenty feet. It wasn't necessary. In fact, I bet they would have thought it to be impossible in that day. The records of his day were all less than thirteen feet up to that time, so he merely visualized the goal at hand and did what needed to be done to set a new record from where *he* stood. And his record endured till August 20, 1920, when a Belgium athlete by the name of Frank Foss set a new pole vault record of 4.09 meters.[3]

What made the difference? Frank Foss looked at the goal differently than his predecessor. He focused intently on 4.02 meters for months before the competition. No need to set his sights any higher than slightly more than 4.02 meters. And because he looked at the goal differently than Marc White, he was able to break an eight-year-old record.

Yes, others tried too but failed. In that eight-year-period leading up to Frank Foss's new record, many believed man had jumped as high as he could jump. Some even supposed that the record could never be broken. And yet today, the record stands a whopping seven feet higher! Why? Because men were not bound to the strict parameters set by others. They put their blinders on and ignored what they had seen and heard and boldly went where no man had gone before!

All these feats are amazing, to say the least. But the most interesting part of the pole vault record is this: Sergey Bubka didn't just break the record once. He actually set the first record all the way back in 1984 in Slovakia. Since that time, he has broken his own record an astounding thirteen times![4] He clearly dominated the sport for several years. To put it in perspective, he had no one to beat but himself for ten years. Despite the lack of competition, he continued to set his sights higher each time he stood at the end of the runway, breaking the world record a total of fourteen times.[5] (Does this guy get it or what?)

One might say that these fine athletes *made up their mind* to break the record and, thus, overcame all the obstacles that lay before them. That's partially true. They did indeed have to invoke the cooperation of the mind. But I suggest that they also had to summon other entities to the party as well.

You see, the mind would be nothing on its own. Remember the story about the piles of brain matter? No matter how well intentioned, the mind could concoct any goal it wished, but without the full cooperation of the body, it would merely be a dream.

Even science would agree that the body is controlled by the mind. So bringing the body into submission in any given pursuit is merely an act of instructing or, perhaps, *insisting* that the body conform to your directives.

Nevertheless, I submit that there is yet another entity that not only must comply with your desires but, in reality, reigns supreme in every endeavor of life. *You*—that is, your *mind*—is actually not who you think it is. It's just a *brain*, a complex thinking and reasoning mechanism.

Although vast and wondrous in its unlimited ability to learn and reason, it is in reality just a complex control center in command of the body. There, I've said it. The mind controls the body, but it *does not* control your life! It is only a temporary control center set in place to oversee the operational requirements of this temporary body. Notice I said, *temporary*. There can be no argument that both the body and the mind are temporary, right? When one dies, the other exits with it! But that's *not* the end of you!

While the mind (or brain) can reason and can even make decisions based on both short- and long-term input, your brain is actually heavily influenced in every decision it makes by a higher power. Listen to this next statement intently! I submit to you that the *only* function of the brain is to control the body and to obey the commands of our number three concrete parameter: the *soul*. (Do you see an order developing here?)

The God of heaven, Creator of the universe, the Author of life, instills within every little baby ever born this *eternal* presence known as the *soul*! In reality, it is who we truly are, and it sits at the core of our being with the central purpose of governing the mind and, in turn, the body.

Without question, we shall all face the inevitable end of this earthly existence. The mind and the body will cease to function, but the eternal being down inside will *never* die! That should be exciting news to every man, woman, and child! You will never die!

Still, the problem that often arises in everyone's life is when the soul loses its authority over the mind and body. All of the sudden, for whatever reason (and there are many of them), things get a bit *inside out*, and the mind and body take over the governing position. In a sense, it's a sort of coup, overthrowing the God-intended central government of our being.

Every creation under God's heaven has an order. Humans are no different. In reality, they might be the prime example of organization. God governs our *soul*, the soul governs our *mind*, and our mind governs our *body*. But when the mind and the body overstep the pecking order, mistakes happen, you make wrong turns, and the human psyche as a whole is turned upside down.

Aiding problematically to this all to common phenomena is the fact that most people don't even realize this transfer of power has taken place within them. They continue to live day to day in denial of the reality that their soul no longer reigns supreme nor has any control whatsoever over the mind or body.

Some of the obvious symptoms of this condition are (but are not limited to) fatigue, anger mismanagement, lack of focus, complacency, depression, lack of drive, low self-esteem, paranoia, and antisocialism. In many cases, we could even add obesity, as well as many other physical ailments to the list.

Most psychiatrists would blame any or all of these conditions on the mind (or a lack of one!) In reality, these inauspicious behaviors are likely the result of the mind making decisions without the ever-needed influence of the soul.

Like any condition, self-proclamation is the first step to recovery. You first have to admit and recognize the enemy for who he really is before you can devise a game plan to defeat him. You might not recognize your condition immediately since losing control of your mind and body rarely happens overnight. It is a slow but unremitting process in which the mind and body begin to gradually tell your soul what they *will*, and *will not* do.

By admitting openly to yourself that you have lost control of your mind and body, you can then begin the method or strategy by which to reclaim said control.

Americans especially are often guilty in regard to living in denial. For instance, most of us have no memory of living in any state but that of being free. We cannot begin to comprehend the reality of losing our freedom to anyone.

Yet today, the threat of left-wing extremists is knocking at our door at this very hour, and most of us are oblivious to this fact or else live in denial of its reality. They threaten our freedoms and even our very right to speak out against the *all-knowing* government! They decide what is *best* for us. From the misguided representation regarding the separation of Church and State to how many children we should have, to what kind of snacks we can eat, to how often we should tan. They now have their finger in nearly every facet of our lives!

What's worse, they've allowed our enemies to sneak in among us through lax border and immigration policies and have thereby put our very lives in jeopardy! Remember 9-11? Don't believe for a second it's over! The chilling truth of the matter is that it's only just begun!

God help us should ever one square foot of this great land be taken from us. Our forefathers were faced with that very scenario and were forced to stare into the inevitable reality of their situation. But in order to right the condition, we first have to admit it has happened. Living in denial will not make it magically go away!

We can hobble along lackadaisically through life, disregarding the signs of impending doom around us, whether in this country or in our own personal life, or we can ignore the norm, think for ourselves, and admit we are losing control, and then, *do something about it*!

Have you noticed how our nation, as well as our world for that matter, seems to be spinning out of control? What's more, the situation we currently find ourselves in is not only obvious but also predictable.

There are a couple of contaminating catalysts that have led us to our looming demise. First, man has *lost control of himself*. Second, man has *wandered away from God*! "Unless the Lord builds the house, those that build it labor in vain" (Psalms 127:1, ESV) Coincidentally, these two states of pandemonium *always* go hand in hand. It is as predictable as having red blotches with chickenpox!

Because the majority (especially those in power) has lost control of themselves, living any way they choose and ruling any way they choose, the inherent result is a failure of biblical proportion. Basically, mass hysteria. The unmistakable truth is, if you live like hell, then your life will go to hell.

Let's get serious. This is not a novel idea, nor is it the brainchild of a mad man. Mankind has battled the forces of darkness from Genesis to the twenty-first century. The ever-present conflict for the liberation from evil has plagued men and women since the dawn of civilization. That's a word we should all likely dwell on continually—"civilized." In every law, every word, every action, every motive, every thought, should we not at least make every effort to remain civilized? That standard alone would change the world as we know it.

Would anyone deny that life is a battle? I submit that the war within your mind and body will be no different. First, you need to recognize the obvious signs that indicate you have been ousted from power. Second, you need to devise a battle plan by which to regain control. I sincerely believe that as many as 80 percent of all humans have lost control of their mind and body and don't even know it! Can you believe that? You're probably saying, "That's no revelation! I know a lot of people that have lost their minds, and I can't think of anyone offhand that has control of their body!" It's a widespread contagion of biblical proportion!

This means that the preponderance of humans on planet earth today are nothing more than zombies—dead to the potentially real and meaningful life that's waiting and available out there for every man, woman, and child. They're simply walking around in a fog, going through the motions of everyday life but rarely enjoying it.

In fact, so drear is their existence that they regularly wish away his or her *one and only life*, with such statements as "I can't wait till this day is over!" "This job can't end quick enough!" or "I can't wait till I retire!" Even worse, ten to twenty million misdirected souls make an attempt to put an end to their earthly existence every year.[6] One million are successful. They lose control to such a degree that they spiral out of control, and the *mind* concludes that there is no longer a meaningful rationale for which to live. Sadly, a coworker of mine shockingly ended his life during the composition of this book.

So many people pass on today, all the while looking further down the road, imagining that for some strange reason, life in the future will be much better than their current life in the present. How sad is that?

One of the greatest misconceptions with that type of thinking is the reality that many of us won't live long enough to see that happiness. No time is guaranteed but the present! No breath is yours but the one you currently hold in your lungs.

If your whole life is spent dreaming of something better, then you'll never actually *live* life! My father used to say that goals are important and that everyone should constantly be seeking to achieve something greater than what they are now. However, he also said that we should always keep our head out of the clouds long enough to live life today! In fact, if we don't do something today toward our future goal, it has little or no chance of coming to fruition.

Remember what we confirmed in the beginning of this chapter? Life is about choices! Every day, from this day forward, you must *choose* to take control of your soul, body, and mind, thereby opening up unlimited possibilities for tomorrow!

Once you are in total control of the soul (first), the mind (second), and the body (last), there is literally *nothing* you cannot achieve! You will actually begin to scare yourself as you see the impossible conquered in your life!

"Dare to dream!" "Think big and act bold!" "Set your heart on something and let nothing stand in your way!" You've likely heard all these great motivational hypes. Don't get me wrong, I believe in every one of them without hesitation.

Humans have accomplished some outlandish, if not, downright bizarre feats over the course of history by simply believing in themselves. However, whether they knew it or not, no one—I mean, *no one*—has ever accomplished anything worthwhile without *first* gaining control of the total human existence. What is that again? Soul, mind, and body!

Hopefully by now you are asking the obvious question: "Okay, how do I regain control of my soul, mind and body?" Well, that's what this book is all about. I'm going to take you through the essentials of physical and mental warfare within yourself. I'm going to teach you the methods by which you not only conquer your mind and body but also put the *real you*—the soul—in check as well.

Once you have control of these three concrete aspects of the human existence, you will become unstoppable! And the best part of all is that these disciplines can literally be applied to any facet of life. It doesn't matter if you're aspiring to be the greatest brain surgeon that ever lived or if you just want to be better, even best, at whatever you currently do.

# Getting the Best Out of Yourself: Body, Mind, and Soul

But first, we have to rebuild you! Remember the six-million-dollar man? For the benefit of the younger audience, he was basically this military guy who was in a terrible accident and should have died, but instead, he became the object of a new bionic technology. His doctor said, "We can rebuild him. We can make him better, stronger, faster!"[6]

That's what this book will do for you! It will make you better, stronger, faster, and even smarter! Now, how literal these things become depends entirely on how literal you take this material to heart. There are no limits!

Let's face your problems together. Let's throw out the old concepts and practices in your life that have clearly been ineffective up till now, and instead, try something completely new and off the wall. What do you have to lose? In other words, if you've been doing something for years and you're still in the same rut, how's that working for you? If what you've been doing up to now hasn't gotten you the results you dream of, then why not change the way you think and do some things you've never done before?

This will also be the least expensive self-improvement program you've ever engaged in. It's not a matter of spending more money. You already possess the potential to be who you want to be, to go where you want to go, and to achieve all those things that, up to now, were only fantasies. If you're looking to blame someone for your failures, look no further than your very own mind and body!

It is you, and *only* you, that determines whether you scale the mountain before you and achieve greatness or stay on the ground, undulating in self-pity.

Join me, as we endeavor to find the *real you* down inside! Let's make an all-out effort to create a *new* you, a *better* you, no matter how old or young you might be.

From this day forward, accept nothing less than the very best within you! Somewhere down inside you is a better person, just waiting to get out! Let's work together, at getting the best out of yourself.

## Chapter Two

# The Soul

What makes us tick? What is it that we all have deep down inside that motivates us to live life each day? What motivates you to get up each morning? The majority would likely say, "Bills."

I've gotten in the habit over the years of setting up the coffeemaker at night so that the first thing I smell when I awake is a fresh pot of java. Psychologically, it somehow gives me a needed boost to know my first cup of the day is ready and waiting. Okay, I admit that once I get the first cup down, it moves from psychological to physiological. "The best part of waking up is Folgers in my cup!"[7]

I am also in an ongoing process of learning new lessons the hard way. Sometime after forty-something, I began to notice how much more difficult it was to get out of bed. For a while, I pawned it off on this activity and that from the day before. Occasionally, I would blame it on a lack of rest. But as time went on, I noticed a pattern developing.

An honest assessment of my youth would reveal that I have put so much wear, tear, and hurt on my body over the years that I am now paying the cruel price of recklessness. My dearly departed mother's words now resound in my ears continually… "Don Jr., don't pick that up, you're going to ruin your back!" "Don Jr., stop running so much, or you'll ruin your knees!" And the best one, "If you keep playing football, one of these days you're barely going to be able to get out of bed!" In the words of Merle Haggard, "Momma tried!"[8] (God rest her wise soul!)

I'm guessing I'm not the only middle-aged person that looks eighty-plus first thing in the morning. I make the Senior Olympics look fast! But regardless of how grueling it might be, we all have to do it every morning, day after day, rain or shine, feel good or not so good, young or old.

Most of us get up routinely out of necessity. It usually takes a few stabs before we get our act together, but nearly everyone will eventually figure out a way to make ends meet. It's imperative that we keep the cycle going in order to assure we have the basic essentials in life, with some occasional extras along the way.

The mainstream adapts to this process early on, and as long as things are flowing fairly smoothly, they persist to contend. But what makes you carry on even when the going gets tough, when things don't go the way you wanted them to go? It's easy enough to see what makes us want to pursue the better things in life. But what keeps us marching even when we don't get our way, when life gets difficult? What makes us prevail when our world comes crashing down around us?

One of my favorite pastimes while out in public, whether at the mall, the hospital, or an amusement park, is the observance of people. There's not a more entertaining show on earth than the human race! Every shape and size you can imagine, every race and walk of life. It is truly a spectacular presentation filled with astounding variety.

A while back, I spent several hours with my bride at a local hospital as she underwent some tests. Many of you are familiar with this arduous process. So I'm sitting there in the middle of this three-ring circus, waiting on my sweet little wife, and I began to make a mental note of some of my observations. As I considered the diversity of lives demonstrated before me, I began to contemplate what makes us *tick*. Everyone there, for the most part, had something physically wrong with him or her. I can't imagine anyone coming there just for fun. (Although it's a great show!)

Like many of you, I've been on the receiving end of medical care on numerous occasions. But outside the obvious fact that everyone was there to find out what was wrong with him or her physically, what other resemblances were paralleled?

First, and most obvious, we were all *humans* or more precisely *Homo sapiens*. Therefore, we shared some common frailties and limitations. Even though we are all different as night and day on the outside, in truth, we are all more alike than you might think.

For example, we all have the same body parts and organs. In fact, many of them are interchangeable. That says a mouthful in itself. Keeping with that same train of thought, we frequently suffer from the same infirmities. Ponder this: how do you suppose the good doctor diagnosed your particular ailment in the first place? Some unfortunate soul had the same or similar ailment before you. I'm sorry to say, it's rare to suffer from something original.

Alongside the physical traits, there are other consonants in each of us that mirror the rest of the populous that are far more intrinsic. For instance, we all have similar aspirations for success and well being as the next man or woman. We long to love and be loved, and we are all, for the most part, in the *pursuit of happiness*, on a quest for the better things in this life, even if some of us are not as proficient at finding them as others.

Finally, the most intriguing peculiarity is the one contiguous trait for which no human can neither change nor stop. Each and every one of us is racing daily against the clock that never stops, toward the end of this mortal plain, and on to the shadowy abyss that lies beyond. We seek to squeeze as much life out of these few years as possible, knowing full well that this will all come to an abrupt end somewhere down the road. These things we all share in common… here.

But out of all of these similarities, the one characteristic that is most awe-inspiring is the latter—the totality of mankind is on the fast track to eternity. Like it or not, want it or not, every last being that is born must eventually face their physical mortality and then their immortality. The very fact that you were born insinuates the necessity that you shall die as well. It is the one inescapable verity of life for us all.

So what drives us? What makes us endure that annoying alarm clock yet again each morning? What inner force keeps us upbeat and consistent in the face of our inevitable finale? It essentially comes down to the definitive question that every human must ask his or herself: who is in control of my life and my eventual destination?

The Declaration of Independence declares:

> We hold these truths to be self evident, that all men are created equal, that they are endowed by their Creator with certain unalienable rights, that among these are Life, Liberty, and the pursuit of happiness. [9]

When Thomas Jefferson dipped his quill and proclaimed these immortal words some 230 years ago, he asserted a profound truth that would level the playing field for every man, woman, and child, from that day forward.

These words, the combined effort of fifty-six God-fearing men, confirmed the assurance of equality not only to the people of their day but, in effect, to every generation to come. Notwithstanding popular belief, it didn't just assume equality limited to race, color, or religion. A closer examination *behind* the ink reveals intent that protrudes far beyond the obvious.

What I believe to be the most important element of this declaration is hardly acknowledged and, to present time, lacks serious notoriety. I submit the clear implication that men are *created* and are *endowed by their Creator* is of far more of significance to our lives than the obvious theme of freedom.

I do indeed concur that *everyone* should be free! No exceptions! (Unless, of course, you are a criminal!) But inasmuch as these men insisted the inference to God's existence right up front confirms that they put far more emphasis on God's intent for man than the king's or any other man's intent for man.

Most will read this document in vague fashion, unconsciously ignoring this small but most important text in order to fast-forward to that which tickles the ears—"life, liberty, and the pursuit of happiness." But the important words preceding the common list of freedoms for which this document is renowned are of far more significance than that which we've been taught over the years.

These men purposely recognized God as the creator of man, thereby assuring not only equality on the surface issues universal to society but, more importantly, confirming first and foremost the *right to life*.

Listen again, "that among these are *life*." So an honest conclusion would assume that *life* is the first basic right of every human! From conception to the grave, God guarantees the privilege of life.

Furthermore, the words "endowed by their Creator" insinuates that they absolve these truths to be of God, not man. They understood a rudimentary truth that has unfortunately been swept under the rug; it is *God* that gives man freedoms. But it's not just the basic freedoms (i.e., liberty and the pursuit of happiness) but, more importantly, life. Therefore, if a man (or a woman) should *take a life*, they have, in essence, robbed God of his most basic gift to man. It matters not if that life is in the womb or of many years. All gifts from God are perfect and, therefore, sacred. "Every good and perfect gift is from above, coming down from the Father of heavenly lights" (James 1:17, NIV)

Another false impression from this declaration comes from the point of view by which people perceive *their* life versus *everyone else's* life. A large number of our population today believe that they are not being treated equally based on their race, color, or financial status. But there is so much more to this term *equality* than the apparent forensic attributes.

Though it is once again God that procreates these, there are in reality deeper elements of man that govern our success in life, far above the absolution from prejudice. It is a fallacy for one to evaluate their own equality based on race, color, or by what they own as compared to others. Equality is not a tangible asset. Once again, it is *not* something any man or woman can give you. Instead, it comes from the inside, way down deep in the soul, and is based solely on the potential of the individual. It is the general lack of understanding this fundamental principle that has caused social unrest of mass proportion throughout the ages.

Notice the difference between those people of any race or color that are successful, and those that are not as successful. (Let's face it. Regardless what the status quo perpetuates, there are successful people of every race and color!)

First, the measure of one's success should *never* be by the accrual of fame or fortune. Though these are what the majority of men and women aspire to, they are temporary at best and often lead to a life of emptiness and disappointment. All one has to do is to look at the number of suicides and drug overdoses in Hollywood to get a clear glimpse into the so-called *life of glamour*.

Surely there are far more intrinsic standards by which to quantify equality. I am convinced that a comprehensive understanding of these communal foundations is the *not so secret* key to "liberty and happiness."

I submit that the aforementioned "inalienable rights" can only come from within and are the direct result of mastering the three concrete elements of our human existence—soul, mind, and body. These three commonalities we *all* share from birth and are in fact the *only* means by which to gain or measure success. The good news is that we all start out with the same amount of each of them. In other words, at birth, we are all created equal! It's what you do with these God-given assets that will determine your own personal life and liberty.

For instance, we are all born inherently *good*. In spite of what some religions try to teach you, no one, absolutely no one, is born with *original* sin. That's simply not biblical. The Old Testament teachings regarding God punishing the sins of the parents to the tenth generation speak from the context of the old law. Deuteronomy 24:16 states clearly God's ultimate intent in respect to man's accountability regarding sin:

> The fathers shall not be put to death for the children, neither shall the children be put to death for the fathers: every man shall be put to death for his own sin. (KJV, Cambridge edition)

Under the old law (or the law of Moses), man had no forgiveness for sins he committed against God. The sacrifices he offered, things like the burnt offerings of bulls and goats, were imperfect. They were merely animals. Their sacrifice was symbolic of the fact that a *blood offering* would have to be made to atone their sin. However, the blood must be unadulterated, without flaw.

From that famous first transgression committed by Adam and Eve in the garden of Eden, it was foretold that a perfect Lamb would eventually have to come to earth to make atonement for man's sin. That Lamb was none other than Jesus Christ, God's only son.

Notice also that Jesus himself alluded to what condition we should aspire in order to appear spotless before God. "I tell you the truth, unless you change and become like *little children*, you will *never* (empahsis mine) enter the kingdom of heaven" (Matthew 18:3, NIV).

Why did Jesus say that? Does he want us all to act like children? I know a few people that never grew up. They are extremely immature. Is that what Jesus meant? I think not! The thought he was communicating was that we should all exude the *innocence* of a child in the acts we commit.

When a small child does something wrong, they often do it out of innocence. They simply don't know better. They are not yet schooled in the basic principles regarding good and evil to effectively differentiate between them. It's not until a child reaches the age of accountability that they can make clear distinctions in worldly matters. That age varies from child to child, depending on their individual development, teaching, and intellect. And the child is the only one that can clearly determine when that moment has come. They will know it in their heart. It's a God-given ability. The apostle Paul alludes to this time in 1 Corinthians 13:11 (NIV): "When I was a child, I talked like a child, I thought like a child, I reasoned like a child. When I became a man, I put childish ways behind me."

Despite the fact that we all eventually need to grow up, there a few childlike characters God wishes us to sustain throughout life. If you're going to act *childish*, then, by all means, exude the more positive attributes.

When a child is hurt, whether physically or emotionally, they are quick to forgive and rarely hold a grudge. They simply forgive, forget, and go on like it never happened. When you commit a transgression, let it be out of naivety rather than malice. These are the childlike qualities Jesus desires us to mirror throughout life in order to remain spotless before God. Remember, "…unless you change and become like little children, you will never enter the kingdom of heaven." (Matthew 18:3, NIV)

Continuing with the thoughts of our forefathers, it would appear that they not only proclaimed the basic rights that every soul is entitled to, but notice also the order in which those rights are written—"life" first, "liberty" second, followed by "the pursuit of happiness." I propose that these wise men not only wrote with intent of purpose but in a descending order of importance as well. Think about it. You cannot experience "liberty" without first having "life." In like manner, you cannot achieve "the pursuit of happiness" without the freedom from restraint that "liberty" affords.

Through prayerful study, consideration, and observation, they adeptly concluded that there is an undeniable order in the universe. Our Father in heaven is a God of unequivocal order. Therefore, He endowed man with the necessities for a successful life. You are born with the essentials to obtain happiness in life. We have God-given equipment! Because God gave it to us, it is perfect. So the problem with men and women never stems from equipment malfunction. As a rule, we more commonly suffer from the mutual ineptness known as user error. Simply put, we don't have a clue how to use this stuff! But it's not from a lack of intelligent design. God left nothing to chance.

Chaos was interjected into the world as a result of man's unwillingness to follow said order. It was always God's desire that man should love and serve him, and in turn, man would be fruitful and prosper. But that love would not come from a father forcing man into submission. To be authentic, it had to come willingly from the heart of man.

Those of us with children can easily understand this concept. We don't want our children to love us because they are afraid of us. We earn their love and respect first and foremost because we are their parents but also because we demonstrate that love through our actions and affection toward them first. Children learn from us by our example. Love is no different. It's a natural response to return affection to those that demonstrate love toward us first. 1 John 4:19 (KJV) says, "We love him, because he first loved us."

It's vitally important that children learn the God-inspired order of life. All too often, we see that children are left to figure life out by themselves. Consequently, they go out in the world upside down. No one ever taught them how to get their own house in order; hence, it's no surprise that they wander around aimlessly, often learning the hard way from mistakes.

Sadly, numerous children come right out of the gate with an ideological chip on their shoulder passed down from Mom or Dad. They are reminded regularly that they have *no* chance at success because *others* are prejudiced against them and will never allow them to do well. So they head out into the world with this heavy chip, never giving success a fair shot, blaming their failure on people they have never known nor will likely ever meet. They often wreak havoc and, in turn, create a burden on society. Rather than *fueling* this extraordinary capitalistic system, they become a *drain* on it. Thus, after many generations of misguided youth, we now find far too few *fuelers* and way too many *drainers*. They were never taught that success has absolutely nothing to do with others! Success *always* comes from within! It comes from the heart.

When is the last time you heard a schoolteacher, Bible class teacher, or parent for that matter, teach a child about the divine structure for humanity? How have we missed this life-centered principle for so many generations? It's been around for thousands of years, you know. The biblical texts referring to self-control are too numerous to list. Self-control is one of the Fruits of the Spirit listed in Galatians 5:22–23 (KJV).

In order to clinch control of the *total being*, it is imperative to maintain an impregnable moral center! Successful living comes from a nutrient-filled soul feeding on the Fruits of the Spirit, centered on a diet rich in self-control. It is illogical to expect the mind and body to accomplish the aspirations of the heart, if the soul lacks leadership skills.

The Zac Brown Band said it best in their song "As She's Walking Away": "My heart won't tell my mind to tell my mouth what it should say."[10] Every move you make, every step you take, every word you say must *never* come impulsively from the mind but rather from your moral center—the soul. For here, and here alone, are your innermost feelings and beliefs. It's that voice of reason, deep within you, that all too often becomes audible *after* the fact.

The great prophet Solomon wrote, "As he thinks in his heart, so is he" (Proverbs 23:7, KJV). In other words, whatever you allow your brain to digest (i.e., images, sounds, reading material, etc.) will come through on the outside. The data that's stored in your mind will consequently influence your heart (soul).

In 1902, the late James Allen wrote in his essay "As a Man Thinketh": "Men do not attract what they want, but what they are." He also said, "A man is literally what he thinks, his character being the complete sum of all his thoughts."[11]

What you allow your mind to feed on, day in and day out, will always effect who you become in your heart (soul). In turn, it will most assuredly seep through to the outside, and there will be no mistaking exactly what kind of a person you really are deep inside. We always bear our true self to those around us in two ways: through our speech and by our actions.

Therefore, it is fundamentally sound that we keep our mind finely tuned to the internal longings of the soul or the *real you* deep inside in order to obtain an internal rhythm, whereby all three parameters of your being are in perfect sync. Is your mind and body in sync with your soul? There's a simple test. Jesus said, "A good tree cannot bear bad fruit, and a bad tree cannot bear good fruit. Thus, by their *fruit* (emphasis mine) you will recognize them." (Matthew 7:16–20, NIV)

If you really want to know what kind of a person someone is, look at the fruit they've borne in the past. Is it good fruit or bad fruit? Pretty simple, huh? What your soul allows your mind to feed on is what your heart will ultimately reflect. It's who the *real you* will become!

Bear in mind (no pun intended) that your soul is in control of your mind. Remember too that your soul is inherently good from birth. The Holy Spirit dwells within you from the moment you are conceived. In fact, Jesus said, "Greater is he that is within you, than he that is in the world" (1 John 4:4, KJV). He's referring to the Holy Spirit living within you versus Satan living in the world.

So in order to overcome the evil influences of the world, God gave you an internal ally that is far stronger than anything the world can hurl at you. It's all a matter of who is controlling whom. Does your soul have dominion over your total person, or has your mind and body stolen the helm from your soul in a hostile takeover, steering you helplessly through life wherever they wouldst go?

If the latter is the case, then your soul is likely sitting idly by, spinning out of control, going down an undesirable road, being fed a steady diet of the "I don't think so's" and the "I don't wanna's!" Again, this condition usually (but not always) starts at an early age. Inasmuch as success cannot be measured by fame or fortune, diagnosis is often difficult, regardless of one's apparent accomplishments in life. Nonetheless, it is a disease of epidemic proportions! Nearly everyone suffers from it in one form or another. What's worse is that it's contagious. All you have to do is to start hanging out with the wrong crowd or lend an ear to the endless streams of propaganda bombarding our airwaves daily by the left-wing media and Hollywood, and before you know it, you're infected!

Without the proper guidance as you age, you will start to lose touch with your soul, following instead, every whim and fantasy the mind and body can concoct based mainly on input from the most prevalent source (i.e., the world). Basically, "if it feels good, do it!" That's the message your earthly vessel would have you believe.

You may get a sense of exhilaration as you first throw caution to the wind. Trouble is, the more you ignore your better judgment, or once again, your soul, the easier it becomes to hush the voice of reason and to boot the Holy Spirit out altogether. But as you have indubitably concluded by now, this is a destructive lifestyle that will inevitably lead you down the path of devastation, shame, and pain.

I'm proud to say that I have never experimented with drugs nor have I ever had an alcohol problem. Opportunities abounded via the influence of friends and relatives. But because of my strong moral core imposed upon me entirely by my loving parents (thank you, Mom and Dad, and may God rest your souls), I just never felt compelled to try it.

However, this doesn't mean that I'm ignorant to the devastation left in the wake of these debilitating devises. I've witnessed firsthand on more than one occasion a mountain of a man standing in the ruins of what's left of his life on the brink of suicide. What started out as a party (the world seems to be obsessed with partying) spiraled slowly but surely out of control into a living nightmare!

I do not mean to imply that I am above reproach. Simply because I have not driven down the more common highway to destruction in no way denotes I failed to find an alternate route on my own. There are various other iniquities to which one might fall prey and with whom I have unfortunately become acquainted.

I know all too well what it feels like to look in the mirror one day and ask myself, Who am I? Or what's happened to my life? Or how in the world did I ever get here? The *world* would indeed be the answer!

It's the world that brought you to this place of misery! Like me, you turned the volume down so as not to hear the inner warnings of the soul. You've wasted many years, running in the wrong direction all the while believing that you really had it together. "Woo-hoo! Life's a party don't you know!" Congratulations! You have now descended to the bottom of the barrel. That's what happens when your life turns upside down. You feel like your moving up. But in a topsy-turvy world, nothing is as it should be. All the while you've been headed toward the bottom because the barrel is upside down.

All of the sudden, life's not so much fun anymore. You might be unemployed, depressed, out of shape, drained of every ounce of energy, lying around the house every day, dreading the ritual arrival of the mailman, delivering further confirmation that your life is spinning out of control.

Like the *Titanic* listing in the calm waves of the Atlantic on a beautiful starlit night, her outer appearance of strength and majesty would have deceived the average onlooker at first glance. After the initial blow, she remained upright for the better part of three hours, despite a 299-foot gash in her hull. Her batteries continued to power an array of a hundred lights throughout the ship that could surely have been seen for many miles.

To the untrained eye, with no prior knowledge of her doomed state, one might have believed, while viewing from afar, that she would have completed her maiden voyage without a hitch. "There's no way she would ever sink!" Isn't that the manner in which she had been billed "unsinkable"?

But a vessel rarely sinks immediately. Rather, it usually sinks one compartment at a time, one floor at a time, as the ominous power and magnitude of the ocean pulls her under, eating her like a colossal sea monster…rivet by rivet, foot by foot, till at last there's nothing left on the surface but a sea of bubbles. Finally, like she was never there, the water glazes over smooth as glass as the moon and the stars reflect off the now ripple-free surface.

For the greater number, life rarely falls apart overnight. More often than not, life pulls us under little by little, one hour at a time, one day at a time, one bad choice at a time, one misguided step at a time. We seldom recognize our listed state until we're up to our ears in water! By the time we realize that we are drowning in the sea of life, there is little, if any, hope of rescue.

Would you buy an automobile that simply steered itself, taking you wherever it wanted to go, without you having any control input whatsoever? I think not. Then why would we want a mind or body like that?

It doesn't take a lot of research to get the big picture of our pathological state. Take a snapshot of any city, small town, or rural countryside. Look closely at the population, young and old alike. Walk up and visit with a person randomly. Go ahead, just any old person, I dare you! Talk to a variety of people from all walks of life. Stir the mix a bit, different races, families, geographic areas.

Start with a general sort of conversation, "shooting the breeze," if you will. Then, ask them a couple of specific questions about what they have gained out of the life they have lived up till now. Inquire as to their feelings about their successes and failures. Then ask the $100,000 question: "Are you satisfied with the overall outcome of your life?"

I guarantee that question will make nearly every person hesitate. Watch as they look away or look down. They're going to have trouble looking at you in the eye. Listen as they hum around, seeking to avoid humiliation by coming across as a failure. No one wants to look like a failure in life. No one! We would all like to believe that we did okay.

Like Frank Sinatra, we may take the fifth and proclaim, "I did it my way!" After all, we are all unique in our approach to life. No two people will go about their education, career, or even their personal life in the same manner. Their lives may mirror one another in many aspects. But if you were to break down the individual steps that each of them took to get there, you would find a pattern as unique in its composition as a fingerprint.

Your study will likely reveal that in at least 80 percent of the people you talk to, there's a sense of disappointment, a desire to have done better in life, a wish to climb aboard Mr. Peabody's WAYBACK machine, so as to go back and do it all over again. How many times have you heard someone say, "If I could go back knowing what I know now, I'd do things differently"?

Even young people are not immune to this life-threatening disease. That's right, *life-threatening*! Wait. Did you just have a déjà vu? Does this ring a bell? Is there something here from your own life that sounds familiar? Are you truly where you want to be in life? Have you achieved all the dreams and aspirations you imagined when you first started your journey? Percentage wise, it is highly unlikely that you are the one in a million guy or gal that emanates a radiant glow of accomplishment and total self-control.

Take it from me, it will change your life. It will change your goals. It will change your direction. It will change your desires. It will change your finances. It will change your marriage. It will change your children. It will even change your religion. In essence, there's not a single aspect of your overall success in life that this debilitating state will not affect immensely! You have to wake up! You have to snap out of it! You're living your life in a fog, wandering around in no particular direction—aiming at nothing and hitting it with remarkable accuracy!

As a young man, I enjoyed a regular exercise routine. Once, after taking a one-year sabbatical (a doctor's suggestion), I started that program again and found that I didn't like it quite so much as when I stopped twelve months earlier.

Exercise, particularly the first few weeks, is often mentally and physically demanding, if not out and out grueling! Regardless of how good our intentions might be, most fail shortly after they start. The average newly founded workout regimen lasts less than a week, and even the best-intentioned individuals are rarely successful beyond the first month.

My wife and I workout on a regular basis at the university gym, just down the street from where we live. It's a modern facility with plenty of square footage, but it isn't large by any sense of the term.

On an average day, the number of students working out at any given time is not too bad. There is, however, one exception. At the beginning of each new semester session, it's so packed that you can hardly walk through the place, let alone work out! You generally have to wait in line to get on a particular piece of equipment. This is extremely aggravating to a veteran as it makes it difficult to keep the heart rate up and get a good workout.

No less than 80 percent of the new students that pack the gym in the first week of the session will disappear by the end of the first month. It's not immediate, but more like a gradual decline at the rate of about 15 to 20 percent per week. I'm certain they all mean well and have great intentions when they start, but they just don't have the necessary control over themselves to make it stick for the long haul.

So we patiently wait (yeah, right!) every five months or so, just biding our time till the crowd narrows down to a comfortable level. Sadly, every student is charged a gym membership as part of their tuition, yet less than 10 percent of the total student population takes advantage of this state-of-the-art facility.

I believe that the particular something they are missing is that same quality we have discussed in detail up to now. Simply put, their soul has relinquished control over their mind and body, and hence, they—that is, the *real person* down inside—no longer have any say over what is accomplished and what is not.

On a side note, I once gave notion to collecting all the slightly used exercise gadgets and equipment scattered out there amongst the well-intended masses and resell them. Can you imagine how much stuff there must be? I would bet that most of it is in pristine condition. Nearly everyone has some sort of exercise gismo in his or her possession. Maybe it's something they saw on one of those infomercials and just couldn't live without or possibly something they bought on a whim while at the sporting goods store. I've often wondered if that old set of concrete weights you see at *every* garage sale isn't in fact the very same set! Someone bought it originally, a long, long time ago and didn't use it, sold it again, and so on and so on and so on.

While I chewed on this idea for years, someone else saw the same opportunity and opened a chain called Play It Again Sports. Guess there was some soundness to my assessment after all!

But during these many regimented years of my life, I've come to know my body and, better yet, my mind quite well. Between studying the Bible and working out, I began to sense a connection.

I might as well confess that I have been an ordained minister for over thirty years. (You're now saying, "I knew it!") I wholeheartedly believe in the words given to us by our heavenly Father. I have preached those basic principles countless times from the pulpit, in dozens of churches, across this great country of ours. And of course (like any good preacher would do), I also sought to live them out in my personal life as well.

I can honestly say that it has been a difficult journey (to say the least) with *limited* success.

I am *far* from perfect and would never consider telling anyone to pattern his or her life after my own. Instead, as opportunities present themselves, I do what I can to lead people into a life patterned after Jesus Christ alone. We too often put our faith in the mere men that don our pulpits. Without exception, we are all just sinners saved by grace, just like everyone else. That's why churches fall apart when their minister makes a mistake. Instead of forgiving, forgetting, and just moving on in the same manner we'd treat any other member, we ridicule, chastise, and look down on them as if they were a god fallen from heaven. Sorry, no gods here. Just men saved by grace who have bared their lives, (and the lives of their families) before the public, in the hopes they might reach some other sinner who has the same problems they have.

How strong the church would become, if we could only get that on straight!

In numerous instances over the years, those same people have come to me, head in their hands, tears rolling down their face, feeling that they aren't good enough, or that they just can't seem to give up the old life completely in order to become spotless before God. In essence, walk the "straight and narrow path that leads to life" as described by Jesus in the book of Matthew.

My approach to helping those that struggle (like myself) is likely a bit less conventional than most ministers. Of course, there is always the methodology I grew up with. It consists of pounding them with what they did wrong, basically shoving the Bible down their throat, putting the fear of God in them in regard to their impending doom should they fail to get their act together. Nothing serious, just hell, fire, and brimstone for the ruthless majority of defiant losers that fall on their face in search of redemption. That was what I thought I was supposed to do for the first few years of my ministry.

But somewhere down life's bumpy road, I did an about-face. (Oh, the irony!) Being humbled before God, convicted by my own sin, even to the extent that I felt like I would never be worthy of preaching again, I did an extreme makeover in the method by which I assisted others with their shortcomings. I no longer felt as if I was in a magnanimous position *over* them. (Like I ever was?) No one can take the wind out of your sails like God can! For the first time in my ministry, I felt compassion for other sinners. To the majority, this may sound like a no-brainer! But I submit from personal experience, that it is likely the one most endemic inadequacy of ministers today.

In a strange way, I began to recognize that our sin somehow made us connected. Instead of reminding them of what God expected of them (something they obviously knew already), I related my sin, assuring them that if God could save someone like me, then he most assuredly could save them.

This is not to say that I never helped to move them away from their wrongdoing. After all, sin *is* punishable by eternal death. I simply reminded them that they were not in this thing alone. The Apostle Paul stated, "For all have sinned and fall short of the glory of God." (Romans 3:23, NIV)

Moreover, I realized for the first time in my life that the expectations God put on me were beyond anyone's reach. Notwithstanding, our aptitude should remain that of continually giving our wherewithal in pursuit of that perfect state. But that in no way alters our likelihood of attaining it.

God knew we could never be perfect like his son. We are undeniably human! For that reason alone, it's just not possible. "Therefore, just as sin entered the world through one man, and death through sin, and in this way death came to all men, because all sinned" (Romans 5:12, NIV)

Did you get that? Also, Christ was the only *man* who went through the same trials as you and I yet didn't succumb to it. "For we do not have a high priest who is unable to empathize with our weaknesses, but we have one who has been tempted in every way, just as we are —yet he did not sin"(Hebrews 4:15, NIV).

So because it's not possible for man to obtain perfection (the only state in which God can accept us), God orchestrated a plan by which we could still obtain forgiveness and, thereby, the gift of eternal life in heaven with him. That plan was Jesus Christ. In turn, God fills us with his spirit as a guide, a sort of *internal compass*, that when used properly, always points us toward home.

While we are on the subject, notice also the final moments of Jesus's earthly habitation: "When he had received the drink, Jesus said, 'It is finished.' With that, he bowed his head and gave up his spirit" (John 19:30, NIV). So Jesus himself required the indwelling of a *spirit* in order to occupy the human form.

Undeniably, I have read at least a thousand times that the Holy Spirit dwells within us. I knew also that the Spirit is a part of the Holy Trinity. In light of this revelation finally sinking into this hard head of mine, I realized that I had to be careful what I did in this body as the body is the Spirit's *temple*.

> Do you not know that your bodies are temples of the Holy Spirit, who is in you, whom you have received from God? You are not your own; you were bought at a price. Therefore honor God with your bodies.
>
> 1 Corinthians 6:19–20 (NIV)

I was aware of His presence. What I had never considered up to that time to any degree was the *internal power* and *potential* insinuated by this Holy Spirit living within me. But like I said, during this regimented time of my life, I came to know myself on a much deeper level. I realized that I am not only human but *spirit* as well. Together, we are one! In turn, this eye-opener revealed some things about *me* for which I was undoubtedly clueless up to now.

For instance, *I* am *not* my body! I know that sounds a little strange. This outer shell that you see is not actually *me*. It's just the transportation for the *real me* down inside. It is the *vehicle*, if you will, that God designed on my behalf to carry the heart and soul known as Don Willingham, Jr. It is exclusive in its design from every other model and comes fully equipped to meet the numerous requirements of survival unique to planet earth.

Consider this, each of us has our own custom designed set of wheels. What's more, I may or may not be happy with my set of wheels. Regardless of how beautiful, handsome, or functional your personal transportation might be, nearly everyone has something for which they are not fond and often seek to improve or cover up the said flaw.

As a rule, humans are obsessed with their outer shell alone. Since it is this part of us that is most apparent to others, we focus all our time, energy, and money on making our wheels as polished as possible. In fact, it can only be described as pandemic! Makeup alone is a nineteen-billion-dollar-a-year industry[12] while annual plastic surgery expenditures top thirty billion dollars![13] These figures do not include our unparalleled indulgence in hygiene and beauty products.

These facts point to an undeniable conclusion: we are completely self-conscious and overwhelmingly narcissistic in respect to our appearance!

In retrospect, it goes without saying that we are far more concerned about the opinion of others in regard to what we look like than what we stand for! It has likely become our most prominent misconception. Our government is riddled with it! Senators, congressmen, and the presidents alike have been found on more than one occasion to be guilty of vanity, posting lewd pictures of themselves online, or purposefully appearing in the media in seductive fashion in hopes of manipulating their persona based predominately on their looks. For these and other atrocities we have shamefully initiated this as the principle method by which we judge the value of others.

But the inclination to redeem our character by external attributes is to no avail after all. For as you know, each and every one of us is trapped inside this shell until we are finally released from it one day by death or the *termination* of this body.

Realistically, this is not a revelation to most of us, but it is the foremost step in gaining control of your life. I am convinced that if we begin to see ourselves for whom we truly are, it will make an overwhelming difference in many things.

First, it will make a difference in how we care for this outer vehicle. Second, it will make a difference in who is control of our vehicle, thereby changing our ultimate potential phenomenally. And third, it will make a difference in how we see and treat others. We will begin to see others for who they *really are* rather than making judgments based on the Shallow Hal perception of what they *look like*.

To more fully comprehend and ultimately encompass the total picture of who we *really are*, we must first break down some of the more common functions we engage in. Think about some of the things this vehicle is capable of and then examine *what* or *who* makes these things happen.

As we confirmed earlier, the human body is capable of astounding feats when one simply puts his or her mind to it! Jesus said in Matthew 17: "No mountain is too high to conquer when one puts his belief in something!"

With that confirmation, we are not only assured success in whatever we put our mind to, but the man or woman of God that *truly believes* in what he or she is going after becomes nothing short of unstoppable!

I tell you that it is futile to attempt to halt the man or woman of God that wholeheartedly believes and accepts the words of Jesus Christ!

Because you have a part of the Holy Trinity living within you, you are, in essence, an *antenna*—a sort of *satellite dish*, factory programmed to be in tune to his calling. Therefore, his words have power. They resonate within you in a homing fashion. And by simply speaking *his words*, his children can summon the awesome power of the almighty God of heaven, and in an instant, literally anything becomes possible!

For centuries, man has suspiciously searched the heavens with the conviction that we are not alone. I want you to know that they are right on the money. We are definitely not alone here on planet earth. Man has this hunch or feeling that there is something more to this universe than this tiny blue ball and the people that inhabit it.

His gut feeling would be fully accurate, if not for the misconception that what he is in search of is an alien life form. Notice the words God carefully chose when describing his creation of the universe: "In the beginning, God created the heavens and the earth" (Genesis 1:1, KJV). Did you read anything in there about other planets or life forms? He was explicit as to precisely what he created (i.e., heavens and the earth).

Unlike some theologians or theorists, I do not believe that there is life elsewhere in the universe. My thoughts on this are simplistic in nature. If there were other life forms with the same intelligence (or greater as some believe) as our own, then that would indicate that they would have the same inherent problem with sin that we have, and in turn, Jesus Christ would be forced to die all over again.

Some might argue that if Jesus died here on earth for the sins of all men, then that would likely cover the sins of men everywhere. I agree. But the Bible never mentions the sins of alien life forms or even the sins of men and women on another planet that might somehow mirror earth. That's a cosmic stretch, to say the least.

I am convinced that what men have been searching for all these years is God himself! They are correct in assuming there is something out there. They're just wrong in their assumption about what or who it is. Man's innate need to search is not unfounded. Plain and simple, it is and always has been God that man is longing for. Like ET (but much more serious), we all have this inner pull to go home!

No matter if you are in the deepest jungle in Africa or standing at the summit of Mount Everest. You may be the only human present for hundreds of miles, but you are certainly not alone! *No one* is alone!

You're not alone because the God of heaven lives within you 24-7. From birth to death, God's Holy Spirit lives within your soul. In fact, that's the part of you that keeps you alive. Without God's spirit, you would die immediately.

The yearning we all feel deep inside is the *supernatural* component of our being. That means we are all born with supernatural ability! That information should give you goosebumps and raise the hair on the back of your neck. You can achieve *anything*. You can become *unstoppable*.

This revelation has changed not only the way I perceived God's view of me, but it also transformed the way I view myself. So how is it that we came to have this awe-inspiring power? Simple. We inherited it genetically from God! Remember? We have God's DNA.

It all goes back to the garden of Eden. (Doesn't everything?) Surely you've heard that story as a child? You may recall from Genesis 2:7 (NIV) that "God formed man from the dust of the ground." And so He did!

Although forming man out of mere dust was, to say the least, a monumental achievement, at that moment, man was nothing more than flesh and bones, just lying there in the sand. He wasn't actually dead because that would be a corpse or the result of death. He couldn't have been dead because he hadn't lived yet. He simply had no life.

God knew He had to do something extraordinary in order to bring His creation to life. Dr. Frankenstein tried it (as the fictional story goes) with massive amounts of electricity. And even though the movie shows the monster eventually gets up and walks around, we know that that is scientifically impossible. If it were not, believe me, someone would own the patent, and science would be all over it.

For thousands of years, man has studied the unique workings of the human body. To watch a man or woman perform the simplistic action of walking across a room seems rather straightforward and unpretentious. But to fully understand the intricate internal mechanisms that come together to make such a movement possible was shrouded in mystery for a very long time. For centuries, the physical potential of man was merely taken for granted.

In time, the curious, but naive early-day explorers (often called madmen) snatched whatever corpse available under the cover of night in an ongoing attempt to more fully identify and understand the body's inner workings. Yet from the crude techniques of these early pioneers to the astute genius of modern physiologists, the *secret* of life continues to elude man, shrouded in mystery to this day.

The enormous strides of modern science are unparalleled, going so far as to grow babies in test tubes and even cloning living organisms. I, in no way, wish to downplay the complexity of their achievements as what they have accomplished to date is beyond fascinating and extraordinary by any standard.

On the other hand, what they have actually done is to take an existing living organism and grow it. (Sorry if this sounds insulting. It's the simple version I'm sure.) But in spite of their tremendous strides, they absolutely cannot take a lifeless pile of tissue and make it live! They have yet to discover the secret to life itself. But in fact, it's no secret at all. It's been right under their noses all this time! The so-called *secret* of life is none other than the breath of God. Look closely at what God did immediately after he formed man from the dust of the ground. He "breathed into his nostrils the breath of life" (Genesis 2:7, NIV).

Incidentally, the fifty-seven elements that make up the human body are also found in the earth's crust. Hmm, interesting? So God formed man from dust, but he just lay there, lifeless. Had God stopped right there, man would have been no more than an inanimate lump of flesh and bones. Something miraculous would have to be done. What he did next was unprecedented, even at this early stage of the creation. God breathed his very own breath into man, and "he became a living soul" (Genesis 2:7, NIV). Two key words of interest here for future reference: *living* and *soul*.

If you doubt the breath within you gives you life, try living without it for a few seconds. The average person will go unconscious in less than a minute. Of course, it is from oxygen deprivation, but there is more to your *breath* than you think. So many people nowadays are obsessed with having *good breath*. I suggest it would be far more significant to recognize that, in a sense, everyone has *God breath*!

You see, we are not only living, but we are *set apart* from the rest of God's living creations. We have a soul! And a soul translates into the breath of God (i.e., "the breath of life"). We have a part of God living within us!

There is no step-by-step description as to the technique God used to bring the animals to life. However, logic would infer that God would somehow have to animate them as well. I offer up the logical contrast between the two. One might give serious thought to the biblical account, closely examining the method by which God painstakingly created both. He formed man (likely with his own hands) versus speaking the animals into existence.

So is it possible that God can actually *speak* life into something or someone? Absolutely! God is life personified, implying the potential of initiating life in many fashions.

Jesus said, "I am the way, the truth, and *life*. No one comes to the Father but through me" (John 14:6, NIV). He was referring to eternal life, but in reality, what is *eternal life*? It is the ability to live forever! Where does that life come from? Through Jesus Christ, God's Son, *life incarnate*.

The significant difference lies in the contrast between man and the rest of creation. The inference is not in any sense a God who merely waves his magical hand and wields his omnipotent power in a cold and brazen fashion. To the contrary, God gives unequalled attention to his *one of a kind* creation.

For the first time, we look through the eyes of a loving father as if starring down at his newborn son in the nursery, so unique from everything else in that, God had indeed "*created man in his own image.*"

He then momentarily drifts back to a few days earlier when he was distracted by a reflection he had seen while hovering over the great expanse of the waters he had just created. It catches his peripheral vision and causes him to pause for several moments and just stare.

He blinks and, once again, gazes upon his child, still lying lifeless in the sand. It was like looking in a mirror! This time, he had outdone himself! But it wasn't enough. In order for this man to truly be like his father, he would need the gift of discernment—the ability to think and reason on his own.

But before God made it so, he sat for a long while and contemplated the endless possibilities that would accompany such a *God-like* attribute. But in spite of the risk, God rolled the dice, gently bent down, put his hand under man's head, and breathed into his nostrils "the breath of life." So uniquely special was this man to God that he shared his own breath with him.

If we were to end the story right there and simply ponder the impact of this truth alone, the resounding implications would be staggering. Please, I encourage you pause here for just a moment or two. You absolutely need to get this! Do your best to digest the weightiness of this astounding revelation: we have God's DNA! That should send a chill up your spine. If that doesn't excite you to your very core, then you are not alive!

It is that *breath* that keeps us alive, that keeps us moving, working, serving, loving, and sleeping until eventually, when the body is ravaged to the point that it becomes uninhabitable (i.e., by trauma, wear-and-tear), then the Spirit of God—the *soul* or the *breath of God*—departs the body, leaving it lifeless once again.

Eight months ago, a friend of mine was diagnosed with a stage four melanoma. He had numerous tumors, and the cancer had spread to several areas of his body. Doctors gave him less than a year to live with the best-case scenario of four years if he would agree to undergo several months of horrific treatments. But after only eight months, his wife called to tell me that the doctors have now labeled him the "Miracle Man." The cancer has all but left his body, and he has now gone from funeral plans to a new lease on life.

The medical world has been astounded on numerous occasions when the body should not have survived, and yet beyond all human understanding, it does!

Quite frankly, this happens for one reason only: the soul did not leave the body. However justified, God was not ready for that person to leave this earth. Maybe his purpose for their life had not yet been fulfilled. Maybe there was some unfinished business somewhere. Only God knows. But beyond all reasoning in the realm of human health and life as we understand it, that person continues to live and, in time, recovers from their trauma.

Here's the bottom line on that: it is God that decides your final day. This must be true, for God is sovereign. In other words, he controls *everything*. However, this does not imply he is always happy with what happens. Case in point, death. Death was not a part of God's original plan for man, but rather, man brought death on his self through sin. "Therefore, just as sin entered the world through one man, and death through sin, and in this way death came to all men, because all have sinned" (Romans 5:12, NIV).

There you have it. Now you know why we die. But know also that God hates death. He despises it to such a degree that he will one day throw it in the "lake of fire" or "hell" (Revelation 20:14, NIV).

The angel of death ultimately takes your life, but every entity in heaven and on earth is in submission to God, including death and even Satan (Job 2:1–6, NIV). So every person has an appointment with death from the moment they are born. "And as it is appointed unto man once to die, but after this the judgment" (Hebrews 9:27, KJV).

No sooner is a person born than they start to die as well. Your date is set: day, hour, second, etc., and there's no stopping it. When we put ourselves in situations of peril, whether by accident or on purpose, God has the ability to intervene in order to fulfill his greater purpose for our lives. In other words, he assures that we make our final appointment with death.

I have conducted many a funeral over the years and have heard friends and family perpetually lament the what ifs. "What if they hadn't taken that route home?" "What if they would have driven instead of flown?" "What if they had just stayed home that day?" The list goes on and on.

But it makes no difference *where* you are or *what* you are doing. When your appointment time comes, death will find you just the same, and I assure you that it *will come* for everyone.

Research the topic of death, and you will discover that there are as many theories about where we go after this life as there are in regard to how we got here in the first place. Science will attempt to explain that which they do not understand with an ostentatious display of verbal gymnastics. (They talk with big words!)

When we don't fully understand something, it is common to circumvent the issue, confusing our audience, throwing out impressive words and data that serve only to cloud the issue further (the politician method). But when the smoke clears, the final analysis will conclude that we still have no pragmatic answer to the original question. We fear that which we cannot understand or predict. The only thing predictable about death is that it eventually comes to everyone. Without a doubt, men and women fear death. In laymen's terms, it is the mother of all unknowns.

The widely accepted synopsis is that man is born, he lives, and then he dies. End of story. Set, match, game. He disappears into oblivion where he is neither coherent nor conscious in any manner. Plainly put, he's just lifeless for all eternity. His life goes away, his body goes away, and in most cases, given time, the memory of his existence goes away as well. What a dreadful thought. So this is it? Seventy or so years (if I'm lucky), and then—*poof!*—it's over? If that's life, then I'll take vanilla!

For this reason, man will hold on to life at all costs. We work thirty to forty years, burning the candle at both ends in order to accumulate wealth. Then, as a result of our labor, we find that our health is ruined, so we will then spend every dime we have accumulated in a futile attempt to regain the health that we had in the first place. How vain and completely transitory are all such considerations. Because of the typical view of death, is it not logical then to assume man would want to live forever?

The only reasonable explanation as to why men and women refuse to admit there is life after death is that it infers we have a soul, and in turn, there might be a day of reckoning. "And as it is appointed unto man once to die, but after this the *judgment*." (Emphasis mine.) (Hebrews 9:27, KJV).

Believe this stuff or not, we all can come together on one certainty—*you will die*! The universal dilemma is this: are you prepared to take a chance on what happens after that? No matter what you believe, it would seem that to err on the side of caution would be in everyone's best interest! Worst case? You die a believer and just stay dead. Best case? You die and don't go to hell. In either case, you can't go wrong!

The good news is that there is a method by which you can be successful in your present life and in your life to come. The *soul* is the life-giving force within the body. Therefore, gaining control of the soul is the most important factor of success in any realm.

So the question is not "Do I have what I need in order to succeed in life?" But rather, "Who is in control of that power, and in turn, my life here and in the hereafter?" Let's examine that for a moment.

If I want a bowl of chocolate ice cream at ten o'clock at night, it's really not my *body* that wants it, is it? My body would just as easily eat a can of tuna fish straight out of the can, if I forced it to do so.

No doubt the tuna would be better for me, but when I eat chocolate ice cream, the taste buds send me a more favorable reaction, so I naturally go for that which is pleasing to the body but not necessarily good for it. (If anyone could figure out how to make tuna fish taste like chocolate ice cream, they'd be rich instantly!)

Now, here's what's strange about this. If I keep putting nothing but chocolate ice cream in my body, it will eventually facilitate a lot of fat, which, in turn, will continue to accumulate, then I will likely develop high blood pressure, possibly diabetes, and who knows what other illnesses will occur simply because I continue to feed my body something that was never good for it from the get-go.

So if chocolate ice cream were not good for me, then why would I eat it in the first place? Simple, it is *pleasing* to the body. But when we get down to the truth of the matter, it's not really pleasing to the body but to the mind. Now we're getting somewhere.

The body has thousands of nerve endings that send continuous messages regarding the body's overall feeling. However, it is the mind that monitors these complex signals and, in turn, interprets their meaning. The mind and body work in tandem to determine those sensations that are most pleasing overall to both. But who is in control of the mind and body? Every entity of our being answers to some other entity.

I submit that the God-given order of our human existence is thus: the body answers to the mind, the mind answers to the soul, and the soul answers to God. But here is where the dilemma begins. Does your soul have complete governorship over your mind and body and, therefore, your life?

Here are a few simple questions to determine whether or not your soul is in control of your life. Keep in mind that your body is your vehicle controlled by your mind.

- Do you like where your vehicle has gone?
- Do you like what your vehicle has engaged in?
- Has your vehicle given your soul a comfortable ride?
- Has your vehicle taken your soul to some interesting places?

If you answered negatively to any of these questions, then what do you do about that? You get *control* of your mind and body. Jump into the *driver's seat* of your vehicle.

Here's the thing. Even though you are not, in reality, *your body*, you are in control of it. (Or at least you are supposed to be.) You're supposed to be in the driver's seat. And if you don't like where you're headed, then for crying out loud, turn the wheel.

It doesn't get any simpler than that folks! If your body is not what you want it to be, then get control of it! True, there are some things we cannot change, but it is astounding just how many things we could change, if we simply forced our will upon our own body. I know that's harder than it sounds. So I'm going to give you some helpful tips that will make your efforts in self-control a bit easier. (We all love easy, right?)

We must go back to the God-given order. To gain control of the body, one must first gain control of the mind. Solomon said, "For as he thinks in his heart, so is he" (Proverbs 23:7, KJV). Jesus said, "For out of the overflow of the heart the mouth speaks" (Matthew 12:34, NIV).

What they are saying is, whatever is in your heart comes out in your speech and your actions. And by the way, there's a difference between your heart and your mind. Your *heart* is the same as your *soul*. It's the deepest part of you. It's who you *really* are. It's the part that's eternal. On the other hand, your mind is the control center for the body. We know this because we've seen what happens when the mind loses control over the body.

But the soul or the heart *always* directs the mind. That's why Jesus said, "Out of the heart, the mouth speaks." He didn't say, "Out of the mind, the mouth speaks" because the mind simply puts into motion the muscles, and the lips translate into language the actual feelings or desires of the heart.

He didn't say mind because while the mind may reason and make decisions on the surface based both on what's happening now and through past experience, it is actually the soul or the heart down inside a person that will ultimately determine what they *will* or *will not* do.

In other words, if you truly have control over your mind in your heart, when choices arise between good and evil, you will do the right thing at any cost.

If you don't, then two things are possible. You are either not authentic in your heart, or you are allowing your mind to override your soul, based merely on surface information.

Let me explain that. The mind makes decisions for the body. That includes the mouth. James said, "We all stumble in many ways. If anyone is never at fault in what he says, he is a perfect man, able to keep his whole body in check" (James 3:2, NIV).

But the mind makes decisions based mainly on what is pleasing to itself and to the body. That may mean the *path of least resistance*, it might mean something that brings *the quickest reward*, or it could even mean that which brings physical *pleasure to the body*. (Remember the bowl of ice cream?) But as a rule, the mind listens to the heart unless the body overrules it. What does that look like?

Let's say that by the normal social standard, you are a good person in everything you do. But the temptation arises to become romantically involved with someone other than your spouse.

When that person comes near you, your body sends signals to your mind. It says, "This is pleasing!" Now, your mind has the ability to reason, and it does so based on two sources: *the signals it gets from the body*, and *based on what is in the heart*. So you have two sources from which to gather information. You have the *physical source* and the *spiritual source*. In essence, the *body* and the *heart*. But in *every* case, the final decision will ultimately be based on what is in the heart. The heart or your *soul* is the strongest governing force in your body. If you are truly grounded in what you believe, you can overcome anything! No limitations! No exceptions!

The determining question as to what you will ultimately do is "Who is in control?" And that always comes down to one thing: "What is in your heart?"

Out of the heart, the mouth speaks! Out of the heart, the hands move! Out of the heart, the feet go! Those things don't come from the mind. The mind simply orchestrates the final movements. But the heart always determines what a man or a woman is capable of doing.

Let's say that you get angry with a fellow human. The brain sifts through stored information based on your present and past experiences with this person. It reasons thusly: "I've had trouble with this person before. This isn't the first time they've talked to me this way or treated me this way!"

Now, based only on surface information, one might retaliate! Seems like the appropriate step considering what is going on at the moment. But the *final* action will inevitably come out of the heart.

If you do not have anger in your heart, you cannot retaliate. At the last second (or hopefully sooner), the heart will send a message to the brain; and if the heart is truly centered where it should be, then the appropriate action will flow naturally out of the body!

It all comes down to being *authentic*! "As a man thinks in his heart, so is he!" Now, can the brain and the body get ahead of the heart? Certainly! We often react too quickly! That's why it is so vitally important to be slow to anger. James 1:19 (NIV) says it best: "My dear brothers, take note of this: Everyone should be quick to listen, slow to speak, and slow to become angry." In truth, we should be slow to everything! It gives your brain time to search your heart. This may be difficult at first, requiring some deliberate thought. But once you become a disciplined driver, completely in control of your vehicle, the appropriate actions will be grounded in your heart. Most decisions in life will be second nature. You won't even have to think about it. They will naturally flow out of your heart and through your extremities.

When the moment of truth is upon you (and it will ultimately come) you will make the right choice automatically. It's just like driving an automobile. You don't have to stop and reevaluate every scenario as it unfolds on the road in front of you. Experience and practice have made driving second nature to you. Your brain need not engage in profound thought. You react instinctively.

All this requires great discipline. In coming chapters, we will pursue an in-depth discussion in the matter of disciplining yourself to do first, what is pleasing to God and second, how you become efficient in getting the best out of yourself.

We're going to become skilled in programming the heart (soul), which will then allow us to control our thought processes (the brain), and in turn move our vehicle (the body) to achieve our dreams and purpose. These disciplines will become your pivotal center, and by mastering them, you will be able to accomplish literally anything you set your heart on.

Jesus said in Matthew 10:28 (NIV), "Do not be afraid of those who kill the body but cannot kill the soul. Rather, be afraid of the One who can destroy both soul and body in hell." Notice that he never mentions the brain.

The reason he put so much emphasis on the soul over the body is because the soul is the living force within you. It's the *real you* down inside. The body may shrivel up and die, but the soul will live forever. Conversely, if the soul dies (in an eternal since separated from the body by God), then consequently, so does the body. This serves as further evidence that the body absolutely cannot live without the indwelling of the soul.

Have you ever heard of a person that drops dead for no discoverable reason? If God indeed owns the very breath within us, does it not then stand to reason that he may withdraw it at will? Remember: death is an *appointment* that every soul is destined to keep. Trying to put some rhyme or reason to death or attempting to align someone's death with some self-construed system of fairness is a mute point. It stands to reason that there need not be any significance to death beyond the fact that your appointment has arrived. Simply put, God takes your breath away.

This verse also reaffirms the vital importance of mastering one's own soul. Through the windows of our eyes and ears, the world will seek to corrupt our inner being by every means possible. Temptation lurks at every corner. Therefore, "be sober-minded; be watchful. Your adversary the devil prowls around like a roaring lion, seeking someone to devour." (1 Peter 5:8, ESV).

A few years ago, my father developed trouble with his heart. We were informed that the medication the doctors were giving him for other ailments had interfered with the natural rhythm of his heart. His doctor analyzed the situation and devised a care plan that included shocking his heart with a defibrillator while he was fully awake. That sounded a bit extreme to the family and, quite frankly, agonizingly painful.

But the doctor explained that in order to knock the heart back into its natural rhythm, he would first have to stop it completely and then restart it.

The biggest fear was that occasionally, they have difficulty getting the heart to start up again. He went on to explain that the odds of that happening were "slim to none."

So they herded the family out of the room and wheeled in the defibrillator. The procedure was amazingly brief. Within twenty minutes, they opened the door and told us we could go back in.

But something strange had happened to Dad in that short time. He lay there in his bed, on his side, just staring out the window, speechless. He refused to converse with anyone. We tried over and over to coax him to talk, but he just lay there, with a glazed look on his face.

This went on for over twenty-four hours till finally, on the next afternoon, I went back to the hospital after work and walked alone into his room. I pulled a chair up beside his bed. Unhurried,

I gently grabbed his hand and asked, "Dad, what's wrong? Tell me what's the matter." Finally, after several minutes of silence, he cleared his throat; and in a soft, barely audible voice, he answered, "Don Jr., everything we believe is true!"

I chuckled. "Well, I certainly hope so, Dad! We've been preaching and teaching this stuff for many a year now, and I'd hate to think it was all a waste!" Then I laughed again.

But I could tell my humor did not set well with him. He wrinkled his forehead, opened his eyes as wide as they could go, and in a raised voice, he said, "No! I mean…what we've been teaching about dying, then living again… It's all true… every word of it!"

These words would seem predictable coming from one preacher to another, but I wasn't sure I understood the full scope of his meaning. Searching for clarity, I asked, "Exactly what do you mean, Dad?"

"Yesterday" he said, "when they shocked my heart and it came to a stop, for just a few seconds… I died! I left my body!" He continued, "In the blink of an eye, I was floating above my body, up there." He pointed upward, to the ceiling. "I was looking down at my own body and watching the doctor and nurses working on me!" He then winced, and with the most serious expression I had ever seen on my father's face, he mumbled, "Don, I was just as much alive as you and I are right now. I just wasn't in my body!" With a shout, he proclaimed, "The soul *does* live on, Don… It lives on!"

I saw tears welling up in his eyes, and in turn, I felt compelled to cry with him. As I patted him on the shoulder, I whispered softly, "Well, Dad, isn't that what we been telling people all these years?"

He replied, "Yes, it is. But it's something entirely different to experience it firsthand!"

What my father confirmed to me on that day seemed so surreal. I knew already in my heart of hearts that it was true, and yet, it brought goosebumps to my arms to even imagine what he had experienced.

The body dies, but the soul lives on! Hallelujah! That can only mean one thing: we are *eternal*! Death is nothing more than a short step into the next realm. We are just a breath away, one second, one missed heartbeat. And it can be triggered by something as small as choking on a chicken bone, running off the road, hitting our head too hard, falling off a ladder, or a thousand and one other possibilities. It matters not how we get there, the truth still remains that we will *all* get there some day!

Every day of your life, you are running side by side with another dimension, and it would frighten you, if you realized just how close this life parallels the next one!

Therefore, it is vitally important to take control of the *real you*, the *soul*, and in turn, steer your mind and body down the proper path in life. And the reason this is so critically important is quite obvious if you think about it. If there really is a soul that lives forever inside each of us, then that makes a whole lot of other biblical truths come to life as well.

That means, there is likely a heaven and a hell. This would also indicate that there would be a judgment day. It testifies that I will have to give an account for the way I've lived while in this body. In bone-chilling fashion, it confirms the prophecy of the apostle John:

> And I saw the dead, great and small, standing before the throne, and the books were opened. Another book was opened, which is the book of life. The dead were judged according to what they had done as recorded in the books. (Revelation 20:12, NIV)

Revelation 20:15 (NIV) says, "If anyone's name was not found written in the book of life, he was thrown into the lake of fire."

Listen to the alarming proclamation from 2 Corinthians 5:10 (NIV): "For we must all appear before the judgment seat of Christ, that each one may receive what is due him for the things done while in the body, whether good or bad."

Sobering, isn't it? Like I said, if we actually have a soul that lives on eternally, it opens up a whole other realm of possibilities. Notice also that Paul refers to the "things done in the body" as a separated experience from that which will happen when we "appear before the judgment seat of Christ." He's giving inference that the soul does leave the body.

One last thought. Just so it sinks in, reread Revelation 20:15 at least three or four times. "If anyone's name was not found in the book of life, he was thrown into the lake of fire." That's translated from the NIV. But read it in any translation you like; the message doesn't change.

This verse alone should make you shutter at the thought of not being prepared. These verses also confirm that where your soul is centered is *the one most important aspect of your existence*. It bares witness to who you truly are, and it will ultimately become the only part of you that will stand before God.

In order to become the master of our bodies, we must first, put the Master in our hearts! God is already in there. We just need to stop ignoring him and, instead, invoke the power he has made readily available to us. So where is your heart centered? Who is in control of your life?

> The *body* of David Livingstone was buried in Britain where he was born, but his *heart* was buried in the Africa he loved. At the foot of a tall Mvula tree, in a small African village, the natives dug a hole and placed in it the heart of this man who they loved and respected. (Wikipedia)

If your heart were to be buried in the place you loved most during life, where would it be?

- In your pocketbook?
- At the office?

- At the lake?
- At the bar?

Where is your heart centered at this very junction in life?

- Out of the heart, the mouth speaks.
- Out of the heart, the hands move!
- Out of the heart, the feet go!

"Where your treasure is, there will your heart be also" (Matthew 6:21, KJV). If you don't have your treasure, it's likely because that is not what is truly in your heart!

Your life has been nothing up till now but a dream of what you *wish* it was. We live day to day on a song and a prayer, fantasizing about what our life would be like "if we could only."

Don't you think that it is time to finally go after your dreams and bring to an end your incessant procrastinating once and for all? If you are not where you want to be in life, you—that is, the real you—deep down inside are the only one that can change that!

Every day, thousands of people board jet aircraft around the globe. They entrust their very life to a science they cannot conceive, to engineers they cannot relate to, to mechanics they've never seen, to fuelers they've never double-checked, to pilots they've never met, to aircraft controllers they'll never hear, over country they have never seen before. Seems like we are all quite familiar, with the practice of being out of control! But in the same light, we are also very familiar with putting our faith in something we cannot see.

Believe that your soul is real. Without a doubt, it is the part of you and I that is most alive! It sits at the core of our being and is in fact that part of us that is *directly linked* to God himself! We all have far more potential, *limitless* potential, at the core of our being than we have used up to now. We just need to learn how to tap into it!

Get in the driver's seat of your vehicle. Grab the controls. It's time to show your mind and body who's the boss! Sit down, strap in, and get ready for the ride of your life. You've gotten this far in life completely out of control. Just imagine the magnanimous and auspicious accomplishments within your grasp once you put the Master in your heart, and, in turn, become the master of your total being! You've settled for mediocrity long enough! You must now endeavor to get the best out of yourself. Ladies and gentlemen, start your engines! "You do not belong to yourself, for God bought you with a high price" (1 Corinthians 6:19–20, NIV).

## Chapter Three

# The Mind

Intelligence, intuition, perception, understanding, reason, thought, cognitive control—these are the most common descriptions in describing the many functions of that mass of gray matter sitting between your two ears. Let me begin this chapter by openly admitting that any attempt to encompass the totality of our most complex organ would be futile on my part.

How can one define the infinite convolution, the idiosyncratic nature, of just *one* human mind in a single chapter? Libraries full of books and millions of pages have been compiled on this single topic, on a continuing quest spanning thousands of years. It is, without a doubt, the most widely studied component of our human anatomy, and yet it remains, to date, the most misunderstood.

Every other organ within the human frame, serves a definitive number of purposes. In fact, the function of some is so minuscule that they can be removed and tossed away, yet the body continues to persevere. But the mind, well now, that's a far different story.

A physical description of the mind is hardly possible. Unlike the numerous other internal allies within the body, the mind lacks a tangible identity. In other words, one cannot put their finger on it. Its merits are far-reaching but measured more precisely by its potential than by intrinsic value. If you were to give the mind a *home*, it would most certainly advertise an address within the brain, for that is where it is contained. Or is it?

In actuality, the mind is the only organ that can break the restraints of the human body and move beyond the conventional confounds of physical limitations. The typical scientist or psychiatrist would likely scarf at my hypothesis. But I shall not be deterred in my quest to enlighten mankind in regard as to how we perceive ourselves as I am convinced that this one obscure faux pas has far-reaching implications. The damage caused in its wake is, in many respects, far more devastating than a nuclear blast.

Since the conception of nuclear arms, we have worried and fretted about the threat of nuclear war (for good reason) all the while creating more havoc and devastation by far, one day at a time, one person at a time, one misguided act at a time, simply by our actions. I am serious when I say that it is wrecking our society and cannon-balling our world.

How you perceive yourself has *everything* to do with how you think, grow, achieve, and succeed in life! It also has everything to do with how you treat others. I am curious as to how many wars could have been avoided if both parties understood and practiced this one principle of Solomon: "For as he thinks in his heart, so is he" (Proverbs 23:7, KJV).

There are two key words of interest worthy of dissection in this verse—the first being *thinks* and the second is *heart*. The obvious inference here would seem to be that *how* we think is of utmost importance, not only in our life in general but, more importantly, as a matter of what we do or do not achieve.

As we discussed in chapter 2, the *heart* is one and the same with the *soul*. In light of this, it would appear that Solomon was most concerned with the thoughts of the *heart* rather than the thoughts of the *mind*. Without a doubt, the final word on morality is grounded deep within the soul. Therefore, what the mind concludes will always and ultimately be tempered by the influence of the heart.

But I submit that a man or woman can never conquer the seemingly impossible expectations that God has put upon them, lest they first gain control of the eyes and ears of the soul, *they* being the *mind* or brain.

From this point forward, we will consider the mind and the brain as one. Although experts in the field might argue that they are not the same thing, I intend (in my amateurish sort of way) to prove that because they are inseparable, they are therefore as one.

The overwhelming majority concurs that the brain has established itself as the control center of the body. However, logic alone would insinuate that it additionally exhibits far-reaching implications beyond the multifaceted ins and outs of everyday operation of our physical compound.

Within its walls lies a vast expanse of neurological functions. While science has identified many areas of the brain considered responsible for basic physical utilities (cognitive functions), there is a deeper aspect to the brain that has no boundaries, save that of our own suppression. If there were an appropriate juncture in the brain worthy of recognition, it would be that well hidden frontier where *brain* and *mind* part ways, and man is freed from his earthly shackles, where the confines and laws of the universe disappear.

It is here that the *heart* and *mind* of man connect. It is here that the soul feeds from the bounties of the feast lying on an elaborate banquet table, spread forth by the mind. Whatever harvest the mind brings to the table is what the soul will feed upon. In like fashion to the body, the soul is forced to make choices between that sustenance that nourishes and the *junk food* from the world that will ultimately "destroy both body and soul in hell" (Matthew 10:28, NIV).

I suggest that it would be illogical to insinuate that the mind and the brain are two separate entities. If you don't believe me, examine if you will the consequences of a mind *without* a brain. You simply cannot have one without the other. But even that is somewhat contradictory.

It has been proven in countless cases that one can lose their *mind* yet retain their brain. If that were not so, that person would lose control of all automated functions of physical existence whenever the mind ceased to cooperate. It is fair then to assume that the brain is the quintessential cornerstone of both mind and body. (If you insist to disbelieve, get a full lobotomy and see what happens.) In this instance, the only entity within us that would persevere is the soul. It remains fully intact with or without the brain. I now leave the obvious conclusion to *your* mind as to where the soul would likely be if indeed the body had no brain at all.

I am not ignorant of the distinctions made by man between the brain and mind. I ask only that you break through the norm and reach beyond the synthetic differentials of modern theory. How you perceive yourself has everything to do with how you think, grow, achieve, and succeed in life. It also has everything to do with how you treat others. I cannot stress this enough. You absolutely have to see yourself for who you truly are.

In retrospect, you must be very much aware of who you *are not*. Psychologists would have you believe that the *real you* is the personality present in your mind. It's the person that flows out of your mind and makes itself present to the general public on the outside.

The mind indeed helps to fashion your inner self through continuous input in the realms of experience and reason. But in truth, it absolutely is *not* the final authority over your being.

It is no coincidence that 80 percent of our society is walking around in a cloud with no idea they are out of control. An epidemic deficiency of fundamental principles has resulted in the predictable madness in which we now find ourselves fully enveloped.

*You*, on the other hand, have the opportunity to release the bonds that are holding you down inside—that are literally breaking your spirit—and, thereby, spring forward, onward, and upward toward the rewards a life of true freedom will afford you.

In our quest for clarity, it might be beneficial to review a definition or two. Most dictionaries unanimously define the word "soul" as the "immaterial essence of a person" or "the spiritual principle embodied in human beings." (Paraphrased.)

Within the context of most definitions, they also insist that while many believe in its existence, there is no scientific evidence that it is real.

Here is where I split the proverbial hair with *them*. Let us quickly review. Over time, man has grown further and further away from his Creator. The *soul* is God's breath in man, and therefore, that part that makes us related to God. The soul is essentially the *blood kin* of God. It contains God's DNA. So when man left God behind, he lost touch with him, thereby cutting himself off from the protection, guidance, and blessings that go with any father-child relationship. This alienation has caused man to make many a flawed decision. In reality, man makes bad choices and, in turn, reaps the benefits of his own mistakes over and over.

But it is not difficult to comprehend why man left God in the first place. Keep in mind (oh, the irony) that Satan's biggest deception to man is that *God does not exist*. He need not deceive us in any other fashion, for by convincing the human race of this one deception alone, man stands condemned before God already. This one mistruth is likely the most common reason man fails and, in turn, finds himself continually in a state of helplessness.

This is a staunch conviction upon multi-generations of parents who have neglected their role as a *spiritual mentor* to their children. Because of our repetitive and consistent failure to model faith in God in our home, it's not surprising that faith in

God in generations of men and women has become so sparse that the majority now readily accepts the probability of evolution over creation. *Faith* is the foundation of our human existence because faith is what keeps us connected to the greatest power in the universe! It's our lifeline to God! Our greatest gift to mankind is our faith!

> And without faith it is impossible to please God, because anyone that comes to him must believe that he *exists* (empahsis mine) and that he rewards those that earnestly seek him. (Hebrews 11:6, NIV)

Faith is also man's part in God's plan of salvation. God has already done his part, by sending his son to atone for our sin. Once again, faith is man's part of the equation. Simply because we can't see God does not release us from our obligation to believe in him. In reality, that's the definition of faith!

> Now faith is being sure of what we hope for and *certain of what we do not see*. (Empahsis mine.) This is what the ancients were condemned for. By faith we understand that the universe was formed at God's command, so that what is seen was not made out of what was visible. (Hebrews 11:1–3, NIV)

Over time, man's faith has diminished to such a degree that his soul has grown far from God. Hence, man has lost all communication with *mission control*. The catastrophic result of this, man's *greatest* miscalculation, is highly predictable! Because he now refuses to admit the existence of God altogether and, instead, places his faith in a manmade theory that God has, in turn, hardened man's heart and allowed him to fail to his own demise. It is not so much that God condemns man, but that man has believed a lie and thereby condemns himself.

Through man's so-called superior intellect, he has set up a parameter that prohibits him from believing in anything he cannot prove by his own standards. In other words, if you cannot identify something through one of the five senses, then it likely does not exist. On the other hand, he has contradicted that same standard in countless other areas of study, including evolution. He doesn't seem to mind guessing how something exists or came into being that cannot be proved, as long as it does not include a higher power to substantiate his claim.

We bestow merit on these *theories* by funding their research for millions of dollars a year, and in some cases, we even reward their efforts with great recognition and prizes. Seems we enjoy patting our comrades on the back for solving the mysteries of the universe, as long as they leave God out of the equation. We can't even solve our most basic problems here on earth but insist to argue over the vast expanses beyond our reach. Go figure.

Man no longer includes his most instinctive parameter for guidance. He has revised the standard so as to require *physical* proof in advance of belief, thereby removing the possibility of supreme intelligence from the picture altogether.

To reinforce his incessant campaign, he now seeks to eliminate any and every reminder of God within his daily environment. He continually pulls at the apron strings of government to write legislation that will, in turn, remove God from our money, from our pledge, prohibit the public display of his commandments, prohibit public prayer, and literally make it illegal to even mention his name.

I believe the paramount violation of accepted social norm in our day is that of *political correctness*. It now directs every affair but is, in reality, the *great bamboozle* of our time! What a crock! It's nothing more than the prohibition to call something for what it truly is! Instead, we tiptoe around the world on eggshells, scared to death that we're going to hurt someone's feelings if we tell it like it is. This practice alone has spun the truth more intricately than *Charlotte's Web*! We are now nothing more than a bunch of over-polite liars! Just remember, no matter *how* someone spins it, the truth is still the truth! And you can't change that.

But it has become overwhelmingly evident that man is no longer interested in the truth. Over time, our minds have readjusted time and time again to that which is *socially accepted* as the standard has changed now too many times to count. They haven't been big adjustments, rather small ones, slowly moving the trend in a more liberal direction.

We *slowly* digested each new morsel of immorality, chewing on it for a while until we can comfortably swallow it, in order to widen the umbrella of our *redefined* freedom, so as to slowly stretch the limits of the *narrow minded*.

Many people today insist that the old standards of morality and truth are outdated, just like our Founding Fathers. This is what happens when you incessantly push God out of the picture. The further from God we get, the harder it is to differentiate between right and wrong and the easier it becomes to justify just about anything.

Case in point: it seems man is far more interested in enforcing the public rights of homosexuals than protecting the public right to pray. Why have the *questionable* agendas of some become law while the most *basic* rights of others are banned?

Gay rights have even crept into the Church as members seek to manipulate God's word so as to leave no one out. (Political correctness again!) They openly condone and identify with every facet of sexual immorality. Hence, we are becoming a modern-day Sodom and Gomorrah. Need we review God's wrath toward these two cities?

In truth, *no one* is left out of the body of Christ, his Church! When I preached, we took anyone, anytime, in any condition. "For all have sinned and fall short of the glory of God" (Romans 3:26, NIV). I propagated an atmosphere free of judgment, abounding in love. We didn't condone their sin but lovingly led them down the road toward repentance, a path we will *all* wear out on life's journey. (They recently built a rest stop in my honor.) But *politically correct* or not, the truth is still the truth! "I tell you no! But unless you repent, you too will all perish" (Luke 13:3, NIV).

Contrariwise, if I were to petition the government for laws that promoted adultery, I'd be laughed out of Congress. No one would ever allow a law that would encourage sexual promiscuity. Oh, really?

I warn you that God is neither deaf nor blind! He hears and sees our actions against Him! The consequence of our mayhem is a world spinning out of control. The standard that man has imposed on himself has caused him to live alone on earth, void of supernatural support, leaning only on his own strength and understanding. Problematically, man's strength and understanding are extremely limited and have thereby perpetrated many a mistake and disaster. It was never God's intent that man should live alone. "Trust in the Lord with all your heart and *lean not on your own understanding* (emphasis mine); in all your ways submit to him, and he will make your paths straight" (Proverbs 3:5–6, NIV).

In spite of the enormous mess we now find ourselves in, I still have faith in what God can do! The total human condition merely comes down to *the way we think*. "Do not conform any longer to the pattern of this world, but be *transformed* by the *renewing* of your *mind*." (Emphasis mine.) (Romans 12:2, NIV) What did I say? We are universally malnourished in the mental sense. Henceforth, the only way to halt the madness is to *renew the way we think*. We will change ourselves first, then our neighbors, then our country, and ultimately, our world.

Having said that, when one looks at the ailing condition of our world, they might be compelled to say that man has *lost his mind!* But take heart because that's just not possible! You cannot *lose your mind*. It is always there, right where you left it. However, it is entirely possible to get disconnected from your mind from time to time or more commonly and far more predominantly in modern society for long periods of time.

When we say that someone has lost his or her mind, what we are really saying is that he or she has *lost touch* with reality. But what is *reality* after all? Who set the norm or standard? What would be considered as *normal* behavior for one person would likely be out of line for someone else.

Case in point: a pro football player and the president of the United States. No one thinks twice when witnessing one team member pat another team member on the behind after a great play. It is a rather *odd* yet widely accepted etiquette. However, if the president of the United States were to use that same pat of approval on members of Congress to demonstrate his enthusiasm over a bill they just passed, people might think he had lost his mind. But that's just not so. Poor taste? Maybe. Wrong time and place? Definitely! But *out of his mind*? Not at all! His mind is right where it has always been. His mind and body simply got ahead of his soul. That's why it is so vitally important to be in the driver seat!

If your soul is consistently steering your mind and body, reflexes will become second nature, and your outward actions will tend to fall more in line with your inward motives and desires. It's nothing more than good old-fashioned discipline! You train your mind, which will in turn train your body to act in accordance to the wishes of your soul.

No two people will ever act or react exactly the same to a given situation. But they will always, most definitely, act according to what is in their heart *if*, the soul is in control. *Lose* your mind? Not likely. Lose *control* of your mind? More than likely!

So the next time you feel like you're losing your mind, just know that it is still there, right where it has always been. You simply need to reestablish communication with it. Don't just sit back and watch your mind run amok, making a mess of things as it wonders aimlessly through life. Intentionally communicate with your mind. Grab the wheel. Get in control. A man or woman that controls the mind gains control of the body as well. The combined potential of these entities is limitless. Once you become the master of your own mind, nothing—I repeat, *nothing*—is impossible to you!

The old cliché "A mind is a terrible thing to waste" couldn't be more on the money. It is likely the most valuable asset of our human existence. Its workings and complexities continue to confound those who study it. After centuries of research, we continue to scratch our heads in regard to the human mind. (Pun intended!) Its many facets are too numerous to identify, let alone, explain.

We are truly "fearfully and wonderfully made" (Psalms 139:14, NIV). In light of the fact that we have part of the God of heaven living within us, it comes as no surprise that we should sport something so complex as the mind.

The mind is a strange, yet wonderful phenomenon. I'd like to reiterate that it exists within a mass of tissue known as the *brain*. It is vital that we get this. Much like the body is the transportation for the soul, the brain is the housing, or better yet, the transportation, for the mind. The mind is actually the inner potential of the brain.

On its own, sitting in a jar of formaldehyde, the brain is nothing more than a pile of gray matter, sort of gushy, not so pretty. And yet within this mound of tissue lies limitless possibilities. In spite of the advances in computer technology, it would still be impossible to completely duplicate just one human mind.

Back in the years when computers were in their infancy, it was once suggested that if science were to build a computer that would equal just one human mind, it would take a building as large as the Empire State building to house it in, it would require as much power as is needed to light up New York City, and it would take all the water from the Mississippi River to cool it while it was running. That's an amazing picture! And yet you have all that expertise sitting right there in your little head.

The capabilities of just one human mind are incalculable. Its wonders are vast, and its facilities are without boundary. Within one's mind, you may travel to distant planets, dive headfirst into a fairy tale land, or as demonstrated in the 1960s, compute the rather complicated mathematics necessary to send a man to the moon and back, with nothing more than a pencil and a piece of paper.

But if there's one thing science has proven about our brains, it's that we all use only a very small percentage of our potential. Obviously, some people use more than others. But even in the most brilliant of individuals, the amount of brain capacity used versus maximum potential computes to only a small fraction.

I've always believed that if a man or woman could truly harness the brain's full capacity, the benefits would be staggering, and *that* person would literally become *unstoppable*. Now, I'm not talking about being *smart*. Intelligence is more than just being book smart. In fact, I would go so far as to say that how smart you are has far more to do with *how* you use the brain than *what is in it*.

I have known some very successful individuals that had little education. They were basically just good ole' boys (and girls) with lots of common sense. They simply used their God-given potential within their own mind and reasoned their way to success. Something you must come to realize about yourself is that unless your mind is in full agreement with and in cooperation with your goal, you will *never* achieve it!

The reason for this is elementary. Your mind controls your body. Therefore, if your body does not move in the direction of your goal (e.g., going to work, writing a book, working out, eating right, playing piano, running for congress, etc.), then you will never be able to accomplish your goal. Make sense?

Let me elaborate. Your soul or the *real you* down inside may have the desire to lose twenty pounds. The amount of weight really doesn't matter, more or less. The point being that it is the *soul* that wants to lose weight, not the mind or body. So the soul instructs the mind to work out a process (i.e., through education and research), thereby laying out a logical plan to accomplish the goal. In turn, the mind will instruct the body to eat certain foods, go to the gym, work out, etc. But unless the mind comes into full agreement and cooperation with the requests of the soul, absolutely nothing is going to happen. A year later, you'll be looking in the mirror at the same overweight physique you have now or worse! The soul sets the standard, and the mind works out the details. But the mind and the soul must *shake hands* on *every* worthwhile project.

Again, it is imperative to separate the *real you* from the mind and the body. Step outside yourself for a moment, and look at what's left. Just a set of wheels with a control center and that's it! Remember that the body will do whatever it is told. It is in submission to the mind, which, in turn, *should be* in submission to the soul. It stands to reason that if you want full cooperation and agreement of the body as well, then you first have to get the same contract with the mind.

It has been said that "a picture is worth a thousand words." But unfortunately, I am not much of an artist. Instead, let me use an illustration or a picture painted with words. I'll go back to the whole *losing weight* scenario, seeing that most of us have been there. But the following information will fit any, and every, goal or desire in your life. Just substitute whatever your own personal objective in place of weight loss.

Everyone has his or her own personal motivation for beginning a workout program. It may be a matter of personal pride, it could be something that someone said to them, or it could possibly be a combination of both. One person wants to lose weight;

another wants to put weight on. I know you both wish you could trade places.

In either case, let's say you're rocking along through life, feeling pretty good about the way you look, never committing to a regular eating or workout routine. You just pretty much eat what you want and do what you want every day of your life.

That reminds me of a coworker I once had that ribbed me regularly about my workout regimen all the while cleaning out the same role of Mama's Cookies every week from the break room snack machine. One day, in the middle of his third bag, he said to me, "I think it's silly you put yourself through all that agony. I believe a person should just eat, get fat, and be happy with who they are!" To which, I replied, "Then you must be extremely happy!"

Most of us are satisfied with who we are on the inside and the outside until someone else criticizes us. You may be convinced you don't care about what others think of you, but that's just not true! Way down deep inside, at the level of the soul, you consciously take in all that information, and you often make decisions based on the cumulative results. I'm not saying that you cannot be happy unless you're thin. That's the great part about gaining control of the *real you*! If that's absolutely who you want to be, then go for it! But the majority of us are not where we are as a result of years of masterful planning and manipulation. To the contrary, it's just the opposite—that is, a lack of any control or plan at all. Our mind and body have become *bullies* of a sort, and we have acclimatized ourselves to the routine of getting pushed around. It's happened for so long now that we kind of get comfortable with it. Or do we?

The first red flag is that your pants don't fit quite so well anymore. They're a bit tight, not too comfortable. You could blame it on that worthless dryer, or the solution could be to just go buy a larger size. Right? That might sound logical. Eventually you've moved up not one, but several sizes based on that same logic. Still, *you* are okay with who you are because no one has influenced your choices up till now but you.

On a deeper level, the level of the soul, you have this feeling about who you really are but even more on who you *long to be*. But up till now, all the input information is from self-awareness. In other words, *you* are your own critic and your main source of input at this juncture (i.e., weigh more, pants are getting tight, tired, bit sluggish, etc.) And for the moment, you may be good with that. Maybe you're okay with being overweight. Or maybe you're just not being true to yourself—the *real you* down in your soul.

Then, out of the blue one day, you run into someone you haven't seen in a while, and the first thing they say to you is, "Man, you've gained some weight!" That remark goes straight to the heart. In an instant, you feel a sense of betrayal.

Why hasn't anyone else brought this up? Why haven't the people I see every day been more diligent about bringing this matter to my attention?

It's not like it's anyone's business, but out of common courtesy, someone should have said something sooner, don't you think? What kind of friends are they if they can't throw a little hint to a buddy now and then?

One of the reasons our daily contacts rarely say anything about the way we look is the same reason you don't realize how much your children have grown over the past year. When you see someone every day, you really don't notice the subtle changes all that much. After all, you're not just walking into work one day suddenly twenty pounds heavier than when you left the evening before. It's cumulative, a few ounces here, a pound there. In time, it's a *whole new you*! In some cases, that's literal!

Another reason no one brings the matter to your attention is obvious. It is truly none of their business. For certain, nothing could be truer. It's not up to us how large or small someone else should be. It's both a matter of personal choice and individual preference.

Furthermore, you and I both know that if a friend or relative ever did mention we were getting a bit chunky (something we probably already knew), we'd likely get offended, maybe even disunite our ties with that person as well. We think we want a heads-up, but most of us humans are far better at giving criticism than taking it, and we're far better at scrutinizing others while avoiding self-incrimination.

So you have now backed up to the mirror, and someone you know has pointed out the obvious as well. This is what is known as a *reality check*. Believe it or not, even though it's often painful, it can be one of the best things that will ever happen to you. It doesn't even have to be about weight. It can be about our attitude, our work performance, our spirituality, or a relationship we are in. Reality checks are a sort of stimulus that everyone needs now and then. They kind of *slap us* back into reality. They often help us see things more clearly. A second opinion is often more honest than our own opinion as well in regard to self.

I'm not advocating that you allow everyone else to influence who you are. You can do whatever you wish with the information others feed you. Take it or leave it. But it is often a good idea to listen to criticism as it isn't always bad, even if it is negative. Just because you don't hear what you want to hear doesn't mean it's not the truth. *You* must decide what criticism is warranted, and the remarks that simply need to be taken with a grain of salt.

It might also be a good idea to consider the source such as your enemies as well as your not-so-close friends and family members might actually be trying to hurt you rather than help you. You should know whom you could trust. In reality, a perfect stranger is often a good source for honest, unbiased information since they have nothing to lose or gain either way.

Let's get back to the agreement and cooperation matter. The soul has taken in all the negative information regarding your weight. With the help of memory, supplied by none other than the mind, you are able to reason as to why you are in this current predicament. Maybe you had your thyroid removed a few years ago. We will address that issue one on one in later chapters. You must not give in to the preconceived notion that just because you have a dysfunctional thyroid or you don't have a thyroid at all, you have to be overweight. It is true that one of the primary functions of the thyroid gland is to regulate the body's metabolism, i.e., all the processes involved in the body's use of nutrients, including the rate at which they are utilized. It also helps to regulate heart rate, temperature, and our overall mood. However, regardless of the unequivocal role this tiny gland plays in weight control, it is still not impossible to establish and maintain a desired weight without it. And I have proof!

It is also possible that you have suffered a loss in recent times that has triggered a state of depression. None of us are ignorant to the fact that people often turn to food as a sort of crutch or comfort.

Remember, you have to come to an agreement between the reasoning of the mind and the desires of the soul. Your mind will give you 101 reasons why you should not lose the weight.

- "It's going to be stressful."
- "It's going to be somewhat painful."
- "You might fail."
- "You don't have time."
- "You have failed at this sort of program before."
- "It might cost extra money."
- "You don't care what other people think. Just eat what you wanted and be happy!"
- And yes, "You don't have a thyroid!"

The list goes on and on and on.

Because of the sympathetic relationship between the mind and the body, the mind will always head down the path of the least physical resistance. Also, never forget the pecking order: the body submits to the mind and the mind submits to the soul. The soul must put the mind in submission. Here's the good, the bad, and the ugly about the ongoing battle between the soul and the mind. The *mind* can be both your best friend and your worst enemy.

When you set a goal in your life of any kind, it is up to the soul as to whether or not you succeed. Your soul can picture the victory. It can see the lifestyle you have always longed to have, and it can envision the pot at the end of the rainbow. But the mind has such an overpowering influence on the soul that it often becomes the most prominent factor in your success.

The mind uses surface information, along with past experiences to formulate a particular outcome. It also is very prone to using emotion as part of its reasoning. What's more, these emotions are usually based only on assumptions. You must learn then to recognize the difference between *what is real* and *what is projected* or conjured up by your very imaginative friend, the mind.

The mind uses logic based on what you have already accomplished in life to determine whether or not the goal of the soul is attainable. It then paints a vivid picture (lifelike) as to the possible outcome. That image is often negative. This is a sort of defense mechanism where the mind seeks to shield both soul and body from failure and/or humiliation. After all, who has to deal with failure up front? It's the mind, of course. Therefore, the mind will go to great lengths to avoid failure of any kind. Absolutely no one likes to fail or be a failure at anything! We are all geared toward winning and success.

I want you to understand that if past accomplishments or logic were determining factors in life's success stories, countless individuals, whose names with which you are quite familiar, would have never risen to the top of their prospective fields. The number 1 determining factor in whether or not you reach your goal is simply how you look at it! Read that again several times until it sinks in. Remember the pole-vault illustration from chapter 1?

The mind will take the goal the soul has handed it, and it will reason thusly:

- "You've never accomplish anything of this magnitude before."
- "It's not going to be easy."
- "You may not have all the knowledge you need to do it."
- "You're too old."
- "You're too young."
- "You're not strong enough."

And here's the greatest obstacle the mind will throw at the soul: *fear*. That fear can be based on the previous items stated (i.e., success and failures), or it can be based on the biggest game stopper: fear of the unknown!

The old saying "It is better to try and fail, than to never try at all" hits the proverbial nail on the head! Many a dream has been lost to nothing more than good, old-fashioned fear! The individual—no matter how capable, no matter how well meaning, no matter how ambitious—never had a dog's chance to win because their dreams were dashed at the starting line by a little voice whispering in their mind: "You can't do it!"

And the number 1 reason the mind believes you cannot do it is fear, mainly fear of the unknown! Simply put, it is scared to go where you have never gone before! In other words, the mind works best in familiar territory.

This is why it is so imperative that the soul gains control of the mind. It is not the soul that sees the failure… It's the mind. The soul pictures success, but because of the ongoing negative bombardment from the mind, the soul often gives up and gives in. Once again, the pecking order is upside down.

If there is any word in the English language that you need to rid yourself of in order that you might reach your dreams, it is "can't"! Don't ever believe the mind if it tells you that you *can't* do something! That's absolutely not true! Instead, replace that word with this one: "can." You *can* do anything you set your heart on! The apostle Paul put it this way, "I *can* (empahsis mine) do all things through Christ, who strengthens me" (Philippians 4:13, NIV).

Did you hear "can't" in there anywhere? He didn't say, "some things" nor "most things" but rather "all things"! And we've already established the reason why this is possible. You have God's DNA! This is the being that set the universe in motion with nothing more than the spoken word. It is that same being that created man from the dust of the ground and woman from man's rib. Consequently, if that same DNA is within you, then I submit that *nothing* is impossible to you as well. It all comes down to *who* is in control. Never allow yourself to fall prey to the negative input from your mind. He/she (the mind) can be a real showstopper!

From the depths of your soul, determine the necessary strategy to reach your goal and then find a nice quiet place to meditate. You will not be alone as you will have your mind and body in tow.

Next, instruct your mind to instruct your body to sit down for several minutes and simply *be still!* One of the things we forget most often in life is to just be still once in a while. As weird as this might sound, you must do this on a scheduled basis, or else, you will get upside down all over again. Remember, it creeps up on you, and you often have no idea that it has happened. Walk circumspectly through life, so as not to be fooled repeatedly. If not, you will continually backslide. It will get a bit easier in time as the more you practice self-control, the more efficient you become at it.

As each new day dawns, there will be a whole new bombardment of negative influences hurled at your mind. They will come from many different directions. It might be something said to you, something you saw, or you might run into one of those frequent emotional upsets in life. This is why it of the utmost importance to train your mind regularly. View your mind-disciplining sessions in the same manner you would view physical exercise. The more often you train, the better your mind will acclimate to making automated responses to the desires of the soul. It will become far less prone to jumping off subject.

*Focus* is a skill that must be acquired, as it rarely comes naturally. The world is full of distractions that continually seek your attention. While it is imperative that you tend to daily life, you must never allow yourself to become completely distracted from your goal. In time, you will master the expertise of multitasking, thereby allowing you to function in daily life, all the while progressing toward your core destination.

Let your soul, mind, and body reunite through rest. Reaffirm to one another your goal(s). Then, once the three of you have sat peacefully for a while, make an agreement of cooperation. In other words, agree that from this day forward, you will work as a team, but that the *soul* has final say on everything.

Afterward, shake hands (mentally that is). Advise your mind that fear is a natural feeling but no longer a deterrent, especially *imagined fear*. There is no reason to allow fears to influence your progress, whether real or imagined. Do this exercise often any time of the day. In most cases, it hasn't even happened and likely won't. So why exhaust the energy to worry about something that lives only in your imagination?

There's no telling how different the outcome would be in many psychiatric patients if medical experts began to work toward curing the soul rather than the mind. I'm aware I will get much ridicule on that one! "Where's your degree?" "Sorry, your name is Doctor who?"

Obviously, my approach would come with the qualifier that one must first believe an individual has a soul before he could treat it. Since so many do not believe in God, it would stand to reason that much of the research in this field is based on something mainly humanistic. It's an irony how we humans study humans in order to cure humans. If someone acts variably from the so-called norm, then they must be abnormal.

Whatever you do, don't act peculiar, or else, someone might have you committed. I admit that there are certain cases where the mind is truly sick. Anything from a birth abnormality to an accident, degenerative disease, drug abuse, and a barrage of other probabilities can cause the mind to malfunction to such an extent that the soul can no longer communicate with it. But is the soul still there? Of course, it is! Is the soul still sane? Most certainly! When that person eventually dies, the body and mind will permanently faint, but the soul will rise unscathed from the ashes.

Any of us could see the ease by which one could lose control of their faculties now days with the less than favorable economy, political woes, the corporate giant's lack of genuine concern for their employees, the false conception projected by the media and Hollywood about *who is cool* and *who is not*, and the list goes on.

Add to that impressive list of anxieties, the usual pressures of home, family, school, and religion, and the cumulative effect of failure in any number of these areas can become unbearable. Life and living are complicated in and of themselves, without competition and attack. But let's face it, that's life, right?

How we deal with all this is the *not so secret* blueprint to becoming happy, fruitful, and satisfied. It's also the best way to keep from going off the deep end, if you know what I mean!

Some people need professional help to determine where their struggles lie, but most will figure it out on their own or just live with it. It's not something you learn overnight and is indeed an art, a balance of sorts, at which we become more proficient as the years go by. Unfortunately, most of our input comes from trial and error, which is better known as learning the hard way.

Surviving life while accomplishing your goals is one of the hardest things you will ever do. If you could only focus on your goal alone, and sort of *turn off* life for a while, you could rock-nroll! But that's not reality. The challenge lies in continuing onward toward your goal on one hand while balancing life with the other.

Let's say I want to become an RN. It doesn't take a genius to recognize that there will be a fair amount of study involved in such an undertaking. Now, let's add another factor. You are married. Okay, maybe not such a big deal, as long as you have an understanding spouse. After all, you might have one hour a day left over that you could spend with them. How about another factor, you are working full time. All right, were now up to heavy studies, stressful relationship, difficult work schedule, and oh yeah, no sleep. Finally, let's add financial shortfalls, and "Congratulations, you're having a baby!" (Sorry, I couldn't resist!)

Most of us are looking at this scenario and are already stressing out, and it's not even ours! (Okay, maybe it's yours?) In any case, you get my drift. When you originally start your goal, it might not seem like such a big deal. We vindicate our goal by saying things like, "I'm just going to nursing school for four years. How hard could it be?" Or how about, "I can go to school through the week and then take weekends off to rest!"

Believe it or not, this is once again your old buddy *the mind*, stepping up to the plate in a feeble attempt to protect your overall person. We call that *rationalizing*, which is just a fancy way of saying making an excuse or trying to justify your cause, even if it's not reasonable or true.

I don't believe at all that every goal has to seem plausible from conception. Most of the larger acquisitions in life seem ominous from a distance. But once you get underway, moving ever closer toward your goal, it becomes more realistic. What once seemed unreachable now becomes attainable.

A thousand-mile journey sounds halfway around the world when you haven't even left the driveway. But once you get five hundred miles down the road, your destination seems doable. Will you drive any less distance in the long run if you look at the thousand-mile journey from the midway point than if you looked at it from your driveway? It's the same distance either way. You just looked at the situation differently. In the future, we will refer to this mirage of hope as "a renewing of the mind." It would do you good to memorize Romans 12:2 (NIV): "Do not conform any longer to the pattern of this world, but be *transformed* by the *renewing of your mind*." (Emphasis mine.) Get used to it as you are going to need a lot of these *mind renewals* in order to arrive where you have dreamed of going in life. While we're at it, from this moment forward, we will begin to refer to your goal as your mission possible or your MP for short.

We all have personal preconceived notions in regard to certain situations. We each have built-in tolerances for dealing with the circumstances of everyday life. However, most are unaware that they possess an internal mechanism as well that is geared toward stretching our parameters in unusual and/or chaotic situations that may arise.

Take for instance, a funeral director. Few people would aspire to perform this rather morbid but absolutely necessary service. But no one would deny the cold, hard fact that morticians deal with death in a much more casual manner than the average person. The same goes for the unusual situations that doctors and nurses often find themselves in. The human body can be quite attractive or, in some situations (though often unavoidable), not so attractive. They've seen nearly every circumstance thinkable, and they have come to understand that all this is a normal part of the miracle of life. While most people would be unable to even stay in the same room, these responsible (and necessary) men and women handle these situations professionally on a daily basis. Never underestimate your mental flexibility.

The same mind control that allows a person to embalm a body, clean a helpless patient, perform a colonoscopy, plumb a toilet, snake a sewer, dump your garbage, clean a port-a-potty, drain the lavatory in first class, gut a fish, clean a chicken, butcher a cow, help birth a calf, examine a horse for pregnancy, artificially

inseminate your pet, clean a kennel, and brush your o
the same mind control that allows you to overcome an
in your life that makes you squeamish.

In order to be what you have never been, you must do what you have never done. This requires that you *wrap your mind around it*! If I want to *be different*, then I have to *act different*. If I want to be a pilot, then I need to start hanging out with pilots, start acting like a pilot, talking like a pilot, etc. Quite frankly, I have to get in the habit of doing whatever it is that pilots do!

Wouldn't you imagine that a stockbroker faithfully watches the markets daily? Any journalist worth his/her salt keeps up with current events, while computer programmers analyze the latest software and hardware. Don't try to reinvent the wheel! Start mimicking who or what it is that you long to be. Successful people are in the habit of doing things other people don't want to do!

This proves that by "renewing your mind," that which once seemed impossible now becomes an absolute! Given time, the mind and body can adjust to literally anything. Never believe there is something you cannot do! It's all a matter of *looking at the situation differently*. Life is a better place because somebody already has!

Your goal may give you butterflies now, but the more you associate it with everyday life (just like your dental hygienist had to do), the more comfortable you will become with it.

While we are at it, from this moment forward, we will begin to refer to your goal as your individual soul purpose or your ISP for short. (You thought I was going to say Internet Service Provider, didn't you?) You may simplify it further by referring to it as your SP or your Soul Purpose. (Pun intended.)

*Warning! Before you plunge headfirst into your dream, take a little while to do some soul-searching. Don't waste your valuable time chasing after rainbows that just aren't there. This is not to insinuate that your dream has to seem entirely realistic before you go after it. It only means that you have to be willing to pay the price for your dream, no matter what the ultimate cost might be.

Ask yourself this qualifying question, "Do I have a *burning desire* for this goal, or is it just another passing whim? (We all get them!) In other words, don't jump on every bus that goes by. Take time to carefully process the *weight* of your goal, considering as many of the implications in your journey to acquire it that you can possibly foresee. Stop for a moment and intelligibly view the circumstances of life in relation to your new direction.

Do *not* use this moment as a means of scaring yourself silly! The primary function of this exercise is to find yourself pursuing only that which you are destined to achieve and to therefore avoid a huge waste of time and energy. If this goal is something that burns down deep within your soul, if it is something that you eat, drink, and sleep every day and night of your life, if you can literally *taste* it, then by all means, get it done!

One final word of warning before we proceed: be careful what you set your heart on! Be certain that your goal is genuine, worthwhile, upright, and unselfish. Examine your motives because one thing is for certain. If you set your heart on something and, in turn, the mind comes into agreement with your soul, you will surely get it! In view of this universal truth, I pray you get your money's worth and that your goal will be worth the price you will ultimately pay for it. (Hint: a prayer or two in advance of your all-important selection might be in order!)

In recent times, the case for hope and change has become a highly popular movement. Under this guise, millions of people became convinced that a pronounced turnaround was about to transpire in America. The predictable dilemma with this scenario was that those same people were deluded into believing that if you merely chant a phrase over and over, something magical would happen.

In the end, it would seem that all the hype was in reality nothing more than an elaborate exploitation of the good and desperate people of this land. For the most part, their intentions were justified. We all realize that something has to change! But until we as people change *ourselves* first, we cannot expect any significant change on a higher level.

A better life is not something that any government can give you. They only have control of the physical properties of your life—things like, lower gas prices, a better economy, and protection from our enemies, just to name a few. But whether or not you are truly happy lies solely within your own soul. No one can take that away from you, but in retrospect, no one can help you with it either. True *change* starts from the heart of a person, and it then creates a domino effect in our country and, eventually, the world.

We have no right to stand around chanting for a handout. We should instead exude an aura of self-confidence and self-reliance in need of nothing more than a *hand* now and then rather than a *handout*. This great country has been adequately sufficient for the masses for over 230 years.

If you found that a once beautiful river had become polluted downstream, leaving no fresh drinking water, what would you do? Would you run around demanding that everyone else give you something to drink? Maybe you should start a chant demanding clean water, all the while looking to someone else to do the actual legwork?

To me, becoming self-sufficient would be the most logical approach. I would forget what *everyone else* is going to do and simply start hiking backward. I would keep hiking till I came *back to the source.* This is the only way you can ever expect to find untainted solutions. Stop looking to the fiasco in Washington to fix your problems. They can't even balance their own budget or pay their own bills. They have proved themselves time and again to be completely irresponsible. If we keep beating the same dead horse for solutions, he's eventually going to come back to haunt us.

If we want to repeat the success that America has enjoyed in the past, then we must do what our forefathers did from day one, and that is to look at the situation differently.

Had they continued down the same mundane path they were accustomed to walking, America would be no different today than any other country. But these brave souls *dared to dream*. They saw the situation differently. They renewed their minds and hence took bold actions that caused, not just a small ripple in the pond but rather a tidal wave around the world.

You have to *think big and act bold*, if you expect to ever make a difference in your own life and the life of others! Stop thinking small. Stop running back and forth over your miserable past, and instead, take control of your destiny. For goodness sake, *get control of yourself*! If necessary, give yourself a good mental slap! (Take your ring off first.) Stop listening to the continual bombardment of negative input from your brain! You simply cannot allow your mind to talk your soul out of your ISP before you even get started!

The mind is a master chef, serving up a delicacy of negative entrées on which you may feast. Go ahead, eat to your heart's content. Everybody else does! But if you do, be prepared to fail. That's just what your mind was hoping you would do.

You might ask why the mind would want you to fail. Simple. If you agree to digress from your goal, it will mean a paid holiday for your mind and body. No strenuous thinking to do, no physically demanding schedules, just couch potato city baby! True, we are not going anywhere in life, but this is so much easier!

While there are countless individuals in our society that need our financial help and support, numerous others have unfortunately jumped on the handout wagon with no intent other than that of taking something from America and contributing nothing in return. Please don't misunderstand me. Everyone needs a hand now and then. But for those that are physically, and mentally able, that's all it was designed to be… *a hand*. It's a bridge to something better; a temporary bond intended to help you hold on until you can get back on your feet again.

And I'm not making a blanket statement, nor am I speaking without adequate knowledge in the matter. You see, my wife and I were once among those in need of a hand from society, and we took it because that seemed to be our last resort at the time. We were so thankful the first month we received our food stamps. We had three little girls to feed and little to nothing in the pantry. We were beyond broke! In debt, out of work, out of money, and an old car that blew so much black smoke going down the road that it looked like we were fogging for mosquitoes! My oldest daughter once asked me if I would drop her off a block from school so that her friends wouldn't see her getting out of my car!

But we never had any intention of taking the help *permanently*. We always knew that this was a temporary fix and that we had a responsibility to our country to support our family, and we now owed a debt to our fellow American taxpayers for their generosity. Because of others, we survived, and with God's help, we looked at the situation differently, picked ourselves up once again, and began to build a new life! That's one of the great aspects of America! You can fail time and time again, yet there is a never-ending supply of equal opportunity for every man, woman, and child! Opportunity abounds in this, the greatest land in the history of the earth, if only someone dares to pursue it!

The difference between those that are down and those who *stay* down is most often nothing more than how they perceive their situation. *How you look at it*—that's what counts when life throws the unexpected your way. The second and most important thing is your response or *what you do about it*! The *choices* that you make from here on out will be the *number 1* determining factor of whether or not you rise to greatness or forever wallow in mediocrity! Success begins with a *fellows will*; it's all in the state of mind! I'm telling you your mind and body can become your ally or your worst enemy! You must get them on your side!

So let's talk about some solid methods you can use in order to regain consciousness and, in turn, reestablish control of your exterior. This input started way back at birth, so we have a lot of making up to do. The only way to break this cycle is to educate your mind in the building profession. It is imperative that you construct a wall between you and the entire negative input from your past. You can't just forget it, but you can act like it never happened! You're going to become such a great actor that you'll be up for an academy award in no time at all!

Since our minds are basically products of our environment or, in essence, what we feed them, it would then stand to reason that we are going to have to begin a steady intravenous solution of the proper nutrients in order to snap us out of our coma. The apostle Paul gives a comprehensive list of efficient sustenance on which to feast in Philippians 4:8 (NIV): "Finally brothers, whatever is true, whatever is noble, whatever is right, whatever is pure, whatever is lovely, whatever is admirable… if anything is excellent or praiseworthy, think about such things."

This is as straightforward a model as one could find. *Before* you ingest a single mental morsel, prequalify its worthiness in regard to its ultimate food value in your quest for *mind control*. Using the aforementioned biblical list as a hard core guideline will save many a wrong turn along the way. If you want the mind and body of a winner, then you have to feed them properly by initiating a routine regimen in the exercise of self-control. It all starts with what you allow your mind to devour!

Do you remember ever hearing the old adage, "He or she is set in their ways"? Like the body, the mind is a creature of habit. I'm certain if you thought about it for a moment, you could think of several people you know that act a bit *peculiar*. There's nothing wrong with that. We all do it to some degree. That's because we are all exceptional in our own right. It would be a boring and commonplace world if everyone were a carbon copy. The very distinctions that make us unique are what make life interesting.

It is also this same quality that introduces new thoughts and ideas that in turn generate *authentic* change and progress.

Because the mind is a slave to habit and since we normally react out of instinct rather than by the influence of profound thought, it is of utmost importance that it be trained to respond appropriately at any given moment.

There are some important mental exercises your soul can train your mind with daily in order to assure you set out each day on the right foot. Remember also that each and every minute of every hour of every day is an opportunity to take yet another vital step toward your ISP.

## Meditation

Begin every morning with ten minutes of meditating on your ISP. It is in this time that your soul will reaffirm to your mind and body the direction in which you are heading in life. Grab your first cup of the day, or bring along whatever it is you drink (nothing too strong, of course), and then start by finding a comfortable nook in your home where you will be unhampered from any outside distractions and/or interruptions. This might be difficult in some situations, but do your best to make it happen habitually. Also, as is feasible, do this at precisely the same time and place every day. The reason for this will be discussed more thoroughly in a later chapter, but for now, set the time and place for this morning ritual in concrete.

Clear your mind of anything and everything that has nothing to do with your ISP. This is *your* time, and it is separate and apart from any other morning activity. With practice, this will become an automatic response, and you will no longer have to coax yourself into doing it. Consider it your first major commitment toward your ISP.

Before your first session, do some interior decorating in the space where you intend to perform this task each day. Design some motivational-type posters in whatever size and shape you desire, and hang them on the wall or walls around this area. Write out your ISP in bold fashion, highlighting the posters so as to get the most attention and visibility. You might also want to set other objects around that relate to your aspiration as well. For instance, if you want to become a pilot, find a model airplane or two that you can place in your space. If your ISP is financial in nature, cut out pictures of what you wish to acquire with your newfound riches or possibly find miniatures of the same.

All this might seem a bit juvenile, but your mind often acts very much as a child when dealing with things it wants. Like a kid in a candy store, your mind will throw a fit any time it does not get its way, if it is not properly disciplined. Visualization is one of the most important things you can do on a regular basis in order to keep the mind believing in the dream. In reality, you do it constantly without being aware of it. When you see an AD on TV for something you just can't live without, it is probably your mind that wants it. If the truth were known, your soul could live without it, and it most likely has nothing at all to do with your ultimate goals in life. Visualize, visualize, visualize! I cannot stress this enough! Unquestionably, you must begin to see yourself where you want to be! If you cannot picture yourself *living the dream*, then it is highly probable that you *will never do it*!

Maybe you would like to bring your Bible or something else that makes you feel confident and comfortable. You might want to open to a favorite verse or reflect on a favorite poem. I do highly recommend prayer as a part of your meditation. Asking your Creator to guide your thoughts and actions toward your ISP is a superior method by which to attain your goals. Without question, it will immediately become your single largest advantage as you are going to need all the help you can get! "If you abide in me, and my words abide in you, ask whatever you wish, and it will be done for you" (John 15:7, ASV).

Aside from meditation and prayer, spend a couple of minutes reaffirming your ISP verbally. Hear yourself say out loud what you intend to accomplish. Do not be insincere or halfhearted. Don't whisper or mumble to yourself. Rather, be firm and insistent in your tone! You need to reassert your goal in a clear, audible fashion. At the end of the ten-minute period, close with prayer, making sure to thank God for what you already have. When in pursuit of something more, we often forget how very much we have at present. Common sense tells us that we could likely live the rest of our lives in our present state in need of little more than what we currently posses. But there's nothing selfish or immoral in wanting more of a good thing as long as we are good with what we receive, and we never forget from whence it came. God loves for us to be successful. What kind of father wants to see his children struggle or grovel through life?

Your daily practice of meditation will seem a bit awkward at first. After all, talking to yourself has never been regarded as a normal habit. (Who came up with that one, and who cares what *they* think?) Most of us do it unconsciously anyway, so you might as well be talking about something constructive and not just venting over matters about which you are frustrated or angry.

Throughout your home, office, vehicle, etc., place visual reminders of your ISP, so every day, you are continuously surrounded by your ultimate destination. From time to time, mention your ISP to friends and family in casual conversation as a way of once again reaffirming out loud your intentions in a public manner. Begin speaking in a future tense, thereby projecting yourself into the fruition of your dream.

This actually does one of two things. First, it allows you to recommit to yourself, and second, it binds you to commit your goal to others. They may not actually hold you to it, but we always feel a sense of commitment when we boast our intentions to those we respect most. Essentially, we don't want to let them down. This is a good thing! You *should be* committed on every level!

You are basically putting yourself in a sort of mental corner. You need to feel confined as if you cannot escape the commitment you have made. You're trapped!

Don't be frightened. The reason you are not where you want to be in the first place is largely because you have always unconsciously left an escape route in the past, in every goal or aspiration. Unknowingly, you made some sort of *trap door* in your plan so that just in case this doesn't work out, you could rationalize your failure. Remember that this is your mind attempting to save face on your behalf. This time must be different. This time, you must ensure that there is no escaping your goal. You have an ISP in life, and it's time you fulfill your destiny!

Finally, you need to realize right up front that your ISP is not likely to happen overnight. Outside of fear, the largest and most common obstacle you will encounter on your way to your goal will be patience.

Generally speaking, we are an *instant* world. We want an instant solution to our country, an instant solution to our job, an instant solution to our finances, an instant solution to our marriage, an instant solution to our teenagers, an instant solution to our health, an instant solution to our weight, and so on.

It is this hunger for instant gratification that has led us to instant breakfast, instant pudding, fast food, convenience stores, one-hour photo (now obsolete for something even faster), high-speed internet, bank loans, credit cards, diet pills, and the ten-minute oil change, just to name a few.

We're in such a hurry that we are willing to risk quality for the sake of speed. We want the quickest route, the easiest route, and the least expensive route all rolled into one. And if we don't actually lose twenty pounds in a month by exercising only ten minutes a day, three days a week with the revolutionary rope on a stick, then we demand a refund! Truer words have never been spoken than these, "Good things come to those that wait!"

If I could give you any advice that will help you to reach your ISP with more certainty than any other, it would be to *slow down*! Just *be still* every now and then. Even God rested on the seventh day, and Jesus walked away from the crowds from time to time in order that he might slow down and, of course, rest.

> Be still in the presence of the Lord, and patiently wait for him to act. Don't worry about evil people who prosper or fret about their wicked schemes. Stop being angry! Turn from your rage! Do not lose your temper- it only leads to harm. For the wicked will be destroyed, but those that trust in the Lord will possess the land! (Psalms 37:7–9, NLV)

> We do not want to become lazy, but imitate those who through faith and patience inherit what has been promised. (Psalms 37:7–9, NIV)

Slow down. Be patient. But by all means, be persistent! You've been *out of your mind* long enough. Today is the day to retrieve what is rightfully yours! It's your mind, so get in there and take it back! It is time once and for all to get the best out of yourself!

## Chapter Four

# The Body

"And God said, let us make man in our image, after our likeness: and let them have dominion over the fish of the sea, and over the fowl of the air, and over the cattle, and over all the earth, and over every creeping thing that creepeth upon the earth."

Genesis 1:26 (KJV)

I doubt anyone could disagree with these prophetic words: "I am fearfully and wonderfully made" (Psalms 139:14, NIV).

Having taken an in-depth look in previous chapters at the awe-inspiring center, the innermost parts of our human existence, the next predictable step would be to more aptly define this outer *shell* of sorts, which, in terms of appearance and functionality, we undoubtedly share numerous similarities.

Much like the varied makes and models of the countless automobiles of the past one hundred years, the basic parts that make up this miraculous contraption we drive around in daily are no different. I mean to say that it takes a particular part to perform a particular job. For instance, it takes a set of round wheels on a motor vehicle in order to move freely in any direction on or off the highway. True, there are other proven methods by which to move the masses, but none quite so versatile as the good old wheel. (Thank you fourth millennium BC people! Though, it would have been to your advantage had you invented the patent first.)

However, there is arguably a system far older, and even more reliable than both the wheel and the automobile for the purpose of moving about. I am speaking of none other than the old as Adam, here to stay, widely popular, all-terrain, never-to-be outsold human body!

Yes, there is no other vehicle to date that is more complex, more versatile, more reliable, and more widely used than that very *set of wheels* you are parked there in right now. It is one and the same with that snazzy little hardtop you sport around town in every day. (Although, some people's top is harder than others!) Yet in spite of all the factory extras, it continues to boast the highest MPG on the road! "Kick the tires, and light the fires." It's the best buy on the market in history. Seriously, can you beat it?

When that old jalopy of yours refuses to start, has a flat, runs out of gas, or whatever the flavor of the day might be, what do you fall back on? Those highly reliable legs and feet, of course!

I consider myself a shade tree mechanic of sorts. If something breaks down, I'll nearly always take a stab at it before paying someone else to do so. Over the years, the hard knocks school of experience has enlightened me as to what jobs are worth my effort, and those that I simply need to hire an expert to do.

But in spite of my jack-of-all-trades aptitude, I have found myself on more than one occasion unable to get that brain child of Henry Ford out of the driveway. But in retrospect, I can nearly always get my body rolling in the morning whether my car does or not. Granted (just like my car), the older I get, the harder it is for me to *get cranking*, but for the most part, I have little about which to complain as I have definitely gotten my money's worth out of this thing. I boast years of satisfied customer experience despite an inadequate in-depth understanding as to how this machine I'm in actually functions.

And the miles, well, who could count them all? Oh, and talking about your money's worth, this baby started out as a lightweight compact and has now turned into a heavy-duty crew cab! When have you ever bought a car that grows larger the older it gets? Tell me pound for pound where you're going to get a deal like that?

I hope you will all agree without question that by every standard, it has been an amazing ride up to this time. (Notice I didn't say *comfortable*!) The places I have been and the things I have done while driving this body around are too numerous to mention. Yet all the while, I was unconsciously multitasking thousands of intricate operations, jointly cooperating with the sole designation to keep *me* moving. I cannot express how incredibly blessed we are that this thing comes fully automated!

Thanks in part to the mastermind known as the brain; the body pretty much takes care of itself. And it's a good thing, seeing that you and I could never keep up with the endless requirements necessary to sustain life for even a single hour, let alone, 24-7, 365 days a year, for years on end.

The following are some interesting statistics that clearly proclaim the improbability of a *manual operation* mode. These many complex parameters of the human body are each and every one necessary for the continuance of life. There are a total of eleven systems in the body:

1. Circulatory system
2. Digestive system
3. Endocrine system
4. Immune system
5. Lymphatic system
6. Muscular system

7. Nervous system
8. Reproductive system
9. Respiratory system
10. Skeletal system
11. Urinary system

All these systems run continually, day and night, from birth to death, each carrying out its individual function in contribution to the whole being. If even one of these complex systems ceases to function, it causes havoc or possibly even death.

There is a biblical account where the apostle Paul describes best the importance of unity within the body.

> Now the body is not made up of one part but of many. If the foot should say, "Because I am not a hand, I do not belong to the body," it would not for that reason cease to be part of the body. And if the ear should say, "Because I am not an eye, I do not belong to the body," it would not for that reason cease to be part of the body. If the whole body were an eye, where would the sense of hearing be? If the whole body were an ear, where would the sense of smell be? But in fact God has arranged the parts in the body, every one of them, just as he wanted them to be. If they were all one part, where would the body be? As it is, there are many parts, but one body." (1 Corinthians 12:14–20, NIV)

It's obvious that God created a set of wheels that could serve every purpose in our life. What's more, it is capable of going just about anywhere, under any conditions.

Just as the body is an extension of the *real you* down inside, man has gone beyond the seemingly inescapable confounds of the body and expanded his horizons through the invention of other vehicles. Through the use of bulldozers, backhoes, cranes, etc., a single human can move loads many times their own size and weight. Through the airplane, man developed an extension that gave the body bird-like capabilities. A ship allows us to tread water at tremendous speeds over vast oceans. And of course, in an automobile, man can travel great distances at continuous high speed, without tiring. Even something so simple as a crescent wrench gives your body much more torque and strength than it has on its own.

In the same manner that tools allow you to accomplish tasks that would normally not be possible, the body itself is an extension of the soul and allows you to navigate, move about if you will so that those physical things which the soul could not acquire on its own become attainable. Without the body, the soul would be nothing more than an entity, alive and well, but with no mobility in this life.

We've seen instances where faulty equipment, either through birth defect or by injury, limits the ultimate functions of the body. However, we have also witnessed what the shear will of the soul can override in regard to the confounding limitations of the body.

I once met a pilot who had no legs yet was a skilled flight instructor. He would stand in the seat and secure himself with shoulder straps. He got in and out of the airplane by swinging by his arms on the wing struts. I have read of other people that draw beautiful portraits and even teach aerobics without arms! I once played football in junior high with a boy that was missing an arm. There have even been one-armed baseball players.

Then there are the bravest of the brave. Men and women who are totally paralyzed, for all intentional purposes, *trapped* inside their own body, and yet through tremendous inner strength and determination, they have become artists, authors, lawyers, stockbrokers, and even write advanced computer software! Their accomplishments stand as a colossal monument upon which are chiseled these profound words: What the mind can conceive, the body can achieve. Don't ever forget that!

But as we know, the mind is, in reality, the *brain*. It can't even live, if not for the brain. It is therefore not actually the *mind* that conceives but rather our *soul* who rises as the true dreamer within us. It's the *real you* deep down inside. It's the part of you that never dies, and it is also the part that longs to live, to achieve, to overcome, and to rise above the status quo! It demands something more than to simply exist.

The Gatlin brothers once put this thought to song so aptly in their number one hit entitled "Done Enough Dying Today." In one verse they proclaim, "Just existing makes dying look easy." How absolutely profound that is! There simply isn't anything that could be easier than *dying*! All you have to do is nothing! You don't have to do a dad-gum thing in order to die. Sure, you might suffer a bit, but if you don't want to live any longer, just do nothing at all, and in time, death will come for you. It is *existing* that is so incredibly challenging at times, isn't it?

Over the years, I have had the duty on numerous occasions to stand at the foot of the bed in hospice and have witnessed firsthand as the body struggles to hold on to life in even the sickest of patients.

We have this built-in mechanism that instinctively kicks into high gear at the very hint of death, doing everything possible to live, to continue to exist, to fight to the last breath within us, regardless of the circumstances. Death is as much a fact of life as birth, and yet when given the choice, we will nearly always choose life. But this does not change the reality that death comes far easier to us than life.

I believe this fact so intently that many years ago, I came up with an original saying regarding my feelings: "The worst part of this is I'm going to live through it!" Isn't that often the case? When disappointment, pain, sorrow, or loss comes our way, is it not true that the very worst part of dealing with the calamity is simply that we are forced to live through it? *Dying* is easy! Nothing to it! It's *living* that is so extremely difficult! It's hard to keep going, especially when your world is falling apart. I know all too well from personal experience that life can get miserably heavy at times. In fact, the word *unbearable* comes to mind!

But never forget that regardless of your current position in life, whether on top or lying flat on your back, you *can* overcome anything! Once you make a contract of agreement between the soul and the mind, together, you will devise ways and means by which to attain any goal and overcome any obstacle! "As a man thinks in his heart, so is he!" It is not up to the body what you will or will not achieve. The body is nothing more than an apparatus. It is at your command, your beckon call, and at your disposal. If one part of the body refuses to respond to your commands, then you must find a way around it. Find a way to move on *without* that part. Improvise! Be creative! But in any case, never allow the body to run your life! In the right to vote category, the body deserves the least amount of input. Stop letting your body push you around!

The next time you are out in public, no matter the setting, stop for just a few seconds and look around. Take notice of the people within your line of sight. Mentally single out ten individuals and take note based only on what you can see outwardly as to their overall physical condition. Centered solely on what you observe, what is the percentage of people that have little if any control over their vehicle? Decades ago, you would have had to have hunted for the one person that was completely out of control. But in today's *instant* society, this element has become the uniform rule. Go ahead, try to find the exception as they will be difficult to spot.

I comprehend that there is more to control of one's self than just their exterior appearance. But would you not agree that in light of modern medicine and the advances in health and science overall that present generations should be more fit than ever? I mean, with the endless resources in the realm of fitness and nutrition alone, we aught to be headed toward a race of super humans, "able to leap tall buildings in a single bound!" Instead, we find ourselves in the midst of super-sized humans, demanding bigger meals, bigger seats, bigger beds, and bigger toilets, just to accommodate the average-sized person.

Despite the illusion that many people paint in regard to their physical condition, much of what we see today is nothing more than a loss of control. To put it in perspective, if our nation's highways portrayed the same substandard driving record as our bodies, they would revoke 80 percent of the driver's licenses on the road! When we look at the *big* picture, it is beyond evident that the majority no longer has a clue how to drive!

Blame it on what you will, but the underlying verity points to a universal commonality. Overwhelmingly, people lack self-control!

To prove my point, let me ask you what your thoughts are at this very moment. "He doesn't understand my problem!" "I have control. I'm just a little off my game right now!" "I can't help the situation I am in!"

Okay, in isolated cases, you might be correct. Some people cannot help their loss of control. But is that really *your* situation? It is far easier to blame your current state on something else rather than address the real issue and in turn be forced to stare into the reality of fixing it. To more clearly address our situation, let us address both the *cause* and the *cure* of these misconceptions.

In layman's terms, the body is very whiny! I can't make it any clearer than that! Your body has thousands of nerve endings and sensors, all corroborating for the general purpose of monitoring the overall condition and functionality of your vehicle. It is comparable once again to your automobile, with gauges, lights, and warning sounds that give an immediate indication should something malfunction. After all, none of these are actually designed to tell you when something is right. Who needs to know that? What we are really looking for is that once in a while scenario when something is *not* right.

As an instrument rated pilot, I've been taught to scan the gauges incessantly from the beginning of a flight to the final moment when the engines are shut down. But I'd bet you would be surprised to discover that pilots are not trained to observe that everything is okay. In fact, it is just the opposite. Because the mind becomes accustomed to the accepted norm, pilots are instead trained to look for what is *not* correct in the cockpit. In the case of flight instruments, this is what is referred to as a *trend*. After all, a good pilot should not expect to look at the instrument panel and suddenly find that the plane is upside down! More likely, he or she will notice a small tendency or trend in (for instance) the altimeter, indicating that, if not corrected, indeed you might wind up in an undesired attitude. This rather minor adjustment in the aircraft's pitch is hardly noticeable to passengers and is the reason why you can sit back, read a magazine, sip on your favorite beverage, listen to music, and even walk about comfortably, all the while soaring across the heavens at 700 mph at 40,000 feet!

Without question, the average autopilot makes hundreds of tiny adjustments per minute, correcting an endless number of trends *before* they become a major issue. Believe me, if you ever rode along on a flight check when we practice unusual attitude recovery, you would immediately appreciate the smooth and upright configuration as the position of choice! These skills are what make a good pilot, and it is his or her ability to proficiently scan and thereby recognize trends in the aircraft's performance that make for a safe and comfortable flight.

There is also another unsafe condition that pilots are taught to avoid that is referred to as *getting behind the aircraft*. Now obviously this is not insinuating that the pilot is actually *behind* the airplane. (That would make it impossible to reach the controls!) Rather, this term is applied to a dangerous situation where the speed at which things tend to happen while flying become faster than the interpretation and inherent control input of the pilot. You are told to always stay ahead of the aircraft (i.e., think and react in advance of the current situation).

By remaining constantly aware of what is coming next, every phase of the flight is an *expected* one. It has also been proven that one error usually leads to another if not corrected; thus, it is extremely important to handle every variance quickly. There's nothing worse than a big surprise when it comes to flying! While you are trained to be ready for the unexpected, there is no excuse for the emergency to be self-induced.

And so it is with people. Just as a pilot rarely glances at the gages and discovers unexpectedly that he is in a downward spiral, you don't wake up suddenly one morning 100 lbs. overweight. As a whole, we all need to become more efficient in the skill of recognizing trends.

In this case, a trend would be the first one or two pounds. But in some cases (like my own), a couple of pounds fluctuation is completely within the norm. But a 10-lb. change would definitely be something worth looking at.

It is an epidemic lack of flying skill (vehicle control) that limits our ability to notice trends as they happen. On the other hand, it is possible that we are fully aware of the trend but choose to ignore its potential affect. Let me assure you that if your 747 commercial pilot had this kind of flippant attitude, you would definitely want to turn down the in-flight meal option!

Trends are the body's way of setting off a warning light or a buzzer in your brain to alert you to a possible problem. If you act efficiently, a tragedy can be avoided. However, if you ignore the warning, one problem will build on another, and in time, you will find yourself spinning out of control!

At first, you notice a slight weight gain, so no action is taken on your part. The next sign something is not quite right is that your blood pressure is a little higher than normal. Within a few months, your back starts to ache, and you may have a bit of a problem walking. (By now, running is out of the question!) Within a year or so, your doctor warns you that your blood test revealed an elevated cholesterol level, and your sugar is less than ideal. What's amazing is that in the majority of cases, we blow these signals off as if we have a faulty, or inoperative gauge, failing to take seriously the inevitable outcome.

Why is it that in the face of death, a cigarette smoker will stuff one more puff around the oxygen tube, in spite of the threat of making matters worse or the definite possibility of blowing themselves to oblivion? We criticize these unfortunate souls that seem to lack a morsel of discipline while shoveling in another artery-clogging meal at the hospital cafeteria. What a weird and unexplainable lot we are!

So let us see if we can summarize all this. We find that we are better educated than ever and thus more proficient are we in the fine art of human longevity, and yet when faced with the grim reality that life may cease to persist, we continue to slowly and painfully kill ourselves till our dying breath? Would you say that is a fair assessment? Let me then ask the obvious question: why?

Once more, I revert back to my pilot training to make a comparison. There is a discernable difference between a trend and an inoperative gauge. You have to assume that you can, in no way, believe what you are seeing or experiencing until it can be verified. Because your inner ear will continually lie to you in accelerated flight, you must become proficient in identification, followed by verification, before any control input is made. You have to take the surface information given to you and compare it with the other back up instruments that aid in identifying if the initial indication is factual.

The body is constantly crying out about one thing or another. In order to become efficient at driving your personal set of wheels you must learn to differentiate between a simple ache or pain versus something more serious. The truth of the matter is that no one knows your body like you do, and *you* are the best judge regarding whether something is truly wrong or not. The better we become at taking care of ourselves, the better equipped we are at recognizing and reacting to our individual body signals.

Because the body has a significant number of sensors and gauges, it often becomes difficult to determine if the warning signs are significant enough to merit a control input. How many times have you gone to the doctor only to discover that what you thought was serious is in fact nothing at all or even *normal*? We are afraid to wait too long for a second opinion, but in the same instance, we hate to take the time, let alone spend the money to find out for certain. And that's just it. Many ailments require subsequent visits and extensive testing before we can pinpoint the problem, let alone, do something about it. But learning the difference between an *emergency* and a *warning* is the key to safe flying.

We've all seen those annoying check engine lights in our cars, right? How many years have you just kept on driving, disregarding that warning sign staring you in the face every time you look at your instrument panel? On countless occasions, I have attempted to get a diagnosis as to what might be causing the light to come on, and I'm still forced to drive with a stuck light, invariably inviting every new passenger to give me the proverbial heads-up, "Hey, did you know you have an engine light on?" Duh! Thank you, wise one! I'm so blessed you sat in my car today just so you could help me avoid certain disaster!

All right, so we don't get a warm and fuzzy every time some well-meaning soul gives us advice on how to care for our automobile. It is true that many of those bells and whistles are worthless as to the overall condition of our vehicle. So with experience, comes the ability to decipher which ones are important and those we can simply ignore.

So it is with this body you are riding around in. It cries out hundreds of times a day. "Ouch! Your finger just got smashed!" "Your left-bottom molar might need attention!" "The ball of your right foot gets sore if you stand on it too long!" "You have a hang nail!" "This pimple is killing you!" "Your right nostril is continually dripping!" "You have a paper cut!" "Your lower back hurts every day!" "You can't get enough sleep!" And my favorite, "You've got gas!"

Gracious, if you listened to every little signal your body whimpers on a daily basis, you would be living full time at a hospital, pavilion, or nursing home! It is time, once and for all, that we learn to recognize the difference between a trend and a catastrophe. In fact, if we would become more efficient as trend-identifiers, there would be far less catastrophes. The whole idea of having an early warning system, referred to as an EWS, is so that we can determine if an input action is actually warranted.

You have surely learned by now that your body is a bit of a baby when it comes to pain and suffering. No sane person enjoys pain. The trick is in learning the art of trend recognition versus the failure to react at all. It would not be desirable to try to second-guess certain symptoms that might be the forerunner to a heart attack or stroke. I personally have been down this road. Initially, I got a thorough check up, heart test, etc., just to prove everything was okay. My doctor found that my insides were healthy as a horse and that an occasional chest or arm pain does *not always* point to a pending disaster. You absolutely want to get a professional opinion on matters such as these, but you cannot get in the habit of running to the doctor every time your body sends a text message to the brain.

The key is getting to know yourself so that you are in tune with your inner self, and you can, therefore, better decipher your own internal instruments. Getting familiar with *you* is the first step to gaining control of yourself. If *you* don't know *you*, then who does? You have to become proficient in recognizing trends in your life. Don't wait till you are out of control before you initiate a control input. You are sort of stuck in your vehicle for life, so you have no choice but to ride it out. The challenge lies in properly interpreting your body's signals.

As I said, the body is a bit of a baby at times. The body is even more apt to take the path of least resistance than the mind. As a rule, the body absolutely abhors physical exertion, so it would stand to reason that exercise is out of the question, which is strange, in that the body was designed to do physical work.

If you were to go back one hundred years, you would find that *everybody* worked in one physical manner or another. The very inference of *life*, insinuated work! Nothing came easy. Somewhere between then and now, we have gradually swung the pendulum toward a sedentary lifestyle. We are much like the civilian masses in the movie *Wall-E* where we rarely lift a finger, except to press a button on a cell phone or video game, and our *growing* population stands as proof!

In our hunger for technology, we stood on the backs of geniuses and allowed the computer world to overtake us. What was once a convenient tool, or neat little gadget, has now become a link to life that we cannot live without. If the electricity ever goes off, we're hosed! The world, as we know it, would come to a screeching halt! It would be a world where you could not fill your car with gas, purchase an item at a store, get your money out of the bank, wash your hands, get a paper towel, or even flush the toilet! We have painted ourselves into a proverbial corner!

The worst of the worst is that if this indeed happened, the majority could never survive on our own. Just the loss of one major utility, such as electricity, would kill off the greater part of our population in a matter of weeks. One would think that in light of this information alone, we would all become *pro-energy*, and stop demonizing energy-based corporations for the simple act of *keeping the lights on*!

Being *green* is a great standard, but let's face it, given the choice of life or death, there would be 100 percent approval to drill here and drill now. Energy is a sort of two-headed snake. We cannot live efficiently without it, yet it could inevitably kill us if not controlled properly.

But who among us is so noble that they would trade their life for *green*? It is impossible to live on this earth without leaving a carbon footprint of some kind. Everyone eats, and everyone excretes. Hey, it's a fact of life.

As we move forward to seek new and innovative methods by which to power up our world, let us not be ignorant of the ultimate choices we might be forced to make one day. Could *you* go back to raising your own food, milking your own cow, raising your own chickens, or slaughtering your own cow and pig, etc.? And how about the millions living in metropolitan areas, what are they to do? Where would they go before starving to death?

We have become a generation of dependen*ts*, putting our very existence in the hands of someone else. The very technology that has made life so grand could, in fact, turn about to become our worst nightmare. So then, it is of utmost importance that you *get control* of yourself so that you become less dependent on others and far more reliant upon *you*.

One of the greatest strengths you possess is the gift of mobility. Those that are physically challenged by illness, age, injury, etc., can testify that the simple act of *moving about* is a tremendous blessing. There is so much about this fascinating vehicle we take for granted.

Years ago, my dearly departed father and I found ourselves elbow to elbow in a men's bathroom one evening at a high school football game. As usual, everybody was just doing their business, keeping to their self, with as little conversation as possible.

Out of nowhere, my dad looked over at me, broke the silence, and said, "Enjoy this while you can. It's one of life's simple pleasures! I guarantee that when you are old, you're going to miss it!"

I was a bit surprised. I chuckled back. "What do you mean, Dad?"

He said, "Going to the bathroom without great effort seems like such a little thing. But as you get older, you begin to understand just what a blessing it is!" Then he started laughing. I laughed too. At least, at the moment! Years later, I began to see that he was such a wise man.

We take so many of the little things for granted when it comes to our body. We think nothing of having to make a second trip back to the TV to pick up the remote control, walking down the short flight of stairs that lead to the basement, raking the yard, riding a bike, and a thousand other daily movements. That is, until we get older. All of the sudden, we see things in a sort of special effect prism, you know, like the one they have in the movies where you're standing still, but everything around you closes in. It's the *reality check* effect!

My wife and I experienced this phenomenon years ago when we moved in our new home. When we first viewed the home, we fell in love with its unique tri-level design. The front door is the only part of the home at ground level. When you open the door, you either have to take seven steps up or seven steps down. It was quite large and beautiful, so we bought it! But as we were moving in a few days later, reality kicked in.

I looked at my wife and asked, "Did we make the right decision here?"

She laughed and shrugged her shoulders. "I don't know," she said. "The more I walk up and down these stairs, the more I wonder!"

Over the years, we have grown more and more weary of the stairs! We've made thousands of trips up and down, and every family member has taken at least one tumble. (Actually, I hold the record!) I can't tell you how many times I've gone downstairs to the den, gotten all comfy in my La-Z-Boy and then remember that I forgot something I needed upstairs. You would be amazed how many things you can simply live without!

The older you get, the more of these *reality checks* you are bound to experience. Adding insult to injury, much of the time the condition is self-induced. This is what you feel like when you allow your body to assert a hostile takeover of your life. You're trapped inside this stubborn, uncooperative, immobile vehicle, completely incapacitated in respect to the normal, everyday functions of existence. Forget the very idea of accomplishing anything extraordinary as "just existing makes dying look easy." In the sense of our potential operating capacity, many of us now days are old before our time.

Getting the best out of yourself starts by getting control of yourself. After all, how could one ever expect to be the best at anything, if they cannot even gain control of their own personal space? I am in no way here to criticize but rather to open your eyes, to encouraged, to light a fire, to push you out of that infernal rut you've been stuck in for so long now. It doesn't matter if you use your body to run a marathon or direct it to the unemployment office to fill out a job application. If you lack the ability to force your body into submission, you will sit around every day watching life go by, getting deeper and deeper into a hole.

Let me ask you something. Are you tired of being pushed around? Are you sick of all the excuses you make for yourself on a daily basis? Are you miles from where you first started out to go? If so, then let's change it! Let's change *you*!

Do you remember that awkward feeling you got inside when you first learned how to drive? It seemed completely unnatural, right? What about the first time you drove a stick shift? Wow, talking about uncoordinated! But now that you have perfected your skills, is it not as much a natural outlet of your inner self as walking or running? The car is just an *outer extension* of *you*. The senses and reflexes that allow you to conquer the automobile are one in the same with the mastery of your body. The body too is an extension of *you*.

If you will learn to think of your body more like a car, truck, motorcycle, jet ski, etc., it will then become nothing more than a natural extension of your mind and soul, moving about to bring the outside world to your doorstep. Envision the vehicle you believe best represents *your* body then see yourself behind the wheel or controls. Rather than seeing your actions as directly connected to yourself, see each move you make as from a third party prospective. You are the outside operator, and you are here to command the vehicle.

Now, think back for a moment with me to the bowl of ice cream scenario. So much of what we do every day has nothing at all to do with what the body truly desires. We basically use this body of ours throughout life to satisfy the inner longings of the mind or soul. Then again, if we first gain control of the mind, then logically it is the soul, or the *real you* down inside in command of your whole self.

With that in mind, we must become captain of our ship, proficiently steering the helm, thereby turning to whatever destination our heart desires. The Bible says, "Take ships as an example. Although they are so large, and are driven by strong winds, they are steered by a very small rudder wherever the pilot wants to go" (James 3:4, NIV).

Like the airplane, it doesn't take but a small amount of control input to make a large correction in the direction of flight. Just one degree makes a huge variance in your final destination.

So the good news is that you don't have to start out big! Begin with only *one* fine adjustment. Then, gradually notice the difference in your life. Start by turning down the sensor sensitivity in your body, becoming more fine-tuned as to what is truly an emergency, or nothing more than a whimper. Demand that your body grow up! Stop acting like a child, throwing a fit every time you don't get your way! Like the parent-child relationship, the *soul* is the *mama* here, and the *body* is the *child*. If you are a loving parent, you will always sympathize with your child, but you will never let them run over you. Force the body to respect the soul. In time, you will discover that you have an affectionate relationship with your body in which it automatically seeks the best interest of every party.

However, unlike your child, the body is a slave to whatever you choose to do but in the same instance deserves your love and respect, as well as an occasional pat on the head (literal or not) and a reward. We will talk more in detail about this shortly.

So let's begin from wherever *you* are in life at this moment. Maybe you've recognized a trend or perhaps it's well beyond that now. Just remember that a trend is the beginning of a much bigger problem and, if not handled immediately, can turn into a catastrophe! Everyone will start from a different place, but at the same time, everyone must start somewhere, and everyone must start now! Procrastination is not your friend! You are only delaying the inevitable. Take it from me. It is much easier to get matters under control up front than putting it off.

Begin each day with your focus time, getting your mind in line with the aspirations of your soul, reaffirming your ISP to the trinity that is you. (I mean no disrespect to the term "Trinity" as used in reference to the Godhead. It is not a holy trinity to which I am referring rather a group of three persons or things, (i.e., the state of being three).

From the moment you awake, your body will begin the morning cry, much like that of an infant. It is at this time of day (as well as late night) that your body will be at its weakest and most vulnerable state. In the morning, it has not fully awakened and has yet to gain the necessary momentum to meet the day. That is the push here—to get enough momentum to get moving and climb the many hills and mountains of the impending day.

At this point, you have two choices: you may either roll over, hit the snooze, and go back to sleep, or you can leap out of bed in a vivacious fashion and shout to the top of your lungs, "Boy, do I feel great!" Okay, maybe you won't get up with quite so much enthusiasm. Though if you tried this method, you would be shocked as to how much better you feel about everything facing you in the coming twelve hours.

The point is that from the very first moment you awake, your body begins to send negative signals to your brain and, in turn, to your soul. "I don't want to get up," "I'm still sleepy," "I don't feel good," and so on. You might as well start right now to get the body in check. I will leave your own personal bed-exit tactics to you, but in any case, be quick about it, be firm, and be enthusiastic! God has just given you a whole new day in which to do whatever it is you wish. This is truly a gift, so let us use it to our fullest potential!

All right, you are now *up*, as we say. So what's next? I believe we are all pretty much alike in our morning routine. We should be in the habitual practices of hygiene, nourishment, and getting dressed. Though some items may tend to be a nuisance, the key is to force your body to accept the choices *you* make, rather than what your body would prefer. Listening to your wishy-washy mind and body is what brought you to your current condition. Enough already! Today is the day you get back in the driver's seat. Grab the wheel early on and make the logical choices in preparation for a healthy and productive day.

Don't worry, your body will not gag on toothpaste nor at the sight of an orange and a bowl of oatmeal. Force-feed yourself if necessary. Most babies don't like what is good for them till you stick it in their mouth. Believe me, if you can get an infant accustomed to eating strained peas, you can get used to anything! It is all a matter of discipline that begins with one small step, one push in the opposite direction, one single *control input*.

It is most important that you develop a cautious technique in regard to focus. By this, I mean to say that you must never look too far down the road. For the first time in your life, you must become shortsighted. You should not allow yourself to look at how far you have to go to meet your ultimate goal. This common error alone has sabotaged more dreams than just about any other factor.

While you originally have to look at the big picture, it should only be for the purpose of establishing your initial ISP. Once you know for certain what it is that you will be striving for, put it in the back of your mind, and don't bring it up again outside of your daily meditation time. The soul will always know what it is you want, but the mind is incapable of handling this much responsibility on its own. Withholding this information daily will make the goal so much more attainable in the long run. Do not remind yourself how far you have to go. It's a field goal blocker every time. Your ISP does not come to fruition overnight but rather one day at a time, one step at a time, etc. So only allow yourself to focus on what it is you will do today. If you accomplish nothing else but that one step, consider your day successful, as you have just finished the most important thing you had to do that day.

Your ISP is not one giant goal but rather a series of small daily goals adding up to the sum of the whole. It will take a lot of mental control to adapt this process, but this one thing will change your attitude and, in the end, your life!

What's more, it works in every aspect of your life. If it's a relationship you are pursuing, take one day at a time, one action at a time. Don't get antsy for something more to happen, but instead, nourish the relationship bit by bit. People that rush into a relationship tend to skip over all the important steps that build a solid, long-lasting foundation. This is evident in the innumerable one-night stands that have become so prevalent in our society today. The accepted norm is to *try on* an individual to see if they fit by *going all the way* in one single step, from the restaurant to the bed! This method rarely works and hardly ever lasts!

No matter what signals your body may be sending your mind, stay in control of your relationship. Don't allow the physical signals your body is bombarding your mind with to overcome your morality or your goal. Do things in a slow but calculated manner, all the while building the anticipation and momentum with your loved one. Also, do it right! That is, do things the way God intended. Remember that God dwells within you, so he is a part of *everything* you do! I promise you the relationship will be far more rewarding and will last a lifetime when God puts his seal of approval on it! Picture your long-term goal with this person; then, break that down into individual daily goals, focusing on every word, every action, and every deed. After all, if you mess up in the short-term, chances are you won't have to worry about what will happen down the road.

Focus is also the key to every other principle of success. It is especially vital in physical exercise. No one ever got ripped in one day. In fact, most do not get ripped in one year. The rationale is this: being fit is the compilation of thousands upon thousands of individual repetitions. You cannot say that any one single rep is more important than another. Nor could you imply that one rep had more effect on your body than another. Muscles respond to repetitive motion. It's like the body is saying, "I guess this guy is going to keep lifting this heavy weight every day, so we'd better get bigger so we can handle it better!"

Your body never responds permanently to a single input, unless it is an injury. This alone disproves the exorbitant claims of the "overnight sensation" infomercials. It just doesn't happen that way. So much damage is done to would-be enthusiasts by empty promises and outlandish claims.

I once ordered a home study course in Judo. (Give me a break. I was only twelve years old at the time!) I saw the well-circulated AD where the bully at the beach is kicking sand in the scrawny guy's face while the bathing beauty looks on in horror. Then, after only a couple of months of study and practice, the situation reverses and the scrawny guy gets buffed up, goes back to the beach, puts the bully in submission, and walks away with the girl! Come on, what young man hasn't dreamed of that scenario?

Needless to say, the course was a complete and utter disappointment. I was able to effortlessly throw my little brother around the room. (Although I could already do that.) But it all went south very quickly when I decided to demonstrate the same technique on my dad who was 6' 2", 220 lbs. He didn't budge, and I ran out of the room screaming, "This junk is a rip-off!"

It takes *extreme* repetitiveness to affect *real* change in your body or in your life, so you might as well settle in for the long haul. No quick fixes, no gimmicks. You didn't get where you are overnight, and you won't get back overnight either!

Not to worry! There is a proven method by which you can overcome this negative fact. If you're suddenly feeling kind of sour about your ability to reach your ISP, then don't! Don't even think about how far you have to go. I want you to start living for the moment. This will not be by the same definition the world has given it (i.e., life in the fast lane, live and let die, etc). You will begin to live life in the *now* but in an intentional, deliberate, and disciplined manner.

As you begin your day, focus only on what must be done *that day*. Once you have mentally assembled the proper course of action, focus from that point forward on smaller increments of success. For example, one day at a time, one workout at a time, one exercise at a time, one rep at a time, etc.

This method should be used in every area of your life. One day at work, one list of tasks to do, one task at a time, one item at a time to complete that task, etc. The old saying "Take one day at a time" is much too vague and is rarely an effective strategy over time. It must be broken down even smaller. Instead of looking at each new day as twenty-four hours you *have to get through*, see it instead in one-hour increments, three twenty-minute sections in an hour, four five-minute sections in twenty minutes, five one-minute sections in five minutes, and so on. With practice you will discover which increment works best for you as everyone has their own unique concept of time. If you focus only on the very next section or slice of life, you will begin to notice that time flies! You will also gain a daily sense of accomplishment as you will be in the habit of completing goals far more often, rather than having to wait weeks, months, or even years for reward.

Many workout programs have failed due to *oversight* or *looking to far down the road* as any other reason. If you have 100 lbs. to lose and you are only a couple of days into the workout, it seems hopeless. But if you only focus on the first exercise, the first rep, the second rep, the third rep, etc., you will be through with that exercise in a matter of minutes and can then start the process over with the next set.

Also, stay off the scales for a while. It will only discourage you. You will physically see your progress in time. Besides, what you weigh is *never* important! It is only a guide. I've known many body builders that never step on a scale. They realize they are heavier than average. They are merely going for a particular look. What really matters is where you personally feel comfortable. Many people can carry a bit more weight comfortably and attractively.

Each time you finish a rep, then a set, then an exercise, then a workout, you have taken a giant leap forward toward your ISP! I call this method *learning to count again*. I have tailored this process to fit my individual needs. You can refine it to whatever extent works well for you personally. Here's an example of a typical exercise set for me:

    Push-ups Intended number of sets = 4
    Intended number of reps per set = 20
    Set Number 1
    Start Count = 1, 2, 3, 4, 5
    1, 2, 3, 4, 5
    1, 2, 1, 2, 1
    1, 1, 1, 1, 1 = Finished set

Do you see how I broke the set down to make it less intimidating? When your muscles are fresh—that is, at the beginning of the workout or at the start of a new set when you are rested—the mind has no problem wrapping itself around twenty repetitions. But as you begin the exercise and the body starts to send unfavorable signals to the brain (crying), you have to readjust your thinking if you hope to complete the set.

Remember that it is your *mind* that needs help, not your body! The body is merely a mechanism. It will do (to the best of its ability) whatever the mind tells it to do. But the mind is sympathetic to the body and tends to immediately stop any activity that causes discomfort.

This is where the soul comes in as head of household and forces the mind to, in turn, force the body one step closer toward your goal. It is true that you must change the way you think, but that change is made in your *heart*, not in your mind. The mind is simply doing its job, putting into motion the desires of the soul. Fortunately, you won't have to concern yourself with the thousands of simultaneous operations physically and biologically necessary to make this happen. Your brilliant brain can handle the task with ease! All you have to do is instruct the mind as to your wishes, and in turn, the mind will instruct the body.

You can now see why this whole control issue is so important to every success in your life. Unlike past methods, you cannot simply force your mind and body to attain a certain long-term goal, without considerable conflict along the way. This is especially true when you have a staggering distance to travel. By breaking your goal down into smaller, more realistic daily goals, you will focus all your efforts more efficiently, and you will never go to sleep at night feeling like a loser or a quitter.

Before we close this chapter, I want to reiterate the basic fact that we *all* start out equal. Each of us is born with amazing God-given potential. We just need to learn how to control it.

Keep in mind that your body has an extreme built-in mechanism to survive at all costs. While you need to get a physical before starting a hard core regimen, once you have a green light, you should not be afraid to push yourself beyond what your body is accustomed to. "No pain, no gain" comes to mind. You cannot expect significant change in mind or body if you are not going where you've never gone before!

Remember that the mind and body only adapt to the *average* activity in your life and no more! It's not like your mind is born with the complicated equations for calculus, nor does your body pack on all this extra muscle just in case. In order to change your mind and body, you have to present a need, but even more than that, it has to be a *regular need*.

With that in mind, each time you start an exercise, do whatever you've been able to do before, then just a little bit more. It doesn't have to be much—just *more*. When you count out your repetitions, do the number you usually do, then one more. If the reps get too numerous, do the same number of reps; but instead, raise the weight by just an ounce or perhaps a pound or two. This is why they call it body *building*. It is not called extreme makeover. The more you move up, the more you build.

In like manner, when you endeavor to learn something new with your mind, study one chapter, then another couple of pages of the next chapter. Take something home with you every time you study. Never allow yourself to say, "I didn't get anything out of that!" Always force your mind to acquire something new, even if it's just one piece of knowledge. All knowledge is pertinent to life, even if it isn't something you are particularly interested in. The point here is to push your mind and body beyond their normal standard of living.

On the other hand, don't get ridiculous. Change comes in small increments. Don't try to beat the system by jumping too far ahead in a single step. Of course you are anxious to succeed, but don't become a know-it-all that annoys everyone around them. I know such a person. They are never wrong about anything, and they always seek to make themselves look smarter than everyone else. No one likes a show-off! Truth be known, *no one* knows everything!

In like manner, don't be the ridiculous show-off that packs way too much weight on the machine or bar, struggles to get each rep, thereby doing every rep incorrectly. If you can't do it right, controlling the weight on each rep in both directions, then it's too heavy! Don't worry about what you believe others are saying about your strength. You're not there to show off but to fulfill part of your ISP!

Most gym rats have no definable goal or goals. They're just addicted to working out and like the results. My wife and I have seen numerous people that have worked out for years yet haven't changed (on the outside) at all. That's okay as long as they feel like they are getting something out of it. In reality, everyone should see some sort of external change as it is the body's natural response to continuous work, no matter what the motion might be.

If a guy works every day breaking rock in a quarry, he can't help but get large forearms and shoulders as these are the two main muscle groups responsible for this motion. If a woman wears Stilettos every day, she will grow stronger calves. I used to know a bricklayer that had one huge forearm on his left arm and a forearm half that size on his right arm. He lifted thousands a bricks a day for years on end, all with his left hand. Even though the bricks were only a pound each, the continuous repetition over the years sculpted his body accordingly. Like it or not, one motion or one movement done in a highly repetitious fashion will ultimately change your body. But the higher the demand is raised, the better the result. However, it does make a difference as to what kind of result you are looking for. We will link particular exercises with specific goals in a later chapter.

For now, just understand that your mind and body already have what you need to succeed. When the chips are down and you don't believe you can go another step, read another page, memorize another verse, pump another rep, perform one more sit-up, or run one more minute. Outside of focus and *learning to count again*, there are a several built-in mechanisms that will get you through these tough times.

One time-proven remedy is adrenaline. We've all heard the story of how an eighty-year-old woman rushes back into her burning home against the warnings of the firemen, puts an 800-lb. piano on her back, and carries it out on the front lawn. Then there are the endless real-life accounts of individuals that have lifted automobiles off crash victims and torn car doors off the hinges. And, of course, we all love the numerous stories of war heroes, forsaking self-preservation, carrying an injured comrade many miles through rugged territory to safety. You call it adrenaline… I call it God-given ability!

Once again, this provides a proven means by which to attain the unattainable in life! Through the proper use and distribution of this one preexisting chemical, we can think deeper, run harder, speak firmer, lift heavier, stay focused longer, climb higher, and learn more intently!

We all have a super-human down inside. Sometimes, they turn out to be a super hero as well! This doesn't just come to us on the spur of the moment, rather it always there, somewhere deep down inside, just waiting to be summoned. So if it's always there, it's just a matter of becoming efficient in calling it out.

I recall a man in the Bible by the name of Samson or "Man of the Sun." Samson was only a man but was granted *supernatural* power by God in order to stand against the Philistine army, as well as perform many heroic feats. He once grabbed an attacking lion and killed it with his bare hands, ripping it to pieces. He is also known for slaying one thousand Philistine soldiers with the jawbone of a donkey. Having defiled God by breaking the Nazirite vow from birth (through the folly of a deceitful woman), he became a prisoner of the Philistines, who gouged out his eyes and put him to work grinding grain. As the Philistines gathered to celebrate their pagan god's victory at the temple, Samson was brought in, put on display, and chained to the main support pillars of the temple. Samson prayed that God grant him back his full strength one more time so that he might seek revenge. God did so, and Samson brought the temple crashing down, killing more Philistines in his death than he had during his entire life.

I know what you are thinking. "Samson received this supernatural power from God." I concur. I would retort that Samson was still just a man, which confirms that God worked through his mortal body to produce this strength. While you may not invoke the full scope and enormity of Samson's strength (although you might), who am I to say to what extent God will lend his strength to any one individual when they faithfully call on his name in their moments of need? The inference remains constant: God lives within you, and you are limited only by your faith in what he can do through you! The Scriptures to back this up are endless, but here are a few of the more familiar verses:

> *Ask* and it will be given to you; *seek* and you will find; *knock* and the door will be opened to you. (Emphasis mine.) (Matthew 7:7, NIV)

Throughout my years in the ministry, many have said to me, "I have asked, sought after, and knocked, but nothing has happened!" To which I reply, "Then do it again!" The key seems to be *persistence*! Listen to the very next verse:

> For *everyone* (emphasis mine) who asks, receives; he who seeks, finds; and to him who knocks, the door will be opened. (Matthew 7:8, NIV)

I don't hear any exceptions in there, do you? And finally,

> You do not have, because *you do not ask God*. (Emphasis mine.) (James 4:2, NIV)

Need I say more?

These Scriptures (and many others) proclaim the unlimited power we may summon by merely speaking words. When we petition the God of heaven in any venture, our true potential goes from natural to *supernatural*!

There are several ways you can make use of this power. First, as we have discussed, you can call it out by trauma. While this can be handy, it's an unexpected reflex, and for obvious reasons, it is *not* the preferred method.

Then there's the *hyper-mode* in which you experience something so exciting that you gain a momentary increase in strength. This would normally occur in a state of euphoria, like when your team wins the championship game, your child is headed to the tape on the last lap of a race, or Publisher's Clearing House shows up on your doorstep with a giant check. All these situations cause an unexpected burst of physical energy that is most often useless, utilized only for the purpose of screaming and jumping up and down!

It is possible, however, to summon this awesome force at will in moderation. If you watch a power lifter, boxer, swimmer, runner, skier, skydiver, etc., just before they compete, they get hyped up, psyching themselves up for what is about to happen. This causes an increase in heart rate, respiration, and yes, adrenaline! Rather than just casually making a cold start, they get pumped up in order to gain more strength, endurance, and even courage.

This method is well-known among seasoned professionals but also works wonders for the less enthusiastic scholar or athlete. Using this concept to your advantage in overcoming a whiny body or a negative attitude will give you the crucial fuel necessary to accelerate through the remainder of each course, section, or exercise. It will also give you the additional strength to push upward beyond your comfort level or zone. The bottom line here is to get excited about what you are about to undertake. Get pumped up! The mind and body perform so much better when they are enthused about the task before them!

Also in association with adrenaline, there is another term that runners refer to as runner's high or a second wind. It can best be described as a *euphoric* sense as the body suddenly skips from near exhaustion to exhilaration! By effectively recognizing the state in which this situation occurs, you may be able to duplicate it many times over. It is important, however, to have patience when using this method as it comes at different times and by different means for most everyone I've talked to. It requires that you not give in prematurely when near the point of failure. But if you're willing to wait it out, you can do an about-face in the latter portion of your study session or workout routine, from retirement to relentless!

All these ideas are in effect *mind games* that you can play with yourself for the sole purpose of overcoming inevitable barriers. There's no shame in doing mentally whatever you must to reach your goal. (I don't believe they're illegal either!) But if none of these techniques make you feel silly or subconscious, hold on cause I've got one more that is sure to make you stick out in any setting.

We have already established in early chapters that the mind is the one organ that is not confined to the body. It is free to move about in any direction it wishes, without the confines of time, space, or reality. So if you have this wondrous portal available to you, then why not use it to whatever means you will?

When you were a child, did you ever imagine that you were a superhero? You probably possessed many super powers as well, with absolutely no limits as to what you could do. Well? (Yes, you know what I am about to suggest!) Why not be superhuman once again? What's the harm? (Other than some handcuffs and a little white jacket!)

I'm not suggesting you wear a cape to the library or gym (although I have seen some guys wear a superman shirt). I wouldn't make a lot of weird sound effects, nor would I leap over tables or weight benches in a single bound! Might I suggest that this mainly be a *mental* exercise? Just imagine yourself to be whatever motivates you best, keeping the hero inside for now till you can actually back it up! Make sure that you retain the ability to separate reality from imagination. As ridiculous as this might sound, it absolutely works! Envisioning your ISP on a regular basis is a palpable part of attaining it. How you imagine yourself getting there is completely up to you!

Finally, I could not close this chapter without hitting on what is certain to be the most prolific argument *against* physical exercise.

1 Timothy 4:8 (KJV) warns, "Bodily exercise profits little, but godliness is profitable to all things."

First, let me say that I wholeheartedly agree with these words! No doubt about it, *physical exercise* is only profitable while here on earth and, therefore, could become a useless distraction if overdone or accomplished for the wrong reasons. If it becomes an obsession in a quest for vanity, then obviously you would need to reassess your motives. Also, it would be inadvisable for the Christian man or woman to spend more time at the gym than they do in daily prayer, meditation, and Bible study.

But this verse has likely been as often misinterpreted as any other. First of all, it did not say "Bodily exercise profits zero." Rather, it says, "Profits little." While so many well-meaning brethren whip this verse out predictably as a means of criticizing those who are disciplined in exercise, they regularly misconstrue its true meaning in order to benefit their particular circumstance. Whether this is intentional or not, I do not know.

As a minister myself, I will admit that it very easy to fall into the trap of interpreting scripture to *fit the need*. It is for this reason that I choose to believe the best of all who have taken the stance that physical exercise is a wasted effort. It becomes particularly interesting when the one standing staunchly on this precept happens to be very much out of shape and has trouble walking up the stairs to the pulpit without losing their breath.

I argue that if the body is the temple of the Holy Spirit and we are made in the image of God, blessed divinely above all creation, put in charge of maintaining this temple presentable before God, then would we not endeavor to do everything possible to accomplish the same?

Arguments have been made from the pulpit for ages in regard not only to wasted time, to the physical damage done by excessive exercise. I've heard everything from "getting hit by a car while running" to "knee replacement due to running too much" as a means to convince the masses that physical exercise is ungodly! Before one casts a single stone, they might assure that *they* too are not guilty of the same sin but in a different manner.

I cannot recount the number of fellowship dinners I have attended where the local preacher was excessively overweight. In more than one instance, I have visited members of the congregation that suffered a heart attack. In the majority of these instances, the doctor concluded that "a lack of exercise" as well as a high fat diet were to blame. In other words, it was blatant neglect of the physical body that nearly cost them their life. You can't tell me that they didn't know they were living an unhealthy lifestyle.

So what does all this insinuate? While exercise can unquestionably be overdone, a *lack* of exercise and the refusal to abstain from overeating, as well as eating that which we know for certain is bad for us, is as much a transgression as the former. If we neglect this temple of the Holy Spirit to such a degree that we *kill* it, are we not guilty then of dying by our own hand, seeing that we are the only party that puts hand to mouth?

There's more research today on the deadly effects of overeating and the sedentary lifestyle than ever before. If our purpose on earth is indeed to "seek and save the lost," then shouldn't we do *everything* within our power to assure that we are as healthy and as mobile as possible? If we cannot seek the lost by our own accord, then we have defeated ourselves in the very work we so earnestly sought and are commanded to accomplish.

I've heard many wonderful sermons in regard to the Great Commission. "Go into all the world and preach the good news to all creation. Whoever believes and is baptized will be saved, but whoever does not believe will be condemned" (Mark 16:15–16, NIV).

These were Jesus's final words to his disciples before ascending to heaven. If truly my charge from Christ is to go, then I must assure that my ability to go is all that I can physically muster. Granted, we can go through the means of many different medias nowadays, but in any case, "go" is a verb inferring motion.

By the cruel hand of age and disease alone, I, one day, will not be able to go any further. But in the mean time, I must do *everything* that *I* can do to prevent either of these foes from hindering my efforts prematurely. I personally would not disparage another for their efforts to stay mobile. Criticize if you like, but be careful also that you have your own temple in the best order you can plausibly assemble before the almighty God.

Let's read that verse one more time from a different translation. 1 Timothy 4:8 (NIV) says, "Physical training is good, but training for godliness is much better, promising benefits in this life and the life to come."

This sheds a whole different light on the matter than the more popular translation. Timothy was a young man, no doubt in the prime of his life and, therefore, physically fit. His intent was not to criticize bodily exercise altogether but rather to confirm that it is only temporary in benefit. He was making a comparison between the *mortal* and *immortal* aspects of our existence.

While the mortal part of our existence is not to be our primary focus, this, in no way, denies the truth that we must first pass through the one to get to the other. With this in mind, let us strive then to pass the present stage with the ability to give God *all* of our "heart, mind, and soul," and yes, our body as well! This attitude alone, the culmination of these three entities within us (i.e., soul, mind, and body), each fine-tuned and sharpened to their ultimate potential, is the only means by which to truly offer Christ our obedience to his final command, "go."

God outdid himself when he created man and woman. In doing so, he expanded the confines of the soul, allowing us to *reach out* from within. What you do with the intricate piece of transportation you've been given is entirely up to you. But what it is capable of doing, well now, that's a different question altogether.

Jesus said, "Whatever you ask in my name, that I will do, so that the Father may be glorified in the Son" (John 14:13, ESV). The key to receiving what you ask from the Father is to ask for that which will glorify God and his Son! Go ahead, I dare you to ask.

Stop sitting around being mediocre! In order to feel good, move about efficiently and effectively, and go after everything else you want in your life, It is important that you put your body into submission. Somewhere down inside, there's a newer, better *you*, just waiting to get out. Stop suppressing your own inner strength and potential! Permanently disembody procrastination! You no longer have any need of it. Have your soul inform your mind, to inform your body that there's a new sheriff in town! Reach down deep inside and get the best out of yourself!

## Chapter Five

# Improving Your Self-Image

I once felt that the most tragic man was the ambitious man who lacked opportunity. After many years, I am now firmly convinced that this is not true. The real catastrophe is the great opportunities of this wonderful world without men and women of ambition and vision who want to embrace them!

> Until you dream, there isn't a mold. Until you speak, there isn't a promise, and until you move, there isn't a path. Do these simple things and you manifest the universe, as you know it. (Author unknown)

We have only to look around us to see people groveling in economic poverty, while opportunity, with her great tasks and rewards of life, eagerly stretches her arms to us as we open our eyes each morning, forgetting and forgiving any neglect of the past. The poet Walter Malone (1866–1915) so aptly said, "Each night I burn the records of the day. At sunrise… every soul is born again." [14]

But having said that, it needs to be said again that for the most part, people are the way they are because that is the way they *see* themselves! It was Shakespeare who observed, "Of all knowledge, the wise and good seek most to know themselves." [15]

But we're not all constituted in such a way that our success in life consists of decreasing our limitations. Is it possible, however, for us to have a clearer conception of what those limitations are so that we can make our supreme business to decrease them?

Most of us are very poor critics of ourselves. We can easily criticize others and discover what is wrong with them, and we can quickly build an argument for our *own side* of the situation. But it is far more difficult to be a *self-critic*—to take the situation in our life and sit down with it and frankly say, "What did *I* do or what have *I* said that has contributed to this situation?"

I have a formula by which I observe all reoccurring calamities in my life or in the life of others. This formula is so simplistic, yet it can be applied to literally every parameter of our world. If something continues to go wrong over and over or if a hurtful or chaotic event happens more than once, then there is likely a *common denominator*. Just look for whom or what is present in every single incident and you will likely find the culprit. Look in particular for a person, place, or thing. But the hardest part of implementing this formula is the ability to be honest in your mathematics and therefore face the often-solemn sum of your equation. For many times, I find that in each and every instance that one common denominator is none other than *me*, *myself*, and *I*.

There is likely none among us who is living up to his or her own possibilities. If you feel like your life is full of chaos, with lots of trouble and worry, just turn the searchlight on yourself. Is there jealousy in your heart? Is there envy or opposition? Then maybe some self-discipline is in order. You've got to clear out those old, festering sores of the heart. Perhaps you've lied about someone. Perhaps you've been unkind. Perhaps you've slandered and gossiped. Perhaps you've been *little* when you should have been *big*.

How can we effectively transmit our ideals into action so that they can have sway in our lives? The answer is, we have to begin in our hearts. When you clear away all that clutters up the channels of the inner *you* and they are cleansed, the head then becomes rarified, with all the old animosities uprooted. It is only at this point that we can begin to effectively trek forward toward new horizons of hope. Clean up your own life and you will find an influx of power to which there is no limit! The mere fact that none of us is living up to his or her best does not preclude the possibility that we can!

The troubled fact that we have to face is that in this complicated world we are living, the very atmosphere is charged with frustration and assault upon unity and harmony continually sows discord. We are in total chaos! And what is true of society as a whole is also true of our little individual world… the one inside us that is so important to us.

The world is basically and fundamentally constituted on the basis of harmony. Everything works in cooperation with something else. In the entire physical universe, every law is intertwined with every other law, and the cosmos is integrated by one harmonic whole. When from any direction discord enters in, trouble naturally arises. What is true of the cosmos (of which we are part) is also true of your life and mine in the little orbit in which we live.

While the majority insists on walking around in a self-perpetuated cloud of denial, men and women of intelligence and integrity constantly observe the *possible self*. This is truly the most effective method by which to move upward in life and is for certain the only honest way to live.

We live today in a world of finger-pointing where everyone blames someone else. We have seen this type of conceded flippantness of late from common businessmen to the commander and chief. The very definition of a leader implies that "one takes responsibility for the people and events under his command." That includes those things for which he *is not* directly responsible. (It sort of goes with the job!) Even the laws in our land perpetuate this concept. If a minor child commits an offense, the parent is held responsible as well. Why? It is for the obvious reason that children are under your authority (or should be!). I have personally lived this reality.

Those of us who have worked in a management position or in a position of leadership know full well that we are responsible for the actions of every person under our command. The company or the military couldn't care less whose fault it is. If it happens under your watch, then, baby, you own it!

If you stop to think about it, the need for management is the direct result of our incompetent nature. If each and every human would merely take responsibility for themselves, imagine what an impact this one attribute would have on our society and, in turn, the world! Management positions would become a thing of the past as workers would become completely organized and self-motivated, completing each and every task throughout the day without the need to be prompted. If something goes wrong with their work, once again, the worker would take responsibility for the situation and rectify it without the need for escalation. The truth is that no one likes to be *managed*, yet by our innate impotence, we demand the same!

Though it is not possible to keep disease, discord, and confusion from touching us entirely, it is possible to keep one's life in such a divine harmony, that the effects of these external pressures upon us are minimal. Constant self-evaluation, and *re-evaluation*, will reveal that there is strength and beauty there—nothing fragile or weak. We change our lives for the better when we begin to rather dwell on the great, positive, creative, and unlimited forces with which we have to do.

Mainstream society is putting an ever-increasing pressure on companies as employees lean harder and heavier on management than ever before. You will only truly become independent in life when you see the inner strength you already possess and begin to rely solely on your own abilities. In every task, every goal, every worthwhile effort, begin to see yourself as *self-capable*!

As a free-climber scales a precipice completely alone without the safety of a rope, every move is entirely reliant upon *self*. The climber becomes fully aware that each and every hold is theirs to verify, and the resulting consequences are exclusive to them alone. There's no one there to check his or her work or correct a mistake. Every climber surely realizes the weight of their decision before taking the very first step upward and, in doing so, takes full responsibility for his or her actions.

Take control of your very next step in life! Each time your foot hits the pavement, let the direction be *intentional*, with full intent in the endeavor for which you are about to embark. Begin to feel the weight of every step you take, and rid your subconscious mind of the concept of a scapegoat altogether!

And while we're at it, just accept the fact that you're going to make a few mistakes along the way. You and I are only human, and with that very definition comes the reality of messing up from time to time. Not all of your decisions will be wise ones, and not every turn at bat will be a homerun. But whatever you do, take responsibility for the choices that you make. Don't fall prey to the spineless examples set forth continually by the leaders of our country, those who stand with conviction on one day only to deny the same at a later date. Hello, we have the video! Saying what you mean and meaning what you say is a part of wearing your big boy pants. You either want to be all grown up with important responsibilities, or you don't! When you hit an obvious fowl ball, take credit for it. After all, you're the one that hit it! Simply walk back to the plate, and try to hit a better ball on the next pitch!

Within this new concept of self-responsibility and self-reliance, set no barriers for yourself! Admit no barricades or obstacles! You really are somebody! I mean that! In fact, I know this to be true because God made you that way, "in his image" and in his likeness! There is much more to *you* than meets the eye.

Having said that, I have a question for you to consider. "Who is your best friend?" If you immediately thought of someone other than yourself, then maybe you should think again. Another interesting question is "What do you think of yourself?" A simple query, yet your answer is staggering because what you think of yourself determines the ultimate achievement of your life. You cannot rise above the concept that you have of yourself. Nothing else will so gear you to accomplish superior results, as the belief in your *own* greatness, and your *own* enormous possibilities! There is no known law by which you can achieve anything successful without first expecting it. You absolutely cannot rise above that in which you can envision of yourself. In other words, if you can't see yourself doing something, then you won't! He who can *thinks he can*! But the opposite also holds true: he can't who *thinks he can't*!

The reason we have to work on our self-image all of the time, is because it is constantly being dented, hammered upon, and bashed in by a plethora of everyday circumstances. Unfortunately, self-image is not a one-time fix, but rather a life-long endeavor. We must continually adjust, then, readjust, in response to the unending, and often unexpected, changes and turns in our life.

As we already confirmed, your self-image today exists because of experiences you've had in the past. But the experiences of the past have not actually made you the way you are, but rather they have made you believe the way you are. All of your thinking, feeling, and acting are consistent with the image you have of yourself.

Maybe you've started selling yourself short. A few failures here and there have shattered your confidence, and you've lost your nerve. Pilots refer to this mental condition as *losing your edge*. You continue to doubt your own ability, or else you focus far too much on the "what if" scenarios in your life, thereby developing a false sense of fear over things that will likely never happen. You need to ask yourself whether you are getting a full, accurate, and honest evaluation of your assets and liabilities. If your concept has grown weak and your self-image is low, it is time you make a survey of your real potential.

There are numerous aptitude tests and trained counselors that can help you "find yourself." But remember that only *you* can reclaim the vision you once had, the desire to create and fulfill yourself. "Dreams?" you say. Yes, but *dreams* are the stuff from which all things materialize.

Life simply cannot be productive, without a good self-image. Life should be happy, vigorous, and rich. God brought us forth to live, not to stagnate. Happiness is a habit, and you can acquire this habit by venturing into the science of properly conditioning the three concrete elements in your life. It starts in your soul, where you dream, hope, fear, grow happy, become sad, remember, envision, invent molehills, and climb mountains. All this then spreads to your mind and body, whether *real* or imagined. All humans act according to what we *imagine* to be true about our self, and the environment around us in which we live. Whether or not it is truly factual is another matter altogether.

The reality is that we build our own self-image through a series of past experiences. How our mind interprets these mental imprints and, in turn, how we react to these experiences is the ever so crucial condition by which we find ourselves bound. Both successes and failures figure into this equation and therefore our final analysis. We also seem to be very heavily influenced as to how *others* react to us. (As if how someone else feels about you will change whom you really are?) The point is that you do have a picture of yourself. Everyone does. It may be false. In many cases, it is. But the important fact is that you *act as though it were true*. This is where the rubber meets the road in your life!

We must then work hard to change the mental picture we have of ourselves, for out of it comes the attitudes of life. All our actions and emotions are consistent with our self-image. We act like the sort of person that we *think we are*. Can you then begin to see the importance of creating a self-worth living with? If your self-image is an enemy, it uses the failures of the past to undermine you and make you a failure in the present.

Make friends with yourself. You must like yourself! You must learn to love being *you*. It's all right to love yourself, to like being yourself more than anything else. We're not talking about mere arrogance that tries to over compensate for insecurity but a genuine, healthy, self-love that is content with being exactly who you are. Of course, we should never be so full of ourselves that we cannot see room for improvement, but we must enjoy being who we are, never desiring the life of another. Your life and mine are just as important and have just as much potential for greatness as the life of any other! God makes no mistakes! You were imagined before you even entered into your mother's womb, and you were created with absolute intent!

Too often we measure ourselves by someone else and convince ourselves of the entirely ridiculous idea that we should be different or like somebody else or even everybody else. We reason, "If I only had that person's body," "If I only had that person's smile," "If I only had that person's charisma," "If I only had that person's beauty," etc.

Why do we feel this way? Your only challenge in life is *not* to rise above others but only to rise above your previous self! Every person on earth is inferior to some other person in some way or another. I cannot hit a golf ball as far as Tiger Woods, I cannot equal Chuck Norris as a martial arts expert, I cannot sing like the late Elvis Presley, and I cannot speak like Sir Winston Churchill. I cannot compare to them in some respects, but may very well outshine them in others. It is mine to respect myself for who I am, where I am, the way I am, to the degree that I cannot change.

But what changes I do make should never be in an attempt to mimic someone else. I am an individual, full of useful and specific uniqueness that only *I* possess. It is our individualism that sets us apart from the rest of creation. You are neither inferior nor superior to your fellow man.

Much of the resentment surrounding the ongoing debate today in regard to discrimination rises entirely from the feelings one group of people have, in regard to what they *perceive* another group of people thinks about them. First, let me reiterate that true freedom is not something any man can give you. Also, it makes no difference as to what *someone else* thinks about you, but rather only what you think of yourself. Without exception, every human, in one form or another, has experienced discrimination at one time or another, from some other human.

While the popular use of this term is used nearly exclusively in regard to race and skin color, its implications are far broader than that and, in reality, touches everyone. But the point here is that success in life is not based on how much other people like or accept you. It is rather based completely on what you think of yourself, and there are thousands of success stories from every race and gender that verify that truth. A person can easily rise above that which *others* think of them, but they will predictably *never* rise above that which they think of their self! In regard to discrimination, one must only concern their self with what they know to be true, *not what others say is true*!

The important thing is to be happy with yourself because that's the only person you're ever going to be! Can you change the image you have of yourself from miserable, unhappy, and negative to positive? Yes, you can! But the way others treat you will have no bearing on whether or not that happens. In the end, your success and failures are the sum of your choices in life. *Choose* to like who you are, and experience the endless opportunities that this one attribute alone will afford you!

But maybe you aren't so fond of yourself at the moment. There are a few things you can do to alter your self-image. First, it is absolutely essential that you forget past failures. Bury them! My father used to say, "The past is a cemetery, not a cesspool." In other words, you should bury the past, not wallow in it! No person has ever lived without problems, and no man or woman, regardless of how successful they may be, could deny having ever had a failure or two along the way. Think only of the past in reference to your successes. Bury your failures, regardless of how many, and think on your successes, regardless of how few.

One of these days, I hope to write a book about nothing other than my failures for no other reason than to observe all that I have overcome in my climb to the top. It will not be published but solely for the purpose of reflection. Believe me, it will be a rather large volume!

Elsie Robinson wrote, "Things may happen around you, and things may happen to you, but the important thing is what happens *in* you!"[16] For it is what happens *in* you that will ultimately change the direction of your life! All the rest of life's bombardments are nothing more than that—a series of asteroids hurled at our outer core that leave dents on the outside only. They cannot penetrate the inner-self unless we open ourselves up to allow it. Seal yourself off from the barrage of daily negativity that others insist to live in, and steer your vehicle unabashedly toward your ultimate destination in life!

An unknown author wrote, "Our doubts are traitors, and make us lose the good we oft might win for fearing to attempt." Far more dreams are lost from the traitor of *doubt* than by the actual failure to attempt it in the first place. In other words, we lose only because we do not believe we can win. If that is your attitude, then I can assure you that you might as well not try at all!

And while were on the subject, let me admonish you to rid your vocabulary of the highly popular, yet truly impotent little word "try." In fact, "try" is the lowest form of commitment! In reality, it is nothing more than an excuse. It is an open door, a back door, and an escape hatch that leaves an emergency exit in every so-called commitment. If you tell someone that you will *try* to do something, you are basically telling him or her that you really don't want to do it at all. "I will" is a totally different concept from "I'll try." The same is true of what you tell yourself. If you mentally concede to "try," you will not succeed. Remember, try is the *lowest* form of commitment! Eradicate that flimsy alibi for good!

When we scrutinize the lives of great men and women, we see their failures (as we are first prone to do), but their history is not so much a history of failures but a history of persistence! So one would have to ask, "Maybe then I can win too?"

Consider this man who was defeated for Legislature in 1832, failed in business in 1833, second failure in business in 1833, suffered nervous breakdown in 1836, defeated for Speaker in 1838, defeated for Electorate in 1840, defeated for Congress in 1843, defeated for Congress in 1848, rejected for land offer in 1849, defeated for Senate in 1854, defeated for Vice-President in 1856, defeated for Senate in 1858, elected President of the United States in 1860! His name, of course, Abraham Lincoln. Care to tell me about *your* failures again? [17]

Isn't it amazing that a man with such a history of failure would eventually be elected to the highest office in the world? He could have allowed his failures, and the ridicule of others, to prohibit any additional attempts at success, dragging his past failures behind him as a prisoner drags his chains. Given this string of unlucky events (although I'm not an advocate of "luck" either), he might have surmised early on, "I am destined to fail!"

We so often become imprisoned by the past, believing somehow that rising above a multitude of failure would be criminal. That's because this is how the world views failure. Let's get this on straight once and for all! Failure is not a catastrophe but rather just one of the many *necessary* steps on the road to success! If you're afraid to fail, you will find yourself frozen in your present situation, unable to act at all! The greatest clandestine truth (although it is actually no secret at all) with which to arm our self-image is to remember your successes, however small, and to erase from memory your failures, however large!

You must not only bare your failures, but you must also stop inventing problems! Worry damages your self-image. Worry is seeing yourself in the light of what *could* happen to you. Worry is imagination used negatively. While it is true that we all do worry and unhappy things do occasionally happen, it is also true that worry rarely makes a difference and only causes us to spend much of today in dread of tomorrow. There's a difference between worry and caution. One is fear, while the other is based on common sense. It is just as easy to visualize yourself positively, thereby creating a future worth living for.

Napoleon Bonaparte once wrote, "The human race is governed by its imagination."[18] Granted, intelligence, talent, breaks, and oh yes *luck*, all play a part, but none of these is as important as the mental picture you have of yourself!

While every position of value in life is important in one way or another, why is it that some people become bank presidents while others sweep the floors? Why do some collect rare art while others collect rare garbage? Why do some students make As while others just get by? The common denominator is usually in how people see themselves. We can think ourselves into disaster or into triumph!

As a child, my father related a comical story that happened to a friend of his many years ago. There was a neighbor of his in Texas that was deathly afraid of snakes. She was carrying out the garbage one morning and left the back screen door slightly ajar. A small snake crawled in and was lying on the back porch. When she walked in and discovered the snake, she was so frightened that she ran next door to her neighbor's house, screaming, "A snake! A snake!" As she entered her neighbor's door, she passed out.

Assuming a snake had bitten her, the neighbor did what any good neighbor would do and called an ambulance. When the paramedics brought her around, they asked her what happened, to which she screamed again, "Snake!" and then passed out for the second time.

She was rushed to the emergency room where doctors were standing by with shots of anti-venom. As she arrived in triage, she came to long enough for the doctors to ask her, "Where did the snake bite you?" whereupon she passed out again!

After an hour or so, she finally woke up long enough to regain her senses. It was at this time that she informed them that she hadn't been bitten by a snake. She had only seen one!

The doctor had been treating her for so long that he now had a predicament. What do you do with a person that's been "anti-venomized" that's never been "venomized" in the first place? Now according to my father's friend, they simply got a snake, and let it bite her! But that sounds like a tall Texas tale to me! It's a fact though that this woman spent many days in a hospital from *not* being bitten by a snake! She had *imagined* herself into disaster.

That's what Solomon meant when he said, "As a man thinks in his heart, so is he." He's implying that we are the products of our hearts and that your present thinking regulates your desires, ambitions, goals, and future accomplishments. You can increase your capability in any of these by simply increasing the concept of yourself.

The story is told of a young man who had enrolled in a self-improvement course. After the first session, he stopped the instructor in the hall and asked if he really thought he could learn to speak, express himself, and be successful. Then came the statement that's so common to most of us: "You see, I've always had an inferiority complex," he said.

It was almost funny. This young man stood six feet seven inches tall and had been a hockey player in Canada. He could have whipped half a dozen men thrown together!

When asked why he thought he had an inferiority complex, he replied, "I guess I've never done anything right in my life!" He went on to say that his father had shown little love for him and had never bragged on him during his childhood. In short, he had always felt that he was a failure in his father's eyes because of constant criticism.

There's no denying that our childhood seems to have an overwhelming influence on our future. In retrospect, many a potential dynamo in life was squelched as a child due to two factors: (1) the parents damaged the child's self-image and (2) the child allowed the damage their parents inflicted to determine their future success.

Case in point: Johnny is four years old. His mother comes to his room and announces, "Johnny, Mother is going to the backyard to work in the garden for a couple of hours. While I am out, you may continue to play in your room. Now Johnny, you are not to get the cookies and milk out while I'm away because your coordination will not permit you to handle them properly at this time. Do you understand?" Johnny nods at his mother although he probably didn't understand anything other than "no cookies and milk!"

But because Mom placed the original thought in his head, after an hour or so, Johnny quietly makes his way to the kitchen. He opens the refrigerator door, drags up a chair, reaches for the milk, sets the milk on the cabinet, climbs up on the cabinet, reaches a drinking glass, pours the milk in the glass, and stands on his tiptoes to reach the cookie jar on the top shelf. (Why are they always on the top shelf?) He then gets three cookies out of the jar and carefully places it back on the shelf. He climbs down, drags the chair back to its original position, puts the milk back in the refrigerator, and walks to the cabinet to retrieve his snacks. All has gone well up to now and is far beyond what Mother gave him credit to accomplish in the first place. He turns to carry the goodies to his room thinking, "No one will ever know!" About that time, the glass of milk slips through his tiny hand and falls on the kitchen floor, shattering in a thousand pieces! His mother comes running in to find her little boy in the middle of an awful mess. Without thinking, she shouts, "Johnny! I told you to stay out of the cookies and milk! Now go to your room and don't come out till I tell you it's okay!"

Johnny goes to his room. But in his mind, that glass of milk is more important to his mother than he is. But he's only four years old and so, he gets over it in a short amount of time.

A few days later, he goes with his mother next door. They have a little boy Johnny's age by the name of Tommy. Johnny and Tommy love to play running games. The only trouble is, this is Tommy's house, and Tommy has made that corner by the big flat-screen, turning around the lamp table and zooming between the coffee table and the sofa hundreds of times. He can do it flawlessly. Johnny hasn't made that trip quite so many times, and as he comes between the coffee table and the sofa, he slips a bit and knocks over the decorative vase belonging to Tommy's mother.

In embarrassment, Johnny's mother grabs him up and shouts, "Johnny, you are the most awkward child I have ever seen! Can't you stand up? You go to the house and straight to your room, and don't come out till I tell you it's okay! I'll deal with you later, young man!"

Johnny does exactly what he is told, all the while believing in his mind that the vase is more important than he is. He then begins to develop a tremendous sense of inferiority.

And so it happened to each of us in one form or another, whether by an overbearing parent, an insensitive friend, or a combination of many other possible sources. Where I have a problem with this whole "blame game" we so often find ourselves in whence we fail is that while our past tends to have an overwhelming affect on our present and future, what *others* think about us has no consequence in relation to who we truly are or ultimately become.

It's easy enough to make excuses (some of which are legitimate) about why we continually fail. But the fact of the matter is that until *you* take control of your own self-image, you will find yourself, like so many others, stuck in an endless cycle of failure, drowning in your own self-pity.

How do you expand your self-concept or enlarge your self-image?

1. You must enjoy successive, successful experiences. This means to tackle jobs and finish them. Each one will subsequently give you needed courage and mental muscle for the next task. Get the feeling of "a job well done!" A winning feeling comes not only from winning but also from giving appropriate credit for the same.
2. Visualize yourself as capable of getting the job done. This means you must acquire the talent of daydreaming constructively. Build a few castles in the air. This is good for you, just don't try to move into them quite yet! You still have to pay for them!

Psychologists tell us that our subconscious mind can't tell the difference between a real experience and one that has been vividly imagined. So *daydream* yourself as a success at whatever you endeavor to be.

Just remember to *love being you*! When you become so pleased with being who you are and when you're so at peace with yourself, then you'll have no difficulty with achievement and no problem getting along with others. (An important trait on the road to success!) You cannot expect others to have confidence in you, if you possess no confidence in yourself. Most people are so unhappy with who they are that they can't imagine wanting to me more of the same. Instead, they seek to be someone else. Enjoy being *you* to such a degree that you constantly strive to achieve more of whom you are already.

So much of where we are headed is shrouded in ambiguity. We really have no idea as to what exact path the future will take. As a result, we write a new instruction guide daily, discovering most of our mistakes only *after* the fact. No one person possesses an entirely correct owner's manual. What's most important is that you are not afraid to take a stab at authorship in your own life. Go ahead, write a new chapter in your life based solely on your imagination, your experience, your technique, your successes and failures! You will discover that most of the time, *your* method is no more wrong than the next man or woman's method.

It's a crying shame that the majority of companies fail any longer to lead in the area of self-importance. Having lost the belief that their employees are far more productive when they develop a positive self-image, they have chosen rather to beat the employee into the ground, convincing them that they aren't good enough, smart enough, or ambitious enough, if they cannot rise to the levels of fellow employees or meet some silly quota based on a computer report or graph. Corporations are "graphing" us to death, thereby elevating the unequalled invention of the computer to the lowest depths of disaster!

We now overanalyze everything! What's more, we actually pay some know-it-all to sit behind a screen everyday deciding who is and who is not measuring up. That is, according to their standard or the standard that some machine has determined to be *normal*. Who is to say that the person that developed such a system is not insufficient also?

We have taken the personal exceptionalism out of our society and replaced it with the "clone technique." Everyone is a robot, expected to mimic everyone else. And you know what? It isn't working. Productivity is at an all-time low! The reason is obvious. When you remove the variables that give us individuality, you have, in fact, removed the very thing that brings about self-improvement, reliability, and trust worthiness. In other words, if a person is faced with falling short due to circumstances that are unseen to the computer graph or lying to save their job, which route do you suppose they will take? In spite of integrity, our instinct of self-preservation will generally kick in automatically, and the majority will do whatever they must do to keep their job.

Many corporations have spent the last several years convincing the individual that they are worth absolutely nothing, and are therefore completely expendable. They give the employee the needed equipment to do the job but no longer invest in the overall attitude of the individual.

Left with no self-worth or sense of value, the average worker is now convinced that their job is on the line every day (which it is) and that regardless of how much extra effort they actually put forth each day on behalf of the company, they will eventually be terminated by a heartless, unimpressed, could give a flip… computer!

We are shooting ourselves in the foot! We really must allow each other to be *different*! It's normal to think differently, act differently, and perform differently. That is the one commonality we all share, and it is the very foundation from which industrialism rose in the first place. Despite the insistence of businesses that "customer service" is number one, their actions are much to the contrary and speak volumes about their actual concern for their consumers.

The personal touch is permanently out the window. They simply want your money, and that's it! From basic utilities to the grocery checkout, no one cares about genuine service or common courtesy but have instead mistakenly believed that we *have to* purchase their merchandise or service. The company that first realizes what they've lost will also then be the first to soar to the top! Wake up, corporate America! You're losing some exceptional people, as well as your valued customer base, due largely in fact to a genuine lack of gratitude and the almighty computer!

In this digital age in which we now find ourselves fully engulfed, we have become more informed but less intelligent than ever. Are we truly more conscious about issues that matter, or are we just more aware that someone had a bad hair day?

The amount of information circling the globe at any given second is staggering, yet one could easily estimate that at least 75 percent of it is mumble-jumble, good for nothing more than to entertain the masses. In fact, we seem obsessively addicted to the drug of never-ending entertainment!

No longer are young people interested in simply going to the park to play ball or hooking up with a few friends and hiking down a local trail. We now look to electronic gadgets to feed our ever-growing need to be amused. It takes only a momentary glance at any one of the thousands of public arenas around the world to get the big picture. Everyone is staring down, whether sitting, walking, or even driving. No longer does anyone simply look up. We are, one and all, mesmerized by these infernal gadgets!

My father used to call the television "the idiot box" or the "boob-tube," relating to the fact that it has some kind of hypnotic trance on the multitudes, forcing us to sit mindlessly before a square box for hours on end, in a "receiver only" mode, offering nothing of ourselves intellectually. Literally, we look forward to spending an entire day, willfully sitting on our backsides, staring into a rectangular glass. But within the past ten years, the power of the force has moved from the TV to the I-Something. We now walk around in a trance, glued to a smaller version of the "boob-tube."

We are also *nosier* than ever before. We want to know the latest gossip on literally everyone, whether good or bad, with no regard as to how it might affect the one that we are talking about. It is a world gone wild! We have lost our sense of substance, like a kid ordering a McDonald's happy meal no longer caring about the meal itself but only interested as to what new toy is inside. We are out of control, obsessing over every new piece of technology and in turn using the same in many damaging and nonproductive avenues. The question is, "Are we truly more intelligent for it, or are we in fact just real good keyboard operators?"

We have been lead to believe that we must rely on machines to make life interesting and fulfilling. What's more, we believe that without this technology, we would be less informed and therefore less intelligent. But actually, nothing could be further from the truth.

It is not possible to fully duplicate the vast intricacies that are *you*. While machines must be programmed for one or more specific duties, *you*, on the other hand, possess an ability that cannot be matched. Out of all the species on earth, out of all the computers, pads, phones, etc., *you* are the only entity on this planet (or as far as we know, in the universe) that holds the title of both *computer* and *programmer* all in one!

Unlike electronic equipment and software that continually requires to be updated by another entity, *you* continually talk to yourself, whether inwardly or outwardly, receiving software updates around the clock at an incalculable rate. Tell me you are not "Fearfully and wonderfully made!" Tell me that *man and woman* are still not the raining intellectual force on planet earth! And that will never change!

If I could draw your mind on paper, I would draw a square. (Not because I think that's the kind of person you are but because that's the kind of pictures I draw!) At the top of the square, I would draw a line representing 10 percent of the total mass, which would represent your conscious mind. At the bottom of the square would be the remaining 90 percent representing your subconscious mind. It is in this lower 90 percent region that most of your thinking occurs, taking in approximately seventy-two thousand images per minute, thereby readjusting the way you think, the way you operate, and your ultimate purpose, every second, of every single day, of your entire life. We perceive, believe, and then behave.

This is where we get the phrase "I changed my mind" from. Listen to those words again: *I* changed *my* mind. It is obvious that *I* refers to *me* and that *my* refers to *me* as well. No one else changes our mind. *You* are the only one that has the authority, the access, and the password to change your own mind. So *you* are both the computer and the programmer all in one. Astounding!

You need to begin to see yourself in a whole new light. For you are far more than the stereotyped image on the outside by which the world predominantly judges you. You must occasionally *step outside* of your body and look back at what is left. Just a shell, a set of wheels, that's it! Without a doubt, it's what's *inside* that makes you special and unique. The problem most of us have is in remembering that we are indeed much more than what we see in the mirror. We have others to thank for this. In fact, when this happens, we have, in essence, allowed someone else to hack into our mainframe! We have unconsciously permitted an outside programmer to redefine our mission, as well as the way we view our self.

In no other area of life (including our personal computer) would we allow someone else to be so privy to our deepest thoughts and desires. It is a security breach of the highest level! When you allow a friend, relative, or even a perfect stranger to reprogram your life, it is equal to handing your car keys over to someone that has never driven before. This is true because *your* vehicle is totally unique from any other. No one else could possibly steer your life effectively if they have no understanding of the many complicated facets that make *you* who you are in the first place. However, receiving positive guidance and direction from someone is totally different from just handing over the keys.

What I'm about to say will shock you. You don't need a computer to run your life! Are you okay? Yes, it's true! Men and women have been living life to the fullest for centuries without it. What you *do need* is a proper self-image! So let's work on that!

If there were one thing you should absorb from this chapter more than any other, it would be the following formula. It was developed by my father many years ago and, in essence, sums up the totality of successful living:

DL = GGE + PS × PSI.

Let me define that for you:

Dynamic Living = God-given Equipment + Principles of Success x the Proper Self-Image.

Now here's something we can get our teeth into!

Notice simply in passing that the multiplying ingredient in our formula is a proper self-image. This is without a doubt one of the top issues we will address in regard to where you want to be in life.

By the time we are eleven years old, most of us already possess a well-developed sense of inferiority, thanks in part to the world and the rest to our own lack of personal awareness.

Perhaps the problem with defining dynamic living or success is that there is no true universal measure for success. But here is a partial answer: children have a way of cutting through to the heart of an issue and showing an unbiased and objective view of things.

An acquaintance once told of an exercise his son was asked to participate in at school. The young boy was told to write a sentence about his family. So after dinner one evening, he went to his room and began working on the project. In a few minutes, he came to his mother with a carefully printed sentence that read, "We are rich."

Well, his mother certainly did not want a sentence like that going around school, so she tried to explain to the boy that though his father worked for a financial institution, it did not automatically mean they were rich. She told the boy that his father did deal with money, but that it wasn't all his, and that his dad's job could be considered similar to many other jobs dealing in other products. The boy returned to his room to try again. In a few moments, he returned with another sentence that read, "We are poor."

By this time, Bill and his wife realized that some further explanation was required. They explained that they were not poor either. Just because you are not rich does not mean that you are poor. Their family was somewhere in between. So the youngster returned to his room for a third try. He finally came downstairs with the sentence, "We are happy." These are the words from a child that tell quite a story about what you and I *should be* looking for in terms of success.

In a child's mind, it didn't matter whether his family was rich or poor. Those are just words. This little boy had perceived that the object of true success and contentment is happiness! While it is true that we're all in need of good health, education, shelter, and a sufficient amount of food, success is not measured by material considerations. It is most accurately defined by a sense of well being derived from the way you live!

Let's return to our definition of dynamic living. Remember that it begins with God-given equipment. As you have probably deducted, I firmly believe that *everything* begins with God! I further believe that he makes all this possible and that unless I remain at one with him, my chances for any *real* happiness and permanent success is very slim indeed.

The fact is that we *all* have this God-given equipment, yet the average person uses only about 5 percent of its total capacity. As we have already confirmed, we each have our own personal computer within the brain that is inhibited only by the limitations we put upon it. This includes a perfect memory. That's right, *perfect*! Now, some of us have a little trouble with recall, but we have a perfect memory just the same.

To my knowledge, nearly every dissertation on memory (if I haven't forgotten) starts with a story of forgetfulness. Here's one that I have heard often. A fellow goes to a psychiatrist and says, "Doctor, I really need help! My mind is going. I can't remember anything for more than a couple of seconds!"

"How long has this been going on?" the psychiatrist asked.

With a puzzled look, the patient says to the doctor, "How long has *what* been going on?"

Okay, I know. Cheap shot. But it's true that every image, every sound, every spoken word that is recorded to memory is available for recall. However, "recorded" is the key word here. Many people cannot remember a particular instance or fact because they simply didn't record it in the first place. Committing a fact to memory requires that the image be imprinted from the moment of influence. If not, it would be like taking a picture without any film or memory chip in the camera. You can snap all the pictures you want, but if you fail to ready your mind for absorption and then *focus* first, it is likely that this one frame in time will never reappear again.

Numerous books and articles have been written on the subject of memory, and even several courses have been published. All the ones I've read about seem to contain the same basic subject matter with only slight variations in method of presentation. (I am not endorsing a particular one over any other.)

There are three basic steps to remembering names, faces, and basic information: (1) concentration, (2) repetition, and (3) association. You first have to be interested enough to catalog the information at hand and to thereby initially focus. You have to *concentrate on it*, *repeat it*, and then *associate* something familiar with it in order to make it easier to locate. I will be the first to tell you that I am bad at remembering names and probably not the best at recalling detail from long ago. However, this does not mean that there is anything wrong with my memory. It simply implies that I am having trouble with recall. It has been a while since I thought about it, or I didn't focus enough originally to imprint a permanent record.

Now, where was I? Oh yes! You have tremendous God-given equipment! You have an incredible body and a genius mind to boot! But having a great body and mind is not enough to obtain true happiness. Remember our formula? If you expect to achieve *true* happiness, then you must first achieve the proper self-image. But a proper self-image is not a factor in the equation, but rather the sum of the whole. In conjunction with God-given equipment, you must add the principles of success. These are basic in nature and have already been discussed to some degree to this point. Here they are:

1. Set for yourself a goal of excellence.
2. Put first things first.
3. Go the extra mile.

Success is not limited to these standards alone, but nearly every other aspect falls under one of these three headings. Let's take them one at a time.

First, set for yourself a goal of excellence. "I tell you the truth, if you have faith as small as a mustard seed, you can say to this mountain, 'Move from here to there' and it will move. Nothing will be impossible for you" (Matthew 17:20, NIV).

Let me begin by saying that the word "excellence" does not infer that your goal has to be special to anyone else. It merely needs to be something that you personally find worthwhile. The reason or reasons for which it is important need only be important to you. After all, you're the one that has to do the work to achieve it, and thereby pay whatever price it costs.

I'm often amused at how predictably we judge others for the amount they give for a particular acquisition. I recently heard of a Russian billionaire's daughter who gave the single most sum of money for a New York City residence. She paid a staggering eighty-eight million dollars! That amount of money would be enough to support countless families for an entire lifetime. Yet what she gave is really none of our business and, I suppose, is only relative to what she or her father believes she's worth.

Would any one of us deny our children an extravagance if we could indeed afford it? Granted there would be a limit, but exactly what dollar amount could you place on the true love you have for your child? (With my finances, it looks like mine is about the price of a new car!)

Our goals are no different. Since it is I that must fork over the full amount (no matter how much it will ultimately cost), it is only I that should concern myself in regard to how much I pay. How much is too much to pay for a particular something? That's a question that only *you* can answer.

I have to admit that while the prospect of scaling Everest sounds intriguing, it is doubtful that I would be willing to pay the price that most have paid in order to stand atop its awe-inspiring summit. For the few who can boast that they have done it, I take my hat off and can only utter the words: "Wow! I don't know how you did it!"

Yet, that is not entirely true! I *do* know how they did it. Maybe not so much in actual technique, but in *spirit*, I can completely relate. At some point in the past, everyone that has ever put a boot to her majestic slopes has had a first-time vision of doing so.

It is highly unlikely that anyone ever climbed Everest by accident! (If so, there's a much shorter route to get around it! Contact me and I'll elaborate.) Every great achievement in life starts with a goal of excellence. It may sound crazy at first, and it might not even sound feasible. But neither of these is a required qualification when it comes to fulfilling the inner longings of the soul.

I'm certain that when telling their friends and family about their intent to climb the world's highest mountain, most were met with some level of criticism and doubt, if not out and out forbiddance! The 29,029 feet would be an easy distance to travel along the ground. In fact, it's just shy of five and a half miles. However, straight up is an entirely different proposition!

I have not only flown a jump plane on numerous occasions but have also parachuted. (Since the pilot is required to wear a parachute, I figured I might as well know how to use one!) Even though I was well into my twenties when I first jumped, my father and mother were horrified at the account! But despite admiration for those who have ascended Everest and my general numbness to heights, I have little desire to put forth the effort to climb a giant rock. There's nothing at all wrong or even abnormal for wanting to do so, it's just not my cup of tea.

And hence we arrive once again around the big circle of life, back to *individuality* and its countless varieties. It is the stuff that dreams are made of and the very thing that makes life interesting to any degree. Imagine if we all did exactly the same things in life. What a boring place this planet would become. But when we turn on the news to discover a "human spider" has scaled another skyscraper without a rope or net or when we watch in amazement as a skilled tightrope artist walks along a two-inch trolley cable miles above the ground, we are intrigued by the astonishing accomplishments of others and are thereby inspired to rise above our own mediocrity.

In spite of the risk, we all set goals for that which challenges our imagination and tickles our soul. If the goal has little or no significance to self, the chances of achieving it decline dramatically. You will only habitually pursue that which brings the greatest since of satisfaction. We may *make* our body get out of bed each morning and show up to the job we cannot stand, but until we arise to hound the *one thing* that fulfills our unique definition of destiny, our heart will not be satisfied, and our life will not be complete. Set for yourself a goal of excellence! It is entirely up to *you*, just exactly what that goal will be!

Second, put first things first. Ephesians 5:15–16 (NIV) says, "Be very careful, then, how you live—not as unwise but as wise—making the most of every opportunity, because the days are evil."

The word "redeem" here means to "buy or purchase," then to "set free." Here it infers that we should recover our time and in turn use it for a more important cause. There is no greater waste in life, than that of wasted time. It is the one commodity there is only one of and once spent vanishes forever into oblivion. Though we are all guilty of this senseless habit, it's evidently crippling and, by life's end, the most obvious reason for failure.

My thoughts on this are thus: if you had more time to pursue your dreams, the chances of success are exponentially greater! In essence, you're not finished in this life till your heart stops beating! It is the clouded notion that we possess an unending amount of time that often leaves us in a deficit in life.

We procrastinate, fail to facilitate, and in general, goof off till it becomes painfully obvious we have not the time to complete our life-long ambitions. This one fallacy is the *one and only* factor that possesses the power to make you fail! The only goal (and the most important one) that you can achieve after death is eternal life with God. But while on this earth, you are bound by the strict confounds of time, which is consistently and predictably unforgiving to the sloth.

To redeem your time means to retrieve it. In other words, you can't take it back, but you can take what is rightfully yours! Be ever so cautious when deciding whom and what you will spend your time on. *Time* is your most precious asset and is therefore the most generous gift you can give anyone. Make certain of your path *before* you step. Assure that the conclusions of your mind coincide with the desires of your soul. This is why it is so vitally important to avoid hesitation toward any worthwhile purpose. Not only is the old adage "The sooner you start, the sooner you'll get done" true but also "The sooner you start, the more time you have left to acquire your goal." Make sense? You're on a set budget. Spend wisely, my friend!

Finally, number 3: go the extra mile. Matthew 5:40–41 (NIV) says, "If anyone wants to sue you and take your tunic, let him have your cloak as well. If someone forces you to go one mile, go with him two miles."

This concept obviously dates back to biblical times, and I have read that it refers to a period when the Romans were ruling over the Jews. In those days, a law was interjected where *any* Roman could demand *any* task, from *any* Jew for a distance of one mile. That was the law—one mile, no more, no less! It is said (although to my knowledge not provable) the Jews were so enraged by this law that they went out one mile in every direction from their home and drove down a peg. I might add that they cleverly named it their *one-mile peg* (which I believe to be brilliant!). Let's imagine what this law must have looked like when applied to the life of two ordinary citizens of both nations.

A Roman soldier is walking down the road. He spots a Jewish man off working in the field. He shouts, "Hey you! Come carry my bag!" Oh! It's so galling... so displeasing!

The Jewish man throws down his hoe, trudges over to the fence, climbs over, snatches up the bag, and grumbles, "Let's go!"

The Jew walks down that old dirt road slightly ahead of the soldier as fast as he can walk. Neither of them says a word to each other. He comes to that one-mile peg, throws that bag down and shouts, "That's it! One mile! You can't make me go any further!"

The Roman reaches down to pick up his bag and thinks to himself what a rude and impolite people the whole Jewish nation must be! Meanwhile, the Jew turns toward home and is quickly out of sight. His temper grows greater with each and every step. He fumes, "I'd kill him if I could!" The wife sees him coming and thinks, "I'd better tread softly tonight!" When his children see him coming, they run and hide.

Now, let's take that exact same law, under the exact same circumstances only this time the Jew believes and applies the principle of Matthew 5:40–41—go the extra mile—in his life. The same Roman soldier is walking down the road and spots the same Jew off working in the field.

"Hey you," he says, "come carry my bag!" Well, it's every bit as galling, every bit as displeasing, but the Jew believes and applies Matthew 5:40-41 in his life.

He runs over and props his hoe against the fence. He then hops over, snatches up the bag, and says eagerly, "Hi! My name is Jason. What's yours?" The Roman is taken aback! He's not used to this type of behavior. Hesitantly, he replies, "Marcus." The two then begin to walk down that old dirt road side by side.

While they are walking, Jason floods Marcus with questions. "How many battles have you been in?" "How many times have you been wounded?" They come to that one-mile peg and just keep right on going.

Finally, Marcus stops and puts his hand on Jason's shoulder. He says, "Jason, you're just too good of a guy to take advantage of. We passed that one-mile peg way back there!"

Jason replies, "I know we did! But I'm having so much fun! I never get any further from home than what you see right here! Please just let me accompany you up to the walls of the city."

When they get to the gates of the city, Jason smiles and gently sets the bag on the ground. Marcus takes off his grooved leather glove, extends his right hand of friendship, and says, "Jason, because of you and your actions today, I think more of the Jewish nation than I ever would have. If you ever need a friend in the Roman army, I hope I'm there!"

Marcus turns and walks away with joy in his heart. Jason runs back home with a spring in his step and a song in his heart all because he believed and applied the principle of the "extra mile." His wife sees him coming and runs out to greet him. The children see him coming and hurry to jump in his arms. His wife says through a grin, "You went the extra mile, didn't you?" He asks, "How did you know?" She replies, "Because it always makes you happier! It always makes you softer! It always makes you easier to get along with!"

Now that we have examined what this principle might have looked like in ancient times, let's imagine quickly what it would look like if applied today. We can use my home as an example.

It's early morning, the alarm sounds, and once again, we engage in what I refer to as the Chinese fire drill. Total chaos! Mom is running around in her housecoat, the kids are late for school, Lindsey can't get in the bathroom because Kara's tying it up, and little Christian cannot find one of her socks! You know the scenario.

But in the middle of all this mass confusion, there is one island of peace and total serenity: me. I'm getting ready for work, buttoning up my coat, when all of the sudden the top button pops off and goes rolling across the floor (likely rolling under the fridge all the way to the back). It always happens at the most inopportune time!

So I bring the coat and button over to my lovely wife and kindly ask, in a low voice, "Honey, would you please sew this button on my coat?"

To which she replies, "What? I don't have time for this nonsense!" She abruptly grabs the coat out of my hands, whirls around, and walks swiftly to the bedroom, spouting off with every step! She fishes out her sewing kit and quickly threads a needle. She then half-heartedly sews that button on, throws the coat back at me, and shouts, "Next time, tell me when it gets loose!"

Before I walk away, she demands, "I need some more grocery money!"

To which I say, "More money? Are you kidding me? What did you do with the money I gave you? You think money grows on trees? Just get by, woman!"

She yells something unkind back at me as I put my coat on and trudge out the door. I stand on the front porch with my head down. On top of everything else, as luck would have it, it's pouring down rain! As I stand there in a puddle of water getting soaked to the bone, I hang my head. I might as well have stayed in bed! I mean, I'm whipped! At this point, there's no hope of having a good day!

Now, let's imagine the same family, under the exact same conditions. Only this time, the entire family believes and applies Matthew 5:40-41, the principle of the "extra mile" to their lives.

Same Chinese fire drill. Mom is running around in her housecoat, the kids are late for school, Lindsey can't get in the bathroom because Kara's tying it up, and little Christian can't find one of her socks! You know the scenario!

But in the middle of all this mass confusion, there is one island of peace, and total serenity: me. I'm getting ready for work, buttoning up my coat, when all of the sudden the top button pops off and goes rolling across the floor (likely rolling under the fridge all the way to the back). It always happens at the most inopportune time!

So I bring the coat and button over to my lovely wife and kindly ask in a low voice, "Honey, would you please sew this coat on my button?" (Just making sure that you are paying attention!) To which, she replies, "Well, of course I will!"

She smiles and gently takes the coat out of my hands. I follow her to the bedroom where she retrieves her sewing kit, gently threads a needle, and begins to painstakingly sew the button back in its place. While she sews, she looks at me and says, "You know, baby, you're such a great man! You work so hard every day for this family, and we really appreciate it! I just want you to know that any old time your button gets loose, you bring it to me, and I'll gladly sew it on for you!" She securely fastens that button, helps me put the coat back on, and gives me a kiss on the cheek that would make you want to slap your grandma!

As I turn to leave, she quietly asks, "By the way honey, could I please have some more grocery money?"

To which I reply, "More money? Of course!" I immediately reach for my wallet, and as I'm thumbing through it, I say, "You know, sweetie, I just don't know how you make ends meet with what I give you! You're definitely some sort of magician when it comes to our finances, and I greatly appreciate all you do in dealing with the bill collectors and all! Here's fifty dollars. No, wait, here's a hundred dollars! Better still, take my credit card!"

As I walk out the front door, my heart is racing joyously! I'm on fire! "You'd better look out, world! I've got a tiger in my tank!" It may be raining, but there isn't a chance my feet are going to get wet cause I'm walking on air! Nothing can stop me today! Why? Because my family believed and applied Matthew 5:40-41—the principle of the "extra mile"!

My father raised me to live by this standard in everything I do. He referred to it as the "and then some" principle. Over the years, I have found that when I live by this faithfully, I am amazed (but never surprised) at what this one little principle will do. Here's what this would look like in your life:

- When your children ask for your attention, give it to them…and then some!
- Do what you would normally do to help your spouse…and then some!
- Perform the work that your boss and company would expect of you…and then some!
- Give a dollar to the guy that's on the corner with a sign every day…and then some!
- Put your regular tithe in the collection plate next Sunday…and then some!
- Do your usual workout at the gym…and then some!
- Give God everything that he would ask of you…and then some!

So there you have them, the three main principles of success. Although there are many more and variations of the same, if you will simply discipline yourself to apply these three little guidelines on a daily basis to you life, you will become unstoppable! There's nothing difficult about them nor are they magical in any way. But what these three pocket-sized generators can do in your life is beyond comprehension to the average person.

But it is only by applying them *faithfully* that one can fully comprehend the magnitude of their impact! The real work in any venture will always be *yours* to do, but it is imperative that you take the built-in qualities you already possess and activate them with an effective catalyst. In truth, many of us already know what we could do to alter our destiny. We simply fail to activate the sequence that would do so. That's precisely what these three directives will do for anyone who dares to initiate them. But like every other aspect of achievement, they will be useless without persistence and consistency.

Hopefully you can now begin to see our formula developing. Once again it's

> Dynamic Living = God-given Equipment + Principles of Success × the Proper Self-Image.

So in order for me to aspire to what we all want in one form or another, that being Dynamic Living, I have to take the God-given Equipment that I already possess, add in the Principles of Success we just talked about, and multiply them both by a carefully constructed Self-Image. Once again (as is the theme of this book), success is a combined effort of the three concrete elements of our human existence: body, mind, and soul. The preceding formula is merely a means by which to coordinate the three.

The latter step in this formula is the direct result of and proportional to the proper application of the first two principles. By disciplining your mind and body (God-given Equipment) with the Principles of Success, you will begin to achieve and ultimately succeed in whatever your soul has moved your mind and body to do, and in turn, the Proper Self-Image should naturally materialize as well. I say *should* because how your self-image eventually looks has a lot to do with how much credit you give yourself for job(s) well-done, and what kind of humility you temper your overall person with, both internally, as well as externally to the world around you.

If you fail to use a proper balance outwardly, or in your heart, you will become extremely conceded, and the resulting catastrophe is both devastating and predictable! "Pride goes before destruction, a haughty spirit before a fall" (Proverbs 16:18, NIV).

It's okay. In fact, it is a *must* to give yourself credit for a job well done. As long as you understand that you are only in competition with *you* and with no one else, then you will continue to succeed, and people will admire you for your accomplishments. But no one likes a cocky individual that throws harsh language around, trying to look tough, flaunting his or her achievements! Most people that display such arrogance are also continually guilty of stretching the truth. I personally know a few people like that. They are extremely annoying, as well as difficult to believe. And let's face it, stretching the truth is one and the same with lying. Although others may tolerate them on a daily basis, no one respects a liar. So by building up their own self-image in a public manner, they have, in turn, lost all respect and credibility from others. That's a lousy trade.

The reason people often engage in such nonsense is quite obvious in that while they may have accomplished something good, it's rarely enough to get the perpetual attention they crave. Their ego deems self-worth insufficient, so they fail to understand that it's the *accomplishment* that's important, not the *recognition* for the same. Hence, they constantly seek everyone else's approval for every little thing they do! They become convinced that without this *false* sense of importance, they no longer amount to anything in the eyes of others.

In the end, they become a big disappointment to themselves. But the truth of the matter is that only those closest to us sincerely care if we succeed or fail, so you almost always absorb the destruction alone. The reason why these egocentric types fail is because they lacked the proper foundation that a healthy self-image is built on in the first place. Show me a bragger, and I'll show you an insecure, immature, disproportioned self-image. I don't know of anyone that likes to be around such a person, and I have personally known many such individuals that have alienated both friends and family with this painfully annoying trait. It's not cute, funny, or impressive, so start from day one to avoid it, or risk losing everything! Love yourself, tempered with the utmost humility, and others will naturally love and accept you as you are in return.

Accept both your successes and failures as mostly a personal matter. As you persist to offer praise for others, that same praise will naturally be returned to you in proportion to your achievement. All too often we seek far more praise than a particular achievement warrants. We all need love and acceptance, but these are gifts to be earned, not expected and certainly never demanded!

All your thinking, feeling, and acting are consistent with the image you have of yourself. We each have a different picture on which to focus, but in every case, it has more to do with what we *believe* we are capable of achieving than any other source.

- "I can't quite smoking!"
- "I can't lose weight!"
- "Eggs make me sick!"
- "I'm always late… It's just the way I am!"
- "I'm a terrible procrastinator!"
- "I can't cope!"
- "I'm always a nickel short and a day late!"
- "Everything I touch falls apart!"
- "I could never be a public speaker!"

- "I'm too short!"
- "I'm too tall!"
- "I'm not that smart!"
- "I've never been good at tests!"

These are all self-images. They may be inaccurate, but they are just a few of the destructive self-images you often hear that people have of themselves. What's strange is that it's just as easy to have a *positive* self-image, as opposed to a *negative* one. It's as if we are beating ourselves up! You surely know by now that there are plenty of other people in the world who are more than willing to do that for you! There's no need to join in the fight!

Now listen to the contrast of a positive (not cocky) self-image:

- "I'm pretty good at sports!"
- "I'm a good cook!"
- "When it comes to looks, I can hold my own!"
- "I stay well informed!"
- "I'm just about the right size for…"
- "I believe I can do anything I set my mind to!"
- "I like being me!"
- "If you need someone you can count on, I'm your man/woman!"
- "My special talent is…"
- "I am aware of the needs of those around me!"
- "I know how to reach my goal and I'm on my way there right now!"

Do you hear the difference? There's no need to lie. Just focus on what you are good at rather than continually focusing on what you're not good at. Everyone has talents and abilities, and there will never be another person exactly like you!

People are continually looking for a better life (i.e., a better relationship, a better job, a better home, a better car, etc). But there's something strange I've noticed. Few seem to be looking for a better *me*. They want to improve everything that has to do with being *me*, except actually improving *themselves*. Since this is one of life's profound truths, doesn't it appear rather fundamental that we constantly put ourselves under the microscope for observation and engage in daily self-analysis, in honesty and humility, regardless of how painful that may be? The majority longs to magically transport their current self into a better tomorrow. But how can we set about to improve our circumstances if we refuse to improve ourselves? Who we truly are in our heart of hearts, has *everything* to do with where we find ourselves tomorrow!

Remember too that *anything* can be changed in your life if your attitude deems it doable! Listen to the *real you* down inside the soul. It's trying to express itself outwardly through your mind and body. If you get your soul in check up front, the mind and body will naturally follow.

A healthy self-image radiates an aura of success and confidence that draws people to you like a magnet. You won't have to actively seek approval, as it will rather flow to you effortlessly in great abundance. Just be leery of how you accept it, allowing gratitude and grace to engender in others a healthy respect for who you really are down inside. While we each must seek to better ourselves daily, one thing should always remain constant: be the person others can count on to be steady and unwavering. Once you see yourself as a *person you can live with*, it won't be difficult then for other people to live with you as well, just as you are. Never attempt to be someone you have no desire to be. Just be you! You might be surprised how popular you will become, once you become popular with yourself. Love yourself, enjoy yourself, and by all means, get the best out of yourself! An unknown author said,

If you think you're beaten… you are.
If you think you dare not… you don't!
If you'd like to win but think you can't…
It's almost a cinch you won't!
If you think you'll lose, you've lost!
For out in the world we find,
Success begins with a fellows will…
It's all in the state of mind.
If you think you're outclassed… you are.
You've got to think high to rise.
You've got to be sure of yourself,
Before you can win the prize!
Life's battles don't always go…
to the stronger or faster man.
But sooner or later… the man who wins…
Is the man… who "thinks" he can!

## Chapter Six

# Staying In Control (Don't Let Go of the Wheel!)

What is the basic *driving force* in life? Philosophers, religious leaders, psychologists, and anthropologists have probed for centuries into the nature of man to find the answer to this mystery. In order to see the proper motivational force for man, let's look briefly at some of their discoveries.

An early anthropologist thought that man's basic urge is *survival.* The will to live is a fantastically powerful drive. However, literally thousands of sane individuals have chosen to risk death in order to reach goals they valued more highly than life itself. Millions have chosen to die in dignity rather than live in shame.

Many years ago (WWII), a soldier was wounded in the heat of battle. His longtime buddy wanted to run to his side, but the commanding officer denied the request for fear he too would be wounded or killed. He defied the officer's order and, dodging mortar fire, ran to his friend, put him over his shoulder, and brought him back to the foxhole. By the time he got inside, his friend was dead, and he himself, mortally wounded. The officer was angry. "Was it worth it?" He shouted sarcastically. "Yes, it was worth it!" The soldier muttered through his pain. He continued, "When I arrived, he was still alive, and he said to me, 'Jim, I knew you would come!'"

There are purposes and people more important to men and women than living.

Sigmund Freud explains that the basic drive of people is the *desire for pleasure*. Yet through the years, humans have been known to forsake physical and emotional pleasure for more meaningful accomplishments. Whether engrossed in an important work or spending their life caring for others, people will often deny self-gratification for a greater cause. So it would seem that the majority are motivated by a force beyond immediate satisfaction.

The great psychiatrist Alfred Adler said that man's greatest will is that of power, and that man, as a whole, will do literally anything to acquire it. But power often leads to futility, frustration, and ultimately an overthrow or downfall from the same.

So if it is not *power* that drives us, then it must be: *the will to live*. This would indicate that we are all strictly motivated by the need to avoid death. We're willing to do whatever it takes to assure our existence continues, whether by submission to a controlling force or the use of our own force. But countless stories fill the history books (like the one just mentioned) of brave men and women who, for the benefit of others or the common good, laid down their life without hesitation. If *the will to live* were our only motivation, it's unlikely so many would forfeit that right.

This is a highly important question in that what motivates you—what turns you on to life—is the most distinctive of personality traits. Is it for no reason that court trials often concern themselves with questions of motive?

The discovery of your own personal motivation dynamic will provide the key that unlocks the heretofore, locked doors of your life! It is the very essence that drives you in everything you tackle.

Many would argue that we are each motivated by something different. In a sense, that would be true if you're referring to individual wants and desires. But whether you realize it or not, we *all* share the greatest motivational factor in life. It's the one thing that motivates us above all others, as this one ominous force moves more people than any other single motivation.

The greatest motivating power in *every area* of relationships, business, employers, employees, customers, companies, parents, children, husbands, and wives is a little four-letter word that may come as a shock to some and a disappointment to others. It's probably not something the average person would ever consider. Are you ready? The number 1 motivating factor in life is *love*! That's right! Love!

Now in order to fully understand the significance of this word in conjunction with our motivation in life, it's important that we first achieve a proper definition. First, what is the opposite of love? Most would say, "Hate." That's what I used to think. But hate is not the opposite of love at all. In fact, *hate* is another dimension altogether. So if hate is not the opposite of love, then what is? The opposite of love is "no love." Or you could possibly define it as "disinterest" or "indifference."

This one motivation is present in every aspect of life, both public and private. For instance, a past survey I once read shows that 68 percent of the people that quit doing business at the retail level did so because of the indifference on the part of those who were supposed to be helping them solve their problem or need. Most of us are familiar with poor service. In fact, despite the insistence from retailers and corporate giants that the customer is number 1, actions speak louder than words, and nothing could be further from the truth.

No one seems to truly appreciate your business anymore, nor does anyone give a *personal touch* to his or her service any longer. It's a cold world out there where the only thing most companies seem to care about is billing the customer. If they're good at anything, it's billing! Now, if they could just *bill the correct amount*, we'd be getting somewhere!

While products and technology compete more than ever for customers, the choices to the consumer are endless. Whether you're shopping at a brick and mortar store, online, or catalog, there's usually more than one place to get a particular product or service.

So if people stop shopping somewhere because they feel the company or personnel are disingenuous, what are they really saying? What they're saying (in a round about way) is that they feel unloved. It's true! If the number one thing people are motivated by in life is love, then it is highly unlikely they will continue to do business with a company that does not love them. Plain and simple!

We're not talking about romantic love although there are plenty of advertisements now days that attempt to hone in on the sexual psyche. "If you buy our sexy cologne, you won't be able to beat the opposite sex off with a stick, and *everybody* will fall in love with you!" That's pretty much what they claim. Why would they focus on our love life? Because they have figured out that every last one of us wants to be loved! (Now we're getting somewhere!)

So if people don't feel some sort of love (i.e., recognition, acceptance, or appreciation), then they will instead feel rejection. That doesn't sound like the kind of feeling a company would want their customers to get.

I'm telling you, if more companies would rethink their strategy of reaching the public, focusing more than ever on making people feel loved, they couldn't count their money! People will flock to love because it's their greatest motivation in life! Just look at the overwhelming number of dating sites and the millions upon millions of lonely people that make up their memberships. It is quite obvious that *everyone* is looking for love!

We are essentially the only species on the planet that has a real need for love. Sure, animals enjoy being loved, but it's not a requirement for their survival. But in the same light, if an animal is loved, then rejected, they will act very much in the same way a human would (i.e., sad, lonely, and depressed). Why is that? It's because once a human, (or in some cases, an animal) has experienced the greatest motivating factor in life, they cannot live without it. It's that powerful!

Take away a child's toy, and in time, they will recover. Take from that same child your love, and they'll become an introvert, losing interest in playing, moping around like they've lost their best friend. We humans often wear our emotions on our foreheads. It only takes a short time around a person to discover they aren't getting the necessary dose of love they need in their life.

Men and women alike have a built-in homing device that automatically seeks out love. I'm not talking about biological. I'm talking about affiliation. This is likely prominent in humans because we are the only species that have a self-image. With this in mind, let's give some characteristics of love that people perpetually seek.

## Understanding

We tend to love people whom we feel understands us, and at the same time, we tend to love people we feel we understand. In our relationships such as parent-child, husband-wife, or just friendships, we say things like, "He or she no longer *understands* me." And that's what customers think as well. "They [the business or company] don't understand my need or problem."

Dr. Hugh Russell, psychologist from Atlanta, says people buy services not so much because they understand the service but because they feel the business or company understands *them*.[19]

So genuine HR (human relations) would be a department that has the ability to relate on a personal level to the individual. It's not the coldhearted automated service often found in large corporations that merely sets forth a set of rules or regulations for employees (or the customer base) to follow. True HR would be an individual or a group of individuals relating to another individual with the understanding that this person is different from everyone else, even different from themselves, and letting him or her simply be who they are rather than forcing them to be who we think they should be.

Really, this is the motive of success, both directly and indirectly. There's no such thing as "company loyalty" on the part of the customers. Build your buildings, buy your stadiums, run your high-dollar cable spots, but people—that's where you get your loyalty from. People who care, people who relate to the customer, people who solve problems and meet needs. There's no such thing as an *unimportant* customer.

At the same time, it's not just the customer that makes a company successful. It's the people *within* that continually make a connection between the service and the people. If you stop relating to people one on one, they feel rejected, unloved and will no longer believe you understand their needs.

The *need for love* drives everything we do, whether consciously or subconsciously. We've all been guilty of saying, "I just *love* their service! or "I just *love* their product!" (Insert your favorite product or service here.) It makes no difference what we desire, there's a since of love in everything we do. We go out to eat at our favorite Mexican food restaurant on a regular basis. But why do we eat at the same place over and over? It's because we love their food, service, or atmosphere. Its no wonder the Bible puts such great emphasis on love!

Love motivates us to patience, kindness, longsuffering, and humility. Coincidentally, love also motivates us to purchase things for ourselves or for others and to give of our means to fill the need of someone else. Proudly, America stands as number 1 in disaster relief and charity efforts around the globe.

It's for these and other reasons that we often think of love as a sort of soft, gushy, romantic type of emotion. But surprisingly, it is love that also motivates men and women to fight or even go to war to defend someone or something they value dearly. Once again, *love*.

All people need to love and be loved. They need to be understood for who they are, what they do, and their overall contribution to family and society, which brings us to our second characteristic of love.

## Acceptance

People *need* to be accepted. Their uniqueness needs to be understood. So often we want a conditional love (i.e., "I love you *if*…"). "I love you *if* you get a haircut." "I love you *if* you get an A in algebra." "I love you *if* you quit drinking." "I love you *if* you lose weight."

"I love you if" is nothing more than exploitation. It's not love at all! It says, "I love you *if* you make *me* look good!" That's my condition in order to receive my love. While we want our children to look presentable (a parent's prerogative), what we may be saying is, "Get your haircut so you won't embarrass us, while at the same time you will embarrass yourself in front of your peers." It's a fine line, and we have to be careful when making the distinction between healthy guidance and acceptance.

People need to know that you're okay with who they are, just as they are. While we want to help those who have an obvious deficiency, it has to be done in a loving way, accepting them first and foremost for who they are at the moment. Since true love is *always* unconditional, it makes sense that everyone needs to be loved *right now*, not after they've made a series of changes in order to merit your love.

In dealing with the public, this becomes a tremendous challenge, as customers won't always say things that are kind or act in a particular fashion according to your training. Experience is likely the best teacher in scenarios where someone acts sporadically, saying or doing something unexpected under the circumstances. People don't always look the way we expect nor say what we expect. But nearly every person that becomes upset with us is secretly crying out for acceptance, whether it be a personal matter revolving around you or a company matter revolving around a service.

Companies that refuse to recognize that their actions, whether directly or indirectly, through their services and employees, are making the customer feel unworthy are bound to get the natural response of retaliation and hate. It goes without saying that simply quoting company policy to a customer is an insincere approach in the quest to prove you genuinely love them.

Love has a limitless scope. Give freely of it, and you will attract much more than what you give. With no other emotion, motive, or desire is the mirror of life so evident. So love motivates us as much as any other motive. Therefore, if you fall into the trap of *not loving* yourself, it is likely that you will become your own greatest enemy! It's okay to dislike certain qualities you exhibit, but any flaw can be changed. That's the great part about getting in the driver's seat in your life. From there, you can steer your life in any direction you care to go! So love yourself just the way you are!

The second greatest motivational factor in life is *fear*. Although we have already discussed this motive in detail in another chapter, it's important that we touch on it again. Fear is likely to be the biggest culprit with which you will have to confront in regard to staying motivated.

Fear is all around us. In fact, many corporations prey upon on our fears on a daily basis. Think about it. We buy a particular brand of toothpaste for fear of tooth decay. We buy insurance for fear of something bad happening and not being able to cover our financial burden as a result. We buy tires for fear we won't have good traction.

Fear promotes action. And companies know this. We live in constant *fear* of what might happen, *fear* of what others may think, *fear* for the position we hold. When properly placed, fear can be a good thing. It often motivates us to action and can ultimately make us a better person.

However, too many people are afraid they will make a mistake or that they won't succeed, even if they try, so in turn, they make the biggest mistake of all—that of doing *nothing at all*! This is a tragic failure of a large majority of the human race. Don't be afraid to fail! To err is human. Just because you fail does not constitute that you are a failure. In fact, failure is nothing more than the honest result of attempting to do something better or different. It's a sign to yourself and everybody around you that you are seeking to make a change in something important.

One of the worst fears you will deal with is that of negative criticism. For some reason, we are deathly afraid of what everyone thinks about us. Your soul has limitless power to make your dreams come true, provided you allow it to work unhampered. Few fears hamper the mind as quickly as that of criticism. It can stop you before you even get started or cause you to quit right in the middle of something worthwhile. And yet it is nothing more than the negative influences of another soul, another person no better than yourself! It is a negative influence from an *outside* source.

On the other hand, it can also be a self-generated fear that comes from past failures. If you had already attempted a particular feat and were less than successful, the mind creates a negative stigma around that action and therefore any future attempts at the same. In this case, you now become your own source of criticism. But it is highly possible that your fears are based on nothing more than what you have *seen* or *heard* from *outside* sources.

It may be criticism due in part to past failures someone has knowledge of, or they might just be putting in their two cents as to your probability of completing the goal based on nothing more than their own uneducated guess! Does that sound like something on which you should base your entire future?

The only entity that truly matters in regard to fulfilling your dreams is *you*! Every man or woman that ever accomplished anything great did so by ignoring external criticism. In fact, you must train yourself to completely ignore every input that might have a negative effect on your progress. Shut it out, and then don't give it a second thought. Mulling over what *others* think about your direction in life is worthless as they aren't going to be the one to pay the price nor reap the benefit. Learn to identify *self-generated* criticisms and insist that your mind become a more positive influence. Ignore all negative criticism, whether *internal* or *external*!

Another motivating factor in life that we all have in common is hatred. Believe it or not, hatred is a strong motivational factor that is not always bad. Hatred of people is a strong source of heartache. We often love things and use people when we should love people and use things. Confusing such priorities defeats many well-intentioned individuals.

You cannot have peace of mind while you entertain the kind of anger that brings you to a desire for revenge, or a desire to injure another, no matter what the justification may be. Great men and women have no time to waste on a desire to inflict pain and suffering on others. If they did, they would not be great men and women!

I once heard about a man, seventy years old or so, who, years before, lost all his money in a real estate venture. Taking advice from a friend, he had borrowed heavily in order to invest in vacant swampland on the assumption that in a couple of years, the land would be in great demand for building sites. This did not transpire, the man's notes came due, and he was forced to watch his retail shoe business sold out from under him to pay the debt.

The friend who had badly advised him also lost money. Nevertheless, this man became filled with hatred toward his friend and said he would get even "if it's the last thing I do!" It nearly was. Five years of hatred left him incapable of even doing business. Meanwhile, the friend prospered and seemed far out of reach of punitive revenge. The man who had lost his money at length eventually lost his mind and had to spend six months in a quiet place in the country surrounded by a high wall (if you get my drift).

However, in his last month of confinement, he was sufficiently recovered to listen to an advisor who pointed out to him that his hatred, and the desire for revenge had done far more harm to him than had been done by losing his money. He was persuaded to forgive the friend who had led him into the real estate deal. He even wrote this man, telling him of his change of heart.

When he went back into business, it was with love for his fellow man and the determination to keep his mind filled with positive, constructive motives. Beginning at age sixty, he built a new career at which he once again became quite successful. But most of all, he has *peace of mind*, the one form of wealth that is indispensable.

Hate constructively. Hate immorality. Morality is not a theological issue; it's a *logical* issue! Immoral living saps energy and wrecks the mind, removing happiness and destroying ambition and success. Hate gossip. Hate bitterness. And in your quest for your dreams, hate procrastination! It is without a doubt a relentless self-generated killer of dreams!

By learning to identify your central motivation, you can regularly revisit your purpose for beginning your journey in the first place. If the motivation is flawed, so will be your efforts to reach your goal. Nothing will affect your results to any greater extent than that of motivation.

But even once the proper motivation has been established, we may find ourselves at the foot of yet another obstacle. My grandma used to call it "stick-to-it-tiveness." Such a wise old woman, she was!

When I was a young man, she related to me her view of people that start something but can't ever finish it in relation to her grandmother's homemade biscuits. She said, "Sometimes, no matter how well grandmother mixed the dough, those biscuits would squat to rise and get cooked in the squat!"

That very much appealed to me as it made sense of the reason we often fail at something that seemed so promising not that long ago. We get all motivated, telling everybody we know about our future conquest. But because of our lack of resistance to negative criticism (both external and internal), we "squat to rise and get cooked in the squat!" In other words, we fail to launch due to the fact that we had everything planned out *except* how we planned on sticking with the program. We all need a healthy dose of "stick-to-it-tiveness" in order to reach our heartfelt goals and dreams!

Every self-improvement course I've ever taken has helped me to some degree—some more than others. But as with any other major change in life, we get fired up, excited about the project we are about to undertake, only to find ourselves a few days or weeks later right back in the same proverbial rut!

As we discussed in previous chapters, the mind and body are highly resistant to change, especially when it involves work or pain. It's sort of like you have to make yourself sick before you can get better.

My daughter recently had her wisdom teeth out due to occasional pain, and the fact is that we had already invested over $7,500 in her mouth up to now. Unfortunately, she became the one out of five statistic that suffers from dry sockets and was told it would take about seven to ten days to subside. That sounds like a lifetime when your lower jaw is throbbing day and night! She knew she did the right thing by getting the teeth pulled as they would have only created worse problems with time. But in the middle of her suffering, she began to experience some "what ifs" in regard to her original decision.

Anytime the mind or body is forced to endure pain, the mind becomes extremely negative and even seeks the shortest route to end the suffering. Remember the path of least resistance? It makes no difference as to the ultimate benefits that the present suffering will eventually provide as the mind is blinded by the string of current events to such an extent that it can't see the forest for the trees.

I wish so much that I could give you an easier route toward the dreams and aspirations of your soul, but as the saying goes, "No pain, no gain." Much of what you will experience en route is not really pain at all but merely the whiny disposition of the mind. The moment your mind senses any discomfort emotionally or physically, it seeks to make a split-second decision to discontinue the activity at hand.

*Anyone* can set goals! There's nothing to it! Talk is cheap, and action is in short supply!

Without a doubt, more exercise equipment has been purchased from the comfort of the armchair than by any other means. Sitting in the La-Z-Boy, with a cold drink by your side, armed only with the remote control, I find it easy to say, "That's just the piece of equipment I need in order to get in shape!" Fortunately, the telephone is also nearby, (infomercial, people love it!) so calling in on the spur of the moment is no problem either. Why people choose one particular type of gadget or scheme over another is beyond me. Most are purchased under the guise of the quick fix. "Just ten minutes a day, three days a week" is all one has to devote to get the body of the supermodel on the commercial. While *any* exercise is better than none, this just isn't reality!

Once again, *ordering the equipment* is effortless (except for the fact that you have to put your snack down long enough to dial or else switch hands). When you hang up, you feel an immediate sense of accomplishment as if, in a strange sort of way, you have already begun the program. I have even witnessed people proclaiming to their friends that they are working out when in reality, they have only ordered the equipment to do so, or they have only purchased a gym membership but not yet attended.

The next hardest step is moving the box full of equipment from the porch to the intended room of use. In the majority of cases, this will be the most exercise ever accomplish with this particular gadget. Many are never taken out of the box, and even more are unboxed but never assembled, or else, they sit in a corner, closet, or garage, collecting dust for many a year. Every garage sale has one or more miracle gym amongst the junk.

These items may seem random at first glance, but in fact, they symbolize much more than that. In nearly every case, these rusty and dusty thing-a-ma-jigs represent broken dreams, empty promises, and failed attempts at an important change in someone's life. They signify good intentions at some point in the past, but now they stand as tombstones, engraved with the dashed hopes of some well-meaning individual.

The same holds true with the countless stacks of self-help books, newsletters, tapes, DVDs, and get-rich-quick courses on everything from real estate to penny stocks. I have a mountain of them! But these too represent a sea of failed attempts to somehow make a positive change in my life. I am certain that most people have the *same pile* and, like me, are grasping at anything that might produce a significant improvement over their current situation.

I feel compelled to use the term helpless here, but that is rarely the case. Most have merely succumbed to the relentless and often-unbearable torture intentionally manufactured by the brain in response to something as insignificant as a muscle cramp or shortness of breath. When it comes to financial gain, the majority halts whatever program they started within the first three months or at the first sign of fiscal discomfort. They never really give it a worthwhile effort.

Oh, that we could throw a switch into the off position for a while, just until we get the mind and body past the initial shock. But of course, that's not possible (not unless you're a monk floating two feet off the floor in a sort of out-of-body trance).

The average (I hate that word) person is forced to endure whatever pain the brain and body can hurl at them, and the only authentic relief one gets is when either one or both have adjusted over time to the regimen. Because this is the most crucial period in regard to your newfound direction in life, it is of utmost importance to seek a method by which you cannot only begin but to consistently persist to endure.

It is my intent to offer you several options that will assist you in maintaining your momentum, and in the very least, keep you from quitting altogether! It goes without saying that talk is cheap, and procrastination is at an all-time high in our society. Just think about the number of people you know personally that continually lament over some goal or another that they have always longed to fulfill but, for some reason, can't seem to it get done! It obviously won't do you a bit of good to get all excited about accomplishing something great if you fail to stick with it or never start in the first place. So let's see what we can do to avoid either of these two crippling outcomes!

First, make an honest assessment of your true motivation in the pursuit of your goal. Determine if your reasoning is honorable and worthwhile. To seek something based on pride or revenge is fruitless, and the attainment of such will ultimately lead to your own demise. Once you've determined that your intentions are noble, you can continue unashamedly, knowing full-well that this goal will only make you a better person overall.

But no matter how good the opportunity to better ourselves may be, we can't take advantage of it unless we are prepared to meet the requirements of any successful venture. Proper motivation is only one of several influences to consider. For instance, timing has as much to do with whether or not we will start and eventually finish a task, as any other parameter. Some of the best advice ever written is found in Shakespeare:

There's a tide in the affairs of men. Which, taken at the flood, leads on to fortune; Omitted all the voyage of their life is bound in shallows and in miseries. On such a full sea are we now afloat, and we must take the current when it serves, or lose our ventures.[20]

We have to *seize* opportunity when it comes our way! "Opportunity" is defined as "a good chance for advancement or progress."[21] The key word in this definition is "chance." Opportunity gives only a good chance for advancement, for there is no such thing as an opportunity that's a lead pipe cinch!

The reason I'm drawing out this definition is that many people don't know an opportunity when they meet it. They are misguided in precept to believe that it has to have some sort of *security* attached to it to make it viable. Failure to recognize a good opportunity in regard to your goal may lead to a breakdown based upon illogical expectations and the actual validity of what you are undertaking. This in turn will demotivate the well-intentioned individual, causing the misconception that there is something invalid in the goal itself when, in reality, they just failed to seize or rather jumped on the wrong opportunity in the first place. In retrospect, there is rarely a deficiency in the *unattained* goal. It just needed the right opportunity and good timing of the same, to head out in the proper direction from the get-go. Understanding what a *real* opportunity consists of is a crucial factor of success from that same opportunity.

For example, some people have the idea that once they join a company, it's up to the company to prove itself to them. While most companies are anxious to prove they have something to offer, the opposite also applies in that an employee must also prove his or herself to the company. Inasmuch as the company is paying you, it stands to reason that they should expect a certain something in return for their investment.

The same holds true for those who order the "latest and greatest" exercise equipment from an infomercial, online, or by mail-order catalog. They are convinced that the promises made through the advertisement will be factual, and that in some twist of perception, the company they bought it from is liable for their claims.

In reality, this isn't entirely the fault of the well-intentioned consumer, as companies offer money-back guarantees—that is, "If for any reason you're not completely satisfied..."

But in truth, this no-holes-barred guarantee does not stand in any fashion as proof that their product does what they say it will do. The consumer merely conceives such based on the fact that the company is "So sure this will work for you" that they are willing to take the chance they could possibly lose their shirts from all the refunds.

It's an old ploy based completely on the averages. All companies that advertise such dribble are in the "bean counting" business. They know the actual percentage of people that will take the time (as well as pay the shipping in most cases) to return their product. Research proves that less than 10 percent of shoppers will actually return their merchandise, even if it is defective or didn't meet the promised level of value to the customer.

Just remember that opportunity is sometimes difficult to distinguish from a scam. However, sometimes the only difference between the two is what the individual *actually does* with the opportunity. In other words, what is your motivation for taking the opportunity in the first place and how motivated are you to give it a reasonable chance to work? Most often, the opportunity is no better than the amount of time and work you put into it.

For instance, it's a proven fact that *any* motion or movement done repetitively (in the correct form) will alter the human body in some way or another. In many cases, this will be a positive improvement. Just doing basic floor exercises in your home will change your health and appearance drastically (I have done it) and is free to everyone! I often encourage people *not* to purchase an expensive gym membership or any workout paraphernalia until they have outgrown the basic floor-exercise regimen at home.

So in this case, the opportunity is there; it just depends on how you apply it as to what actual benefit you will ultimately get in return. The same holds true in just about every other opportunity in life. This is why all companies insist on posting the final disclaimer (usually in a low voice, or in small print) "Your results might vary" or "These results are not typical." Either the person on the commercial really didn't get that near-perfect physique from the equipment they're demonstrating, or else, they understand that the results will vary greatly depending on how each person applies what they have in their hands.

A young man was being shown through one of the most famous art galleries in Europe. He continued to make shallow criticisms of one masterpiece after another. Finally, after he had made a particularly inappropriate remark, the guide could take it no longer, and drawing himself up to his full height, he said, "Sir, these masterpieces are great works of art! They're not on trial... *You* are!"

It's the same with opportunity! Your boss is not on trial... *You* are! Your teacher's not on trial... *You* are! Your equipment, routine or program is not on trial...*You* are on trial! And if we're not careful, we may not recognize an opportunity because of the nitpicking that we do until it's gone!

John Greenleaf Whittier wrote, "For all sad words of tongue or pen, the saddest are these, 'It might have been.'"[22] Literally *everyone* has opportunities. It's sad if we are too busy to notice, too timid to take advantage of them, or worst of all, if we're not willing to put in the extra work that's always required to see them through to their full potential.

We fail sometimes to take advantage of obvious opportunities because of some *alleged* handicap. Each of us has something we believe to be to our disadvantage. The key is to carry on toward your goal and never mind what someone else *appears to have* that you don't, or in most cases, you can't have. We each must proceed only with that which *we* possess. After all, that's all we have to work with, so why stew over it? It's a fact, that those with the greatest handicaps often get the most out of life. They look at life as being more precious than the average person and therefore tend to focus more on that which is good in their life rather than that which is not.

We are always inventing reasons why we cannot continue the fight. For instance, I often hear someone lament, "I haven't done any better in life because I didn't go to college!" But almost everything you can learn in college is available at the public library, or better yet, online. Shakespeare was a grammar school dropout! Handicaps don't prevent us from winning the race; it just makes it a little more difficult. History is filled with men and women who proved that the human spirit can meet *any* challenge!

This may sound like just another pep talk, but it's a fact that the spirit a person has determines the *quality* of his or her life. It's not only a matter of always looking on the bright side, but it's also a fact that those that refuse to let their present situation get them down are also the people that most successfully proceed to their dreams.

The reason for this is quite simple. People of action never sit around waiting for opportunity or advancement to fall in their lap. These rare individuals aren't asking for a handout! They instead insist to *seek out* the necessary ingredients that are required to take the next step in the formulation of their goal. While in search of opportunity, they are keen in perception so that when it happens to come their way, they take advantage of it in a timely manner. The *pursuit* of opportunity will, in itself, create more of the same as once you head in the general direction of your dreams you will naturally encounter paths that relate to your ambition.

How many times have you heard someone say, "He's so talented…He would be a rich man if he only had the opportunity?"

It's pretty common for people to sit back and wait for the breaks. They nourish a myth that an important person will someday recognize their talents, and they will be propelled to the top like a movie star. But for every star that is discovered in this way, there are hundreds more that get to the top, only after years of hard work. "It usually takes years to become an overnight success!"

I'm telling you all this in order to prepare you for the inevitable circumstances of which you are about to encounter. *No one* is immune to them! No matter how determined you may be, you will inevitably hit a wall of opposition to your progress. That wall might originate from an outside force, such as finances, legal documents, licensing requirements, or a number of other humps in the road. But more than likely, the wall will be self-imposed, originating in none other than your *own* mind!

While recognizing authentic opportunity is extremely important, it's only the first step toward accomplishment. There are several phases you will encounter along the way that must be dealt with in order to keep your momentum constant and to avoid a complete and utter failure.

Francis Bacon said, "Chiefly, the mold of a man's fortune is in his own hands."[23] The next time you hear yourself say, "I'm waiting for my big break," see to it that what you are doing daily is actually working in the general direction of the same so that your words and actions express the same sentiment. It's not uncommon to hear someone say one thing, yet never really do anything about it or else do things that work in opposition to their words.

If you're the kind of person that does a job well and you are disciplined to some degree, you will likely find that opportunity is looking for *you*, and so in return, you inevitably find the kind of opportunity you are looking for. Plainly spoken, you get what you work for.

You might say, "But I know a person who has worked for years for a promotion but never got it!" or "I've been trying to lose weight for years! I've tried every diet and exercise plan out there, but none of them ever worked for me!"

To which I reply, "That's because it doesn't matter how hard your friend worked and then didn't get promoted, and it doesn't matter how many different weight-loss routines you tried and failed at." The question of the hour would be, "Did you both *really* try?" In your friend's case, it would sound like they did but have failed to get the recognition they deserve. In *your* case, however, it sounds like you didn't work hard enough or, as in most cases, did things contrary to your commitment or likely quit way too soon.

These statements might sound presumptuous, but the reason I can make these assumptions without knowing either one of you is simple. If you are certain your friend has done *all* they can do to reach their goal yet hasn't accomplished it yet, then it's just a matter of time before they do. That is, if they continue to put forth an honest effort and explore *every* avenue. This means they might have to step outside their comfort zone and go somewhere they feel uneasy traveling to. This could infer a different geographic location, another company, another position, or even more education. There's definitely a missing link somewhere in the equation. For the honest, hard-working, and determined individual, success is not a question of what but merely a question of when.

As for you, it's obvious that if you continue to fail at every program you start, there's a missing link as well. Remember that when something continually goes wrong time and time again, you must look for the common denominator. Could it be that it is *you*?

If others have lost weight or built muscle using the same program, then there has to be a reason you're not gaining the same level of success. The human body is fairly predictable—that is, a certain reaction to every action. The level to which it reacts is based mainly on the level and consistency of the input. In reality, the number 1 reason people fail at weight loss and exercise is simply a *lack of consistency*!

I know some folks that are on a perpetual diet and exercise program now and then. If you think about it, that's an oxymoron, which would indicate their program is doomed to failure before they even start. A big part of the problem is that their diet consists of eating the right meal every day or two, restricting their meal to a can of tuna or a salad, then the very next day or even the very next meal going hog wild! They even justify their actions outwardly with statements like, "Okay, I did really good yesterday, so I deserve a reward!" or "I starved myself at lunch, so I can eat a little more at dinner!" In these cases, the individuals stated goals and his or her actions contradict one another.

I realize that many weight-loss programs work on a point system, thereby allowing you to eat pretty much any food in the right proportion. Great! The prevailing dilemma is that many people don't follow the rules specifically when it comes to the particular program they are on.

You must realize that these programs are designed to be successful, only within a specific set of rules. If you break the rules, you can't expect to get the same results as you would when you follow them. Success is *rarely* based on blind luck! Rather, success comes from a sequence of carefully taken steps in a particular order.

That's why it is vitally important to map out your strategy *before* you start toward your goal. How many times have you looked back after arrival only to realize that you could have saved yourself a lot of effort by taking a different route? This is true in travel, and it's also true in life! Winging it never works well and will only cause you to waste a lot of time (the one thing we cannot replace), running around needlessly in the wrong direction.

If you diet one meal and pig out the next, if you exercise one day and skip the next, or if you just start and stop randomly every day of the week, *nothing is going to happen*! In a few cases, the people I know have even gone in the opposite direction, gaining even more weight *after* they end a diet.

There are a lot of reasons why this might happen, but mainly it is because their body is geared in the starvation mode, then suddenly shifts into the glutton mode. In both instances, your body is storing up calories in case of a famine. It actually takes several days or even weeks to prep the body to burn sufficient calories to lose a significant amount of weight. But if you gear your body toward the idea that there is no longer as much food available as there has been previously, it will begin to burn far less calories and therefore continue to do so even *after* the diet is ended. Obviously, if you are suddenly eating more than you have been, it's not desirable to have the same slow metabolism you had when you were dieting. In fact, just the opposite is needed at this juncture. This process will continue until the consistency of daily food intake soothes your systems concerns in regard to starvation. In every case, consistency plays an all-important role in what your ultimate success will be. (This should be a no-brainer!)

It matters not what kind of dream or goal you are pursuing. Consistency is the most important key to achieving it. Your mind is no different from your body. It automatically responds to whatever stimulus it is most familiar with. So the mode (action and thought) that is most consistent in your life is also the mode in which your mind and body will predictably operate. They are both creatures of habit.

In the same manner that a rock climber can overcome heights, an overweight person can overcome cravings, a smoker can overcome addiction, a salesman can overcome fear of rejection, a slothful person can overcome laziness and procrastination, etc.

Every mental or physical effort we attempt in a new direction will be met with some level of resistance, depending on the severity of change to the average daily routine the mind and body are accustomed to.

It is obvious that you cannot seize opportunity by *sitting on your hands*! Just as in the skill required to master a martial art, every move toward your goal must be a calculated one. Every action must be intentional. No energy or effort is wasted. Each motion, no matter how small, is a part of the overall action. Become a master at acquiring your goal. Envelop your total person, body, mind, and soul, in knowledge and skill to such an extent that every movement is automatic!

When opportunity knocks at your front door, you won't be out in the backyard searching for a four-leafed clover! Instead, it will be expected. You knew it was coming because you have taken the necessary steps, put out the necessary work, and endured the necessary pain to *force* your dream into the world of reality.

The idea of being in "the right place at the right time" is not an honest perception. The deep-seated reason why someone fell into success is not due to his or her location. If they hadn't been the kind of person that the particular opportunity fit in the first place, then it would not have mattered where they were at the time.

Others might have arrived to the same location and never received the same opportunity. That's because most opportunities fit only certain individuals who are already prepared to accept them (i.e., they're interested in that field to begin with, they've studied or trained in this area before, or they've all the preexisting qualities to fulfill the required obligations associated with the opportunity in the first place).

If a school affords me the opportunity to become a nurse, but I have yet to even start on the basics, then this opportunity would be better fitted to someone that has already acquired all the requirements leading up to the clinical portion of study. Either person could make the opportunity work, but it would be more advantageous for the latter due to their previous diligence toward preparation in this field. The same holds true for most career opportunities. Highly motivated individuals are ones that take as many steps as possible on their own in advance of opportunity. The opportunity just makes the trip sweeter.

Give one person the chance to make a million dollars in a proven system, and they'll fall flat on their face, losing whatever capital they had to begin with or making no return whatsoever. Give that same opportunity to another person, and they will succeed. Neither of them had formal training or education in this direction up to now, but one of them had some of the necessary qualities to seize the opportunity, follow the steps as precisely laid out, and consistently stick with the program to the end.

Jesus tells of three such investors in the parable of the talents found in Matthew 25:14–30 (NIV):

> Again, here is what the kingdom of heaven will be like. A man was going on a journey. He sent for his servants and put them in charge of his property. He gave $10,000 to one. He gave $4,000 to another. And he gave $2,000 to the third. The man gave each servant the amount of money he knew the servant could take care of. Then he went on his journey.
>
> The servant who had received the $10,000 went at once and put his money to work. He earned $10,000 more. The one with the $4,000 earned $4,000 more. But the man who had received $2,000 went and dug a hole in the ground. He hid his master's money in it.
>
> After a long time the master of those servants returned. He wanted to collect all the money they had earned. The man who had received $10,000 brought the other $10,000. "Master," he said, "you trusted me with $10,000. See, I have earned $10,000 more." His master replied, "You have done well, good and faithful servant! You have been faithful with a few things. I will put you in charge of many things. Come and share your master's happiness!"
>
> The man with $4,000 also came. "Master," he said, "you trusted me with $4,000. See, I have earned $4,000 more." His master replied, "You have done well, good and faithful

servant! You have been faithful with a few things. I will put you in charge of many things. Come and share your master's happiness!"

Then the man who had received $2,000 came. "Master," he said, "I knew that you are a hard man. You harvest where you have not planted. You gather crops where you have not scattered seed. So I was afraid. I went out and hid your $2,000 in the ground. See, here is what belongs to you." His master replied, "You evil, lazy servant! So you knew that I harvest where I have not planted? You knew that I gather crops where I have not scattered seed? Well then, you should have put my money in the bank. When I returned, I would have received it back with interest."

Then his master commanded the other servants, "Take the $2,000 from him. Give it to the one who has $20,000. Everyone who has will be given more. He will have more than enough. And what about anyone who doesn't have? Even what he has will be taken away from him. Throw that worthless servant outside. There in the darkness, people will sob and grind their teeth."

There are a couple of things quickly that I want you to get from this parable:

1. Opportunities for growth are not always equal in their amount but are no less important to the outcome.
2. The reward for properly investing your time, energy, and money is the same, whether the amount equals what someone else gained or not. The amount is only significant in relation to your effort and expectation. If both are at a reasonable level, then so also will your reward be. Never forget that whatever price you pay for your goal is significant to you alone. No other human can relate to the intrinsic worth or value of your personal dream.

Another great attribute of the parable is that, with or without training, everyone has individual qualities that are suited to a particular task. All that matters is *how* you apply those qualities.

I once worked with a common housewife who had never worked in sales in her life. In fact, she had never worked outside the home in any capacity. Within the first six months of employment, she became the top salesperson in our office of 160 representatives, outperforming seasoned businessmen and women trained for many years in the art of salesmanship. She maintained that level of production for over five years. She earned every award, plaque, trip, and bonus possible in her time with the company. She was the best I have ever seen at multitasking and had a memory second to none.

In time, managers would come to her to verify company procedures and to review training material. She could talk to a customer on the phone, surf the net, shop online, file her nails, and type notes in the necessary systems simultaneously. She was amazing to watch.

"Just a housewife?" you ask. I say that with the utmost respect for what housewives *really* do. But a housewife with hidden talents and abilities that were obviously God-given. Outside of what her parents had taught her growing up or from experiences in life, she had no other source.

My point is that *everybody* is suited for something. Some might be suited for one thing better than others, but we all have the ability to apply what we already possess down inside and accomplish anything we set our heart on! That means *anything*! I've always been of the frame of mind that, if someone else could do something, then so could I! I'm just as capable as the next guy or gal! I simply have to put what I already have into motion, combined with what I will acquire in route to my goal. It's in there… You just have to want it bad enough to release it!

So how bad do you want this special something? Is it truly just a dream, or is it the burning desire of the deepest part of your soul? I've never known anyone that *truly* desired something they couldn't get it. Remember the poem from the previous chapter: "Out in the world you'll find… success begins with a fellows will; it's all in the state of mind!" What state is your mind in?

The opportunity you so desire is probably in your hands right this minute. You just haven't recognized it yet. It might already be in your reach, or it might just be a phone call or e-mail away. It might be a Google search away or maybe just a suggestion or hint away. Most goals fail *not* because they were never realistic but merely because we never acted on them!

Since your greatest motivational factor is love, it's time to put your love for yourself to the test. Do you actually love yourself enough to do whatever it takes to make your dreams come true? Do you love yourself to the point of paying whatever the price might be?

When a parent gives an expensive gift to a child, they don't do so with a focus on how much it costs. They rather give the gift, regardless of the cost, based solely on their love for that child.

That's what makes Jesus's gift of the cross so incredibly awesome to all of us. Despite the cost, he gave up everything, suffered humiliation, torment, and the pain and shame of the cross, in order to fully demonstrate his love, and his Father's love for us. This is by far the greatest example of actions speaking louder than words in history!

The New Testament tells us,

> You see, when we were still powerless, Christ died for the ungodly. Very rarely will anyone die for a righteous man, though for a good man someone might possibly dare to die. But God demonstrates his own love for us in this: While we were still sinners, Christ died for us. (Romans 5:6–8, NIV)

It's one thing to *say* you're going to do something great but an entirely different concept to see it fulfilled through your actions.

James 1:22 (KJV) says, "But be *doers* (emphasis mine) of the word, and not hearers only, deceiving your own selves."

Did you catch the word "deceiving" in that verse? That is precisely what you're doing when you *say* one thing and *do* another. You're not only deceiving those around you by saying something you're not serious about following through on, but more importantly (and to greater detriment), you are deceiving yourself!

## Visualization

I purposefully saved the most common motivation in any self-help manual till last in order to make a full contrast between the two types. Most people only know of one type of visualization: that of putting your goal before you in as many forms as possible. If you have a picture, hang it where you can see it all the time.

Still another popular method is to write it out. Vividly describe exactly what your goal or dream looks like and each step on how you plan to get there. Carry these with you in some form. Look at them often! If it's a new car you want, go look at cars. If it's a new home, go home shopping, even if you can't afford to buy just yet. If it's to become a pilot, hang around the airport. It you want to be a doctor, go to the hospital regularly. Visualize, visualize, visualize!

Finally, one of the greatest motivations that I have found in my own personal experience will in all probability *not* be found in a textbook. We will simply refer to it as "Type-2 Visualization." Once I share it with you, it will become evident why any psychologist worth his/her salt might tell you to avoid it. In truth, I myself would rarely recommend this technique except when used properly or in the direst of situations. You may already be saying, "That sounds exactly like my situation! I'll do anything!"

I understand that we get a sense of helplessness in regard to reaching our goals and dreams, especially when we've tried the same old modus operandi time and time again to no avail. At this point, people become desperate and will often take measures that are either out of character or dangerous!

I suppose it would do no good to tell you at this point that there is always *hope*. These are easy words to tell someone else but difficult to swallow and definitely not very filling, if you are on the desperate end of things. So I won't waste your time or the ink and paper it would take to do so. Instead, I will give you an extreme alternative.

I would never refer this method to the newfound dream seeker as the aforementioned techniques should work quite nicely for the passionately motivated individual. Admittedly, at times there are desperate situations that require drastic measures!

Under no other circumstance would I propose the following practice be initiated save that of desperation. If you feel you have *honestly* (be truthful) done *everything* I have recommended up to now to stay motivated and have failed or if you are to the point of giving up altogether, then go ahead, break the glass, and pull the alarm! The following lifeline is for you! (I would rather see you stoop to this level than fail!)

In each and every instance up to now, I have encouraged you (as any good motivator would do) to look at the bright side, focus only on the positive, and to never take your eyes off your goal. You will remember that I just told you to never focus on negative input, whether internal or external. Well, now I'm going to tell you to do just the opposite!

You heard me correctly! If you get to the point where you absolutely cannot stay positive, then *don't*! What I mean to say is, if all else fails, turn around 180 degrees and look at where you came from. In reality, this is nothing more than reflection. There's no better way to compare how good you have it now or, for that matter, how good you will have it when you finally arrive than by looking back at where you started.

For some of us, we may not have to look too far back to see where we took the first step. In fact, you may still be standing in the exact same spot as when you began your journey. This would normally indicate that you merely failed to act. But that might not be true in every instance. You may feel that you gave your very best effort to the cause but buckled under the negativity and weight, making it impossible to get to your feet in the first place. Some goals and dreams are tougher than others.

The total distance you have to travel to get there best measures the difficulty of your particular goal. Your attitude and motivation also directly affect the difficulty level as well. But it goes without saying that some people will have a far shorter distance to travel in their quest to better themselves than others.

I once again allude to the pilot world as I am quite familiar with it. I recently went in pursuit of my lifelong dream to become a commercial pilot. But since I had already been a private pilot for thirty years and already possessed an Instrument Rating and a Multi-Engine Rating (requirements of the commercial certificate), my trip to completion would obviously be much shorter than someone just starting out that has never flown before.

In the same respect, if your goal is to lose 20 lbs., that feat would be far easier to accomplish than say a person that needs to lose 100 lbs. Make sense?

Unless you're just the *most chipper person in the world*, the distance to the goal will always have some bearing on whether or not you believe you can get it through the uprights. The farther out it is, the more difficult it becomes, and the more you will doubt your ability to hit the target.

It is in the darkest hour of your life, flat on your back, with nothing further to lose, that you possess the most power to change! That "nowhere but up" feeling you have down inside is one of the most powerful forces for change on earth!

The soldier on the battlefield fights harder than ever when it appears that all is lost. The player on the field plays with everything he or she has within them when they're down by just one score, with less than a minute on the clock. Suddenly, they don't need a huddle or time between plays to rest. They run one play after another without a break until they nearly drive the opposing team in the ground. You're angry! You're full of newfound adrenaline and determination! You're not going down without a fight! Strangely enough, this power existed within you all along. It just takes the proper motivation to bring it to the surface.

Let negativity propel you forward like a great rocket! Feed off the disgust you have for your own situation! This might just be the extra push you need to get out of your proverbial rut! It's a last-ditch effort but extremely effective when used correctly.

Often we see ourselves in a sort of "third party" way. We walk around in life, staring through the windows of our eyes, never looking at whom we truly are inside and out. We've mentally developed some predetermined picture of ourselves that is rarely honest or accurate. It's more who we *want* to be than who we really are.

So here goes! Stare at yourself in the mirror. See your reflection in a storefront window. Stop ignoring your reflection! After all, it's you! There's no better reality check! Not looking at yourself won't change who you are. Take a long, hard look at yourself. Don't just look at your body. Stare deep into your eyes, the windows of your soul! Take an *honest* and thorough assessment.

Is this who you intend to remain? If your goal is physical change, look at your body. For every other goal, look yourself in the eye. Don't paint a false picture. See the harsh reality of yourself in a candid fashion inside and out. If you have to, pull up your shirt! Turn around as well! Can you see your reality?

Look into your soul! Get angry! But instead of taking your anger out on someone else, use it toward something positive. You can be angry (sheer determination) and still do everything in love at the same time. It is possible!

Jesus drove the moneychangers from the holy temple with anger, with chords in his hand as a whip, turning over tables. But in reality, He did it because he loved his Father, and he loved the ones that were sinning as well. Anger is okay when used proportionately with love.

If you'll learn to be properly motivated, the next twelve months will be the most amazing year of your life! Changes are going to take place without and within that will revolutionize your existence!

By all means, *dream*! But in the meantime, get your head out of the clouds long enough to do something positive today toward reaching that dream.

If you will find a way to make love, hate, fear, and visualization work effectively in your life, you will finally know firsthand, how sweet it is to get the best out of yourself!

## Chapter Seven

# Bringing It Home

We have mischaracterized freedom. Because the whole of society lacks a moral center, we have now stretched the laborious endeavor of our forefathers to encircle everyone and everything. *Right* and *wrong* are no longer concrete barriers but have instead become variables that are conveniently repositioned, like orange traffic cones, depending only on how we interpret a given situation. Under the guise of freedom, given time and the right angle, *anything* may now be construed as "okay."

Numerous countries around the world look upon our freedom with lust and rightfully so. But few understand the enormous weight that comes with it. Freedom is a two-edged sword, with the ability to eliminate those that oppress us or destroy the one that wields it.

History reveals the somber reality that freedom and democracy have ruined as many nations as they have helped. When restrained to certain boundaries, these tools will build a nation from the ruins of the 1930s to the superpower of the 1970s. But when taken for granted and thrown about here and there like some cheap trinket, it will, in time, bring that same nation to its knees. From here, what becomes of this great land of ours depends entirely on the very thing that got us here in the first place: "The hearts of men and women."

Choices. When you think about it, that's really all that life consists of. We make hundreds of them a day, countless thousands in a lifetime. And the unique characteristic of these priceless chattels is that they never run out; they are renewed at the dawn of each new day, and everyone has an equal amount of them.

Two people can even be given the identical choice. But the way they each perceive the underlying opportunity will determine the methodology behind their ultimate decision as to how they will *spend* this one ever-so-precious commodity.

Oddly enough, most persist to toss them aside as some worthless piece of garbage, exhibiting ignorance as to their priceless intrinsic value. They may very well be the greatest of earthly assets given us by our Father in heaven. For within each singular choice lies immeasurable power and potential for greatness.

The man or woman who wields them wisely will rise from the ruins of failure and destruction to the lofty heights of life's greatest honors and accomplishments. They are all that stand between mediocrity and triumph.

Charles Kettering once said, "I expect to spend the rest of my life in the future, so I want to be reasonably sure of what kind of future it's going to be."[24]

No one has better or worse choices than anyone else. They are level and equal in value and can be exchanged or tendered for any currency or purpose. You can cash them immediately or use them as venture capital toward a greater future purpose. They only run dry upon the death of the proprietor.

The entire reason for why you are where you are in life at this very second is based on choices *you* made in the past over a span of days or years. Oddly enough, we often arrive in the future surprised to find ourselves in a particular situation when in reality, it is often our own series of choices that have intertwined with one another to bring us to our current state. You might say that we brought it on our self. Though some choices seem to be forced upon us, it is *not what happens to us* but rather *how we react to it* that matters. In actuality, those *reactions* to life's continual obstacles and arrows are called choices.

Life lays out multiple paths before us each, and every day, the number of which cannot be fathomed. By a *single* choice, we determine which path we will walk down at a precise moment in time and thereby alter our present and future course forever!

Therefore it is of utmost importance—vital, to say the least—that we choose *carefully* and *deliberately* as many roads have no exit ramp. Once you start in a particular direction, it is often difficult to back up or turn around. Choose wisely we must, for today is where the past and present meet and is the only place in time that we humans can live. So what we do in the present has everything to do with changing both our past and our future in one singular blow.

Although the past cannot truly be changed, our current and future choices function as a means of overlooking it, if indeed the path we are now on is evidentially better than the previous one. This not only facilitates a more positive outlook for us but also serves as a sign to others that we have changed for the better.

Your life will be subjected to no greater influence than your very next choice! You can choose to wallow in mediocrity or break the bonds that currently hold you and soar toward the pinnacle of success and freedom from whomever or whatever your particular captor may be.

A prisoner encased in concrete walls may be bound in body, but beyond that, no restraint can hold him. For behind the vast channels of the mind stands an eternal soul with unlimited potential and eternal life, restricted only by its own ability to control the mind and body's very next choice. He or she can choose to change their life for the better to whatever degree is possible, or they can remain shackled within themselves, thereby being imprisoned twice over!

We who are free dare also to dispose of our daily choices without an ounce of remorse. We nonchalantly cast aside our most valuable asset, believing that what we are about to do has no bearing or weight on tomorrow. We say things like, "If I don't like what I'm about to do, I'll choose something different later." But tomorrow is not guaranteed nor is another opportunity to change.

Through the annals of time, men and women have selected from a superfluity of choices the direction in which they would travel, and by that, the destination to which they would ultimately arrive. From history, we can easily determine that some of these contenders were famous for less than desirable reasons. The great Pharaoh of Exodus, Judas Iscariot, Bonnie and Clyde, Al Capone, and Charles Manson, among others, jar a particular feeling of negativity upon the mere mention of their name.

Yet no one is to blame but themselves for their individual selections in life and their resulting direction of travel. From the age of accountability to the edge of their grave, any one of them could have abruptly halted their journey, bringing it to a complete standstill, turning then 180 degrees toward a more honorable future. But as in the case of Pharaoh, when given the opportunity by God, through His servant Moses, to do the right thing, his hardened heart (soul) could not overcome the habitual force of its negative tendencies and nature. He was no longer in the driver's seat in his life. His soul had lost control to such an extent that he no longer had any control over his mind and body.

In my feeble effort to bring it all home in this final synopsis, I feel compelled to divulge as much knowledge as I can muster toward this singular and final verity. As I contemplated the vast differentials from which I might bring this collection of chapters to a close, I felt a tremendous burden in doing so in a manner that would greatly emphasize the enormous importance of what I have attempted to give you, the reader.

I assure you that this work has not been a *reckless* nor *casual* undertaking on my part. I take very seriously the responsibility imposed by the stroke of each key, and from the depths of my heart, my *only* intention from the very first letter has been to awaken the vast numbers of potential successors to the innumerable awards awaiting *anyone* who dares to rise, pursue, and conquer!

Through much prayer and deep thought, I concluded that there could be no more powerful message in closing than that of the hidden potential within each and every personal choice.

Though in a casual manner I have glazed over the surface of this subject in previous chapters, this narrative might be chronicled as incomplete lest I elaborate on the same before we part, with finite clarity.

No greater challenge lies before us at the stroke of midnight, than that of what we each will do with the inevitably proceeding twenty-four-hour period. We *exchange* each second, each minute, each hour, each day, each month, and each year of our life, for whatever we chose to purchase just a split-second in time before the current moment.

It is by these choices that we currently live, breathe, and have our very being in the present. They each claim a part of shaping and permanently inscribing our history, as well as the current moment in time in which we now find ourselves living. And if left unaltered, those same choices will also pronounce our destiny, driving the final nail, painting the final portrait that will portray the combined pages of history that belong solely to us, which are unremittingly cataloged with our name on it for all eternity.

Upon drawing our last breath, the choices will end forever! No more changes will be made, no more chances. Only one thing remains: "For Heaven and Earth shall pass away, but my words shall not pass away" (Matthew 24:35, kjv). Of all the millions of choices we will make, the choice to *follow Christ* will be the one that makes the greatest difference, both here and hereafter.

It will make the greatest difference here as it will change our perception of life, guiding us in turn toward better, godlier choices here on earth. It will make the greatest difference hereafter based on the promise Christ has made in his Father's holy word for those who hear, believe, repent, confess, and are baptized into his blood. "Neither is there salvation in any other: For there is no other name under heaven given among men, by which we must be saved" (Acts 4:12, KJV).

All of these requirements are found repetitiously throughout the New Testament and can *only* be taken as a whole. Jesus confirms this just before His ascension to heaven.

> Then Jesus came to them and said, "All authority in heaven and on earth has been given to me. Therefore go and make disciples of all nations, *baptizing them* in the name of the Father and of the Son and of the Holy Spirit, and teaching them to obey *everything* I have commanded you. And surely I am with you always, to the very end of the age." (Emphasis mine.) (Matthew 28:18–20)

Everything would mean every, single command. I have listed a few of the many individual Scriptures that confirm these truths, at the end of this chapter.

But it is imperative for you to understand that none of these are actually choices. Yes, you may choose to follow Christ…or not. But the weight of your actions should be prefaced with the following stone cold truth in mind. These are commandments!

You may ask, "Who has the right to demand my obedience? After all, didn't God create this life for me?"

Yes, he did. But it was *never* his intent that man should live apart from him. And by the way (in case anyone missed it), Jesus has "all authority in heaven and on earth"! That gives him the right to ask whatever he wills of us.

Personally, I have never believed that these commands are all that difficult to submit to. People make a far bigger deal of this than it really is. It takes less than ten minutes of your life to submit and obey and is little to ask in exchange for the life God blessed you with, let alone for the price that his Son traded for that same life.

I am very much aware that some will read this chapter and immediately begin to lament of their tormented existence, along with all the reasons why they can't make better choices. I'm not ignorant of the horrific suffering which plagues our world daily. Not a second goes by without some evil perpetrated upon the innocent. For you, I am praying! In fact, I can even do something else. I can sympathize and, in some instances, empathize as well.

While your individual situation and hard knocks may vary from my own, it goes without saying that few of us will escape the bounds of this world unscathed. And before we get into comparing our individual sufferings, it might be good to first ask the question: "How much happiness is *normal*?" How much of the time should we expect to be effective and contented?

We hear a great deal of talk these days about what is *normal*. People want to know what the normal weight is, the normal height, the normal level of income, intelligence, and so on. But many times this preoccupation with being normal can lead to some very real abnormalities.

Nowhere is this more evident than in the area of *happiness*. A large number of people are desperately unhappy today because they have become wrongly convinced that they ought to be happy all the time with never a setback. They have come to believe that to be frustrated, discontented, or anxious is some kind of indication that they are *abnormal*. They think (and this is amazing but true) that it's normal to be happy almost all the time, without a worry or care, with no problems or frustrations. This, they think, is the only *normal* way to be.

This in itself is abnormal though it's easy to see how one could get this impression. Part of this distorted perception is caused by TV programs, movies, and advertising. The housewife sees a model that has every hair in place, has not a line in her face, whose clothes have not a wrinkle, and whose surroundings (a mansion or yacht) indicate a super-abundance of money. That frozen picture is, by implication, what life ought to be like.

When a man sees a television show of some bright young executive with a ripped body, going straight to the top of his company with little effort or failure, then he goes home to his model-like wife (whose on the yacht or in the mansion) there is a natural tendency to believe that he himself, is somehow inadequate.

We then see famous personalities in very idealized and unreal situations. They throw money around on bizarre and outlandish purchases that are well beyond the *average* person's reach. We see the stars on the red carpet, waving to the crowds, having their photos taken repeatedly, then getting into expensive automobiles with other famous people. And they all look eternally happy; they give the appearance of complete fulfillment and well-being. (Even though we know from the tabloids and talk shows that this couldn't be further from the truth!)

You need to realize that some unhappiness, feelings of inadequacy, and occasional anxiety are the most normal feelings in the world for everybody, including movie stars and supermodels! And it is only by recognizing these feelings, that they are *normal*, that we can rise above them, overcome them, and concentrate our energies and thoughts on more positive actions.

The dimensions of our personality have been examined for some time, and many conclusions have been drawn about what it takes to have a *healthy* (there's another word I love) personality. Some of our everyday emotions like fear and guilt can be traced to how we see ourselves personally based on other's appraisals. In other words, a person may feel they are a certain way due to what people have told them or how they have reacted to the particular personality traits of others.

We also base who we *think we are* based on who we would *like to be*. We sort of live in a diluted sense, believing at times that we are someone we aren't. We project our imaginary character to the world, but we know in truth it's not who we really are. At least, not yet!

We may even live by mistaken reputation where we project the reputation we long to be seen as, all the while living a secret, somewhat diabolical reputation in private. In other words, people say wonderful things about us that aren't true based on the watercolor painting we display to the public eye and ear. This is dangerous, however, in that it only takes a tiny rain in our life to wash away the temporary vivid colors, thus revealing the rather dull, unattractive-self beneath. I personally know several men and women that wear elaborate watercolors every day of their life.

In fact, the latter extreme is likely the one we Christians struggle most with, and the world is on to us! Though we do not pretend to be above reproach, it's true that we often lead double lives between the church and the world, work and the world, and even, our family and the world.

There are those that might want a child to think they always act in a certain manner that would leave a good impression, even though it's not who they really are. In like manner, we might want to appear intelligent around coworkers, spouting off about something we really don't know anything about, sort of buffaloing our way through a conversation we should have stayed out of in the first place for obvious reasons. Another common use of this character trait is when a person falsely projects their personality to someone they're dating or seeking to become friends with as a front to advance the relationship on a lie.

All these traits are nothing more than a means by which to stretch the reality of our actual life to mirror some image we have imagined to be *true* happiness and contentment. But it's almost certain that even these picturesque illusions would be flawed in some manner as well if brought to reality.

You might as well face the fact right now that everyone has bad days, everyone has drama, everyone has trauma, and *no one* is perfectly happy all of the time! This is evident by one reason alone: *sin*. Because of sin, now, no life is picture-perfect. It's not entirely your fault, but we are all contributors to it.

But here's the rainbow in the thunderstorm of life. Regardless of your extreme circumstances, I assure you that God has given you (yes, you) the very same built-in equipment that he has given all the rest of us. Everyone I know has a body (whether fully intact or not), they have a mind (whether fully in act or not), and they certainly have a soul (fully intact for certain). I know the latter to be true based on the fact that you're alive!

With these three concrete elements, you may go wherever your heart desires. It's only a matter of proper control, the deliberate command of your inner and outer being that will determine the summation of the being that will be forever known by your name.

I too have had a pretty fair share of pain, suffering, and anguish. (Life's negative gifts.) I likely have as many viable excuses as the next man or woman as to why I should simply throw up my hands and give up for good! Regretfully, I have come close to doing just that on more than one occasion. After all, isn't *quitting* just about the easiest thing anyone can do? Sometimes, it actually sounds logical! But of course, there's really no way to quit completely, save the avenue of death.

Many have opted to end it all. What a sad and bitter pill their life must have been. I mean that! To come to the point where you know longer even want to exist. As I stated earlier, I recently lost a coworker to such an act and even discovered that my Christian college Greek professor had surprisingly succumbed to this bitter end as well. You might as well know that I have been there too. I think we have all thought about it but fortunately came to our senses.

Please forgive me for the very personal accounts of my life that I am about to attempt to articulate. I do so only as a means to relate to each of you, no matter what your reality or past circumstances might be. I want you to know that you are *not alone* in your suffering, struggles, or pain. Such is life. That's why I long for the next life with eager anticipation! We are promised that the things of this earth shall pass away. That includes pain, suffering, and yes, even death.

A long and fruitful life is wonderful but only if it is truly *fruitful*. I pray that you will bear a sufficient amount of *good fruit* so as to make the bitter fruit of life go down a bit easier.

## Sherry Ann

I was twelve years old. Our family was living in a small central Missouri town, in the parsonage, just next door to the church building where my father was the minister. There were four of us kids, Sherry, Terry, Don (me), and Jon. Mom and Dad seemed to have gotten a kick out of making our names rhyme. Nonetheless, life was pretty simple then. We were a close-knit family, full of God, and love for each other. Church was all we knew. It was our life. Everything we ate, drank, or slept revolved around church. We even developed our own gospel quartet in our family, each of us singing a different part, serenading ourselves as we traveled from place to place. Those were *good* and wholesome times, rich in meaning and priceless, to say the least!

I can honestly say that I have *equal* love for every member of my family. I have never felt more love for one over the other. That holds true to this day. However, I would be lying if I said that I didn't have more in common with one over the other. I believe this is a common trait within the family unit. For whatever reason, we seem to relate better to one parent over the other, one sibling over the other, etc.

Again, it's not that there's a measurable difference in how much you love each of them. It merely stems from the fact that we are all either very much different, or very much the same. Friends and family have a lot in common in this regard.

For many reasons, my brother, Jon, and I were very close. We spent the most time together by far, and thereby shared many common interests, and in turn, the most memories. If we weren't playing outside, we were playing music together, or simply laughing our heads off as we made shadow puppets on the wall at night with our fingers. We just genuinely enjoyed being together.

Then there was Sherry. She and I undoubtedly shared the same sense of humor. We'd go on for hours with our silly celebrity imitations. She would do her best Lilly Tomlin (i.e., "One ringy-dingy, two ringy-dingy") and I would answer with my best John Wayne. We'd have mom and dad in stitches all the while driving our other siblings up the wall! We also shared a love for music and sports.

Maybe there was something special in her being the eldest daughter, and me being the eldest son. I never really gave it much thought. All I know is that Sherry and I enjoyed being around one another and rarely needed help being entertained.

Terry and I rarely speak to this day. I am deeply saddened by this and have tried many times to reconcile our differences. Seems we are both extremely hard headed, and we each tend to push the other's buttons, whether intentionally or not. We also have very different views toward other members of the family, our childhood experiences, etc. That being said, I love her greatly, and would give nearly anything for our relationship to be mended. Our family has shrunk drastically over the years and therefore it is a shame that we cannot make the most of what family we have left among the living. In any case, I have resided to finally accept it for what it is. I suppose some fences can truly never be mended. Regardless of what she might believe, I love her equally, without exception.

But for all the problems, all the heartaches, and all the shortcomings, we were no less a family than any other family. We moved every year or two, but I can say without a doubt that we made a deep impact everywhere we went, and friends were rarely in short supply.

During our first year in Missouri, the whole family was awakened one morning, around 2:00 a.m. by some sort of commotion. It was coming from the girl's room. Then there was a loud crash, followed by a thud. I can remember running into the room behind my mother and father. There on the floor lay Sherry Ann, my older sister. It would appear that she had fainted, clearing several items from atop the dresser on her way to the floor.

Mother fell to the floor on her knees, cradled Sherry's head, and began screaming over and over, "What's wrong, baby? What's wrong?" About that time, Sherry came to. "I feel sick at my stomach," she said. Mother quickly helped her to her feet and headed down the hall toward the bathroom. Sherry was clinging to her, barely able to walk.

No sooner had they reached the bathroom door than Sherry began to throw up violently! But she didn't vomit her supper from the night before. She threw up massive amounts of blood. She continued to throw up continuously for a minute or two. Unable to reach the toilet, she unwillingly painted the floor, walls, and shower curtain with her blood.

Mother was screaming, "Call an ambulance!" My parents would have picked her up and driven her to the hospital but were afraid to move her as they had no idea what was wrong. They didn't know if she had some sort of internal injury, and by moving her, it would make it worse.

They stripped Sherry of her blood-soaked nightclothes and wrapped her in a sheet. It seemed as if the ambulance was taking a very long time to arrive, seeing that we were just across the street from the hospital. In fact, we lived on Hospital Road.

I'll never forget the anguishing minutes (nearly thirty) waiting for medical personnel to arrive. Mother ran to the door, opened it abruptly, and just stood there in the night on the front porch, wringing her hands, sobbing huge tears, and screaming, "Where are they? Why is it taking them so long?"

I reached up and gave her a reassuring pat on the shoulder. "It's okay, Mom," I said. "They'll be here in a minute!" But secretly, I was worried too. I may have only been twelve years old, but I knew for certain this was getting more serious by the minute.

The ambulance was a welcomed sight as they finally arrived in the parking lot that we shared with the church as a driveway. They unloaded their equipment while Mother tugged at them to hurry. Once inside, they evaluated Sherry's vitals and determined that her blood pressure was low, and her heart rate was weak. This was no surprise under the circumstances. They quickly loaded her in the ambulance and drove the short distance to the hospital within a couple of minutes.

My parents followed closely behind the ambulance, then rushed into the hospital, clinging to Sherry's hand. As traumatic as this scene may have been, I guess I never really understood its full impact till years later when I had children of my own. There's nothing worse than when your child is sick or hurt! What a horrible experience this must have been for my mother and father!

We were later told that the local doctor had taken over Sherry's examination, and within hours, it was determined that she had a bleeding stomach ulcer, situated on a blood vessel. That explained the large amount of internal bleeding.

He advised my parents that this type of surgery was difficult and beyond his scope of expertise. He asked permission to fly in a specialist from the hospital in Kansas City. My parents agreed, and by late afternoon, the surgeon had arrived.

After another thorough exam, the surgeon concurred with our doctor's diagnosis. He told us that this type of surgery was risky with a fifty-fifty chance of survival at best. By this time, the lobby was filled with church members, all in prayer, giving Mom and

Dad as much consolation as was humanly possible, reassuring them, "God is in control."

Although fifty-fifty was better than nothing, it's not the sort of odds a parent wants for their child.

And so, the surgery began. Many hours went by without word. We all stayed huddled together, praying without ceasing, waiting for those large double doors to open, anticipating any sign that would indicate that Sherry was going to make it.

By now, my parents were completely wrung out! Their faces were full of anguish and sorrow. I could see the immense pain in their tear-swollen eyes. Finally, the doors flung open, and through them walked the surgeon. He walked over to my parents, sat next to them, and put his hand on Dad's knee. He said, "Mr. and Mrs. Willingham, your daughter came through the surgery pretty well. At this time, she is stable. We'll know more in the next twenty-four hours, but at the moment, I believe she's going to make it!"

The waiting room exploded into cheers! No sweeter words could have fallen on our ears! Our prayers had been answered! The Lord is great and faithful and had heard our cries for mercy!

They put Sherry in a room that, coincidentally, faced our home across the street. From the front window of our home, we could look across the long front lawn of the hospital, now fully covered in deep, green grass, and stare into the window where Sherry now rested. It was early June, and her sixteenth birthday was just around the corner on the twenty-eighth.

We each took a turn going in to visit her. But before I went, I asked Dad if he would mind taking me to the local jewelry store so that I could pick out a nice gift for Sherry. He obliged. The store happened to be owned by a member of the church. He was very sympathetic and extremely helpful in showing me through the glass cases within our budget.

For some reason, my eyes lit up when I got to the display case full of necklaces. There, in the very front, in a pretty little velvet-lined box, was a large ivory-like question mark, hanging from a gold chain. I don't know why it struck my fancy as being something Sherry would enjoy. It's even stranger if you think about what it represented: "the question mark," a sign of uncertainty? I really didn't think about its meaning at the time.

I enthusiastically told the jeweler, "I'll take that one!" He smiled, removed it from the case, and walked to the cash register. He then put the box in a sack, handed it to me, and said, "I'll bet this will make your big sister feel much better!" We thanked him and left.

Dad drove me straight to the hospital. To this day, I remember Sherry's face as I walked in the room. She was sitting up slightly, with the biggest smile you've ever seen!

"Hey! How are you doing, Don Aubrey?" she asked. (Aubrey was my middle name, given me from my father's middle name. I was a Jr. and was honored to wear my father's name.)

"I'm doing fine, sis. How are you feeling?" I asked.

"I'm doing just fine, Don. The doctor said I would be out of here in no time!" She smiled at me again. Sherry had a happy, bubbly sort of personality, always laughing, always positive.

I walked to the edge of her bed, handed her the jewelry box, and said, "I got a little something for you. I hope you like it!"

Her eyes lit up as her smile grew bigger. She slowly opened the box, pulled the necklace up by the chain, as she exclaimed, "Oh, Don, how beautiful!" I immediately smiled, breathing a sigh of relief. I didn't know how she would react to such an odd, let alone, inexpensive gift. "I love it!" she exclaimed ecstatically. She'll never know how much her simple act of gratitude meant to me.

We visited for about twenty minutes before the nurse came in to run me off, insisting that Sherry needed some rest. But before I left, Sherry asked if we would mind bringing Pepe (our family poodle) to the window of her room later that day. "Sure!" I said. And with that, I gave her a hug and told her that I loved her.

That afternoon, my sister, brother, and I took Pepe to her hospital window. She waved at him and called to him, and we waved his little black paw back at her. Pepe was just another member of the family. Everybody, including my hesitant father, had come to love him dearly. The sight of Pepe was good for Sherry. It brought another smile and clearly meant a lot to her.

Later that evening, Mom and Dad sent my younger brother and I over to my friend Greg's house to spend the night. My parents were staying round the clock at the hospital, and we were too young to leave alone.

My buddy Greg was my closest friend, and in fact, he still remains near and dear to me to this day. We only see each other every eight to ten years, but it's always as if I never left. I can remember Jon and I playing with Greg and his brothers, as if nothing was wrong in our little world. After all, the incident was coming to an end, Sherry was going to be okay, and soon, life would return to its normal ebb and flow.

But the next morning, while we were eating breakfast, the phone rang. Greg's mom answered. I recall her troubled tone of voice and the serious look on her face. She hung up and turned to me. "You need to get dressed quickly, sweetie. Your father wants you back at the hospital as soon as possible!" she said.

"Okay," I replied. I wasn't too concerned. Dad probably just wanted my brother and I to come back to visit Sherry again. Greg's mom drove us to the front parking lot of the hospital. I can still recall that scene vividly… nearly forty years later.

Dad was walking down the sidewalk that led from the front door of the hospital. He walked over to the car to greet us. He was slumped over, as if he'd just gotten some sort of bad news. Tears ran down his face as he took my brother and I into his arms. By this time, Terry, my next to the oldest sister, had joined us.

Dad cried out loud, "She's not going to make it!" These were not the words I had expected.

I asked, "What do you mean, Daddy?"

He repeated, "Sherry's not going to make it! The doctor said she's taken a turn for the worst, and she only has a few hours to live!"

I hugged Dad tightly and said, "Don't worry, Dad. She'll be all right! The doctors aren't right! Sherry's going to be okay!"

I'll never forget the intensity of Dad's look as he stared me squarely in the face. The next few words from his mouth went straight to my soul, "She's not going to be all right, Don Jr.! Sherry's going to die!"

I still could not come to grips with that reality. I just new that somehow God was going to pull this thing off and that Sherry would *not* die! When you've never experienced death, it is difficult to accept the concept and scope of its reality and resulting finality.

We walked into that all too familiar waiting room. Once again, it was packed with many members of the church. They were all sobbing around my mother, each taking a turn at hugging her, reassuring her of their love and support for our family.

Mother then looked at Dad and said something like, "I have already been back there, but I can't go back there again! Can you go?"

"Yes," Dad said, "I will go be with her."

And so he did. My father sat by her bedside for several hours, holding her hand, and weeping with as much restraint as he could muster under the circumstances. Dad later relayed the account of his final moments with Sherry. "She opened her eyes and turned toward me," he recalled, "with a big smile, she said to me, 'Dad, don't worry. I'm not afraid!' Then she closed her eyes for the last time, squeezed my hand, then she was gone."

Dad came back to gather the rest of his family around him. We stood together, arm in arm in the waiting room, weeping for many minutes, as members of the church surrounded us and prayed with us.

We walked down the hall, past our family doctor, who was leaning against the desk at the nurse's station in the hallway. As Dad looked up at him, the doctor quickly hung his head and just stared at the floor. It would later be discovered that although Sherry was originally doing fine the day before she died, we were told our doctor took her off the stomach pump prematurely before checking for bowel signs (as I understand, a common practice after any type of stomach or intestinal surgery) and began feeding her a regular diet. The cold, hard reality set in: Sherry had died from food poisoning. It was very much avoidable had the doctor known what he was doing.

I will never forget that *long* walk down the *short* roadway from the hospital to our home. For some reason, it felt like several miles. We were all side by side, weeping aloud, in shock from what had just happened. Six of us had gone to the hospital, but only five would be coming home. There was now a painfully permanent hole in our family unit. Just four days earlier, Sherry was sitting on the couch in the living room just before bedtime, watching TV with the family, visiting, and of course, laughing.

I suppose the reality of it all had still not set in on me. I, like the rest of the family, was numb from the sequence of events and their unforeseen ending. It was not yet possible to believe she was gone—that is, until we visited the funeral home later that night.

I was the first to walk into the room where Sherry's body lay in state. The second I saw her, it all hit home! I broke down into tears as Father and Mother, Terry, Jon, and myself hung over her lifeless body. There, around her neck, was the question-mark necklace I had given her just a couple of days earlier. I was delighted she was going to wear it for eternity.

The visit to the funeral home was an overwhelming reality check for me. Up until this moment, Sherry's death was a distant story. My last memory of her was one of life and laughter. It was impossible for me to know her up till now in any other way but *alive*. But at this moment in time, talk and rumors came to an abrupt halt as reality hit me between the eyes! The horrifying certainty of the moment instantly ended my denial. It was true... Sherry was dead! We stayed there for at least a couple of hours. It was extremely difficult to walk out the door that evening and leave our beloved Sherry behind.

A couple of days later, as we were getting dressed for the funeral, Dad asked if I had seen Mother. I had caught an earlier glance of her and told him that she might be across the parking lot at the church building. The funeral home had just delivered Sherry's body, and I thought I saw Mom walking that direction. Dad asked me to go over and check on her.

Once again, another horrific scene would be permanently inscribed in my memory. As I walked through the front doors of that little church building, I caught my first glimpse of Mother. She was sitting in a folding chair that she had dragged over beside the casket. She had pulled Sherry's hand out and was holding it tightly and wailing to the top of her lungs, "My baby! Oh... my baby!" I will never forget the shrill tone of her moaning. It was as if it was coming from the very depths of her soul. Yes, I'm certain that it was! I would never witness this moment with the two of them again, mother and daughter, holding hands for the very last time.

I walked up slowly to her, put my arms around her, and began to cry with her. "She was a good sister," I whimpered.

"She was a good daughter, a good girl all the way around," Mom cried.

That little central Missouri town would see the biggest funeral it had ever seen that day. People stood outside as there was not enough room to get them all in. A Greyhound bus pulled up on the road out front. Down its stairs came all the members of the youth group from the Twenty-Ninth and Yale Church of Christ in Tulsa, Oklahoma, where we used to live and where my father had formerly preached. Sherry had once been a member of that group and could sing alto like an angel!

As the funeral started, the youth group began to sing all Sherry's favorite songs. That was all it took to make the whole family burst into tears once again. And so we continued through the entire service.

That afternoon, under the warm Missouri sun, we buried Sherry beneath a tall oak tree, in one of the most serene cemeteries you've ever seen. On her tombstone my parents had inscribed the words that best fit this beautiful young woman's legacy.

Over the next several months, we were daily forced to stare into the hospital window directly across the street where Sherry's final moments of life were lived out. Looking through our front window or just walking out the front door, forced us to relentlessly relive the worst nightmare of our lives.

Even sadder, little Pepe would cross the street daily for months after Sherry's death and stand on his hind feet below the window where he had last seen her. Sometimes he would just lie down on the grass below the window for hours at a time, confused, but patiently waiting for Sherry to appear at the window once more. Eventually he would give up and walk slowly with his head down, back home. It broke our hearts all over again to see him go there each day. But one day, months later, he suddenly stopped going to the window. I think he finally figured out that Sherry wasn't there anymore and that she was never coming home.

Mother would eventually have to move across town. There were too many heart-rending memories in the parsonage. Sherry's death would affect each of us in a different way, but the same. But Mom and Dad would never be the same again. As one could imagine, it made an understandable personality change in both of them. I suppose none of us were ever the same after losing our precious Sherry Ann.

As I said, I never realized at the time how hard Sherry's death hit my parents. Years later, while preparing for a sermon on Adversity, I unexpectedly ran across an article my grandmother had saved over the years. My father used to write a weekly commentary entitled "That's What the Bible says" for the local paper. It was obviously religious in nature, and this was my dad's first newspaper article after Sherry's death. Surprisingly, this was the first time I had ever seen it. He had written this column for years but was unable to continue for some time following Sherry's death.

Even after the years of space between her death and now, I could not read my father's words aloud to the congregation without breaking down. Therefore, at the end of the sermon, I asked my wife to do so. In order for you to fully wrap yourself around what happened, I'd like to share an actual copy of this article, written by my father, with you.

I apologize in advance for the fuzzy nature. After all, it's quite old.)

# Getting the Best Out of Yourself: Body, Mind, and Soul

THAT'S WHAT THE BIBLE SAYS...

## "SHE KNEW SHE HAD A SAVIOUR"

Fully three months have passed since our darling Sherry Ann passed from this life, only two weeks before her sixteenth birthday. Concerning this heartbreaking episode that has robbed our home of some of its sunlight, I have had little to say and I have written nothing. A hundred times I have tried to put my thoughts on paper but adequate words would not come. I longed to write words that would match the beauty of the life and the sweetness of the memory but such words are not to be found in the human tongue. Indulge me then, in this feeble attempt.

In the gospel of Mark Jesus said, "Suffer the little children to come unto me; forbid them not; for to such belongeth the kingdom of God..." In this context, Jesus informed his disciples that in spite of the importance of the work he had to do, he always had time for those trusting little souls who possess the characteristics of the heavenly kingdom. Sherry possessed those characteristics. She is home with her Redeemer.

In Sherry's life heaven swung low. In her life there was something of the other world which I often recognized as standing in marked contrast to my own rough earthliness. I loved her and she love me and it softened and subdued me.

But why did God take her? I needed her. Her mother needed her. Terry Jan, Don, Jr. and Jon needed her. Why didn't he leave her here to bless her family and others? We so miss her gales of laughter; her unbelievable humor and wit; her constant smile; her thoroughly Christian sensitivity. Does God in his total loveliness rob us of all of this? Why did he not hear my prayers to spare my child? Could not God have touched Sherry and healed her?

Reason intervenes. Faith intercedes, at this point. What is so bad about a momentary sickness which returned Sherry to God compared to the prospect of a life lived in a hard and unlovely world? Don't we always ask him to spare our loved ones. None of our loved ones would ever die if he answered all of our requests. A moments reflection reveals that such a course would not always be an act of mercy. The God who delivered Peter could have delivered James. We must leave all such matters to God with the assurance that all he does he does in love.

Sherry is still living. She is with the Lord. She is cared for. Over in Paradise she is comforted by the Lord who blessed children while he visited among us.

Sherry is spared all earthly sorrow.

Sherry is awaiting our coming. We miss her so very much now. The pain and emptiness in our hearts has not disappeared. It shall perhaps never disappear in this life. We weep because our hearts were entwined with hers. But we dry our eyes when we consider that she is out of the reach of all evil. We cannot remain filled with anguish when we ponder that she is eternally secure.

Sherry will not arise in three days as Jesus did. But because he did, she shall be given an immortal body Thank God for his love and power.

Under a large tree her body lies in the peaceful Missouri sod. Her soul is with the sweet redeemed of all the ages. On the simple green-marble headstone are inscribed these words which summarize her brief, lovely existence:

Sherry Ann Willingham<br>
1957 - 1973<br>
"She Knew She Had A Saviour"

—Daddy

243

And so it happened, thirty-nine years ago at the writing of this book. I've gone back to that town a few times over the years. And every time I go there, I take a stroll through that little cemetery that holds so many precious memories for me. There, frozen in time from a world that is constantly changing, is Sherry Ann's grave.

Lying beneath a huge oak, now ten times the size it used to be, is the old headstone that still has her faded, weather worn, high school picture on it. And even though I know what her tombstone says, I once more read the inscription that my parents had chiseled on it so many years ago:

"She knew… she had a Savior." And she did! *That's* why she told my dad she wasn't afraid. She *knew* where she was going. I have consolation in knowing that heaven is surely a much brighter place because of Sherry Ann Willingham!

I'm coming Sherry. Wait for me, please! Rest in peace, dear sister.

## Mom

No other relationship in life can come close to, nor equal, that of your beloved and precious mother. Regardless of how much you love your father, siblings, and even your children, the love you have for your one and only mother is incomparable in depth and substance. It's not that you love the other family members any less, it's just a different and unique sort of love, when it comes to Mom.

Many years in the ministry, along with the loss of a daughter, bankruptcy, and the constant moving around, had finally taken its toll on my parent's marriage. Understandably, they had both changed. It was clear for some time that their marriage was in trouble, but as they say, "Who is the preacher's preacher?" Few would ultimately come to the aid of these two devoted disciples who, for nearly 30 years sacrificed their own desires in order to come to the aid of others.

I will never forget the Sunday morning Dad called me to tell me they had separated. I was in my church office going over my sermon for the morning. It broke my heart and I found myself crying uncontrollably. I tried my best to reason with Dad, to convince him to "give it another try." But it was too little, too late. Dad was finished. In fact, the day he walked out was the very last time Mother would ever see his face this side of Heaven.

What's worse, the church was pretty much through with them both as well. The elders where I preached forbid me to ever quote my father from the pulpit again. So all of the sudden this man of God was no longer a valid source of wisdom? How do you tell a son *not* to idolize his father? I was both hurt and angered at this directive.

Instead of encouraging my parents, praying for them, and helping them to reconcile, most would use this as an opportunity to talk badly about them behind their backs, and to ultimately banish them from church work for many years to come. It would take many years and a denominational change before dad would be allowed to grace the pulpit again. If that's godliness… I will kindly pass!

At the age of twenty-seven, I was living in Dallas, Texas. I was married with one baby daughter, Kara, who was one and a half years old at the time. My mother was living on her own at the time in a small town about seventy-five miles south of Dallas, near Cedar Creek Lake.

She was working for Walmart in the bustling metropolis of Mabank, Texas, just a few miles from where she lived. The job paid only minimum wage, but somehow, Mom found a way to live on it. I went to visit her regularly, spending time on her front porch in the evenings, laughing and lamenting of days gone by.

She would always insist when I visited on taking me to coffee in the morning. She literally knew everyone in town, and this was her time to meet and greet the locals. The drinking of coffee was just an excuse to go there.

I didn't have much money in those days, and even though Mom could rarely afford to eat breakfast, she would always order a full breakfast for me, despite my arguing with her. She would say, "Now, you've got a long drive back to Dallas and a hard day at work! You've got to fuel up! And don't worry," she'd say, "I'll just have them put it on my tab, and I'll pay it at the end of the month." She was a good mother.

She had purchased a modern four-bedroom home and furnished every bedroom merely in the hope that some day all three of her children would come to visit at the same time. She talked often of that day with great enthusiasm. Unfortunately, that day would never come. But I loved to watch her dream about it. It brought great hope to her. It was obvious that she missed her family with every fiber of her being. That alone kept me coming back regularly though I would have come anyway.

Over a five-year period of living in the same geographical area, we became very close. It was fall, and she was nearing her first holiday season in her new home. The holidays had always been special to Mother. When we were small children, she spent the better part of two years, sewing a fall tablecloth just so she could bring in the cold weather in a festive sort of way. It featured horns of plenty full of every fruit and vegetable you could imagine. Every object was covered solid in sequins to match the correct corresponding color. It was beautiful, and I always looked forward to seeing it come out just before Halloween.

Each holiday exuded a festive spirit and an abundance of unique decorations, always making home for us kids, warm, enjoyable, and rememberable. And of course, there would always be plenty of food to match the holiday as well. Mother was an awesome, Southern cook!

It was around this time that Mother transferred at Walmart from the clothing department to the snack bar, believing she might enjoy it more, seeing that being in the kitchen was her forte. She had only been at work a few weeks when something happened. It seemed so small at the time, but unknowing to all of us, it would change her life, and ours, forever. Talk about how one small choice can affect your life!

While lifting a heavy soda canister behind the snack bar, she pulled a groin hernia. She knew right away what had happened and went immediately to her manager to report her injury. Unfortunately (boy, would I like to find this guy), he believed her to be faking, and sent her home without pay. Of course, they provided no insurance coverage either, so Mother was forced to deal now, not only with the physical pain, but with financial woes as well.

The next couple of months would be tough for her. Although my sister and I did our best to reach out to her, neither of us was doing well financially. But of course, when it comes to family, you would naturally do all you could do to help.

She initially moved to Rapid City, South Dakota, to live with my sister. She was excited at first, but soon, she decided that she missed Texas and came back home. She tried to get whatever employment she could but was having great difficulty working due to the hernia. She retained an attorney on a contingency basis to sue for her disability, but the manager continually refused to give in to her needs and what she rightfully had coming to her.

I pleaded with her several times to move in with my family in Dallas, but she really didn't want to leave her home. I understood, but eventually, necessity took over, and she was forced to come to Dallas through the week. I promised her we'd find some kind of job there Monday through Friday, and she could then go back to her home on the weekends. Again, she seemed excited with this suggestion at first.

I'll never forget her grand arrival into Dallas. She had an old yellow Cadillac, given her by my father for Christmas many years prior. It always reminded me of a giant banana! It was a beautiful car in its day but was getting old, and she had rolled the odometer over a couple of times by now. She was constantly having mechanical trouble with it, and I had worked on it more times than I could count.

There were two modes of transportation my mother was deathly afraid of: motorcycles and airplanes. I owned a motorcycle and had a pilot's license.

I waited for several hours on her but never heard anything. When her expected arrival time had passed by an hour or so, I jumped on my motorcycle and headed down the highway to look for her. Sure enough, not ten miles from my house, was Mom's bright yellow Cadillac! She had the hood raised and was standing on the shoulder of the road in front of the car.

I went to the nearest exit and circled back to get her. You should have seen her face when I arrived. It lit up like a little child. She was laughing and grinning from ear to ear!

I parked and got off the bike. "I am so happy to see you!" she screamed. "I've been here almost two hours and couldn't get anyone to stop!" Keep in mind that these were the days before cell phones.

"Well, I'm glad they didn't," I said. "You never know who you're dealing with nowadays."

She then said, "My car stalled again, and I have no idea this time what's wrong with it!" (It later turned out that she was merely out of gas.)

"Hop on, Mom," I said through a grin and pointed to the motorcycle.

"You want me to get on that?" she asked. She grimaced as her mouth turned into a huge frown!

"Come on, Mom, you've got no choice! Besides, it's only about ten miles to the house," I coaxed.

She reluctantly nodded and then slowly climbed on the back behind me. "Hang on tight, Mom!" I shouted. "The traffic's pretty heavy, and I don't want you to fall off the back!"

Then, off I went with her screaming every foot of the way, her arms clinched so tight around me that I could hardly breathe! All of the sudden, I started laughing uncontrollably. Mom looked aggravated with me at first, as if I was making fun of her. But then, she started laughing too, softly at first, then an all-out belly laugh, all the way home! She later admitted that she was only laughing because she was scared silly.

Mother seemed so happy to be in our home. I just knew this was going to get her going again until she could get what was legally hers from Walmart. But sadly, barely a week later, I came home from work one afternoon to find a note on the table. It read, "Dearest Don Aubrey, thank you so much for your love and hospitality, but I really am homesick and feel I must get back to my home in Malakoff. By the grace of God, I will find a job there soon or get my disability going so I can have surgery. Please forgive me for not waiting to tell you this in person, but I wanted to beat the nightfall. I will be in touch soon. I love you with all my heart! Mom."

My heart sank. Of course I was disappointed, as well as a bit frustrated at her, as I wanted to help her get back on her feet. But this was not a bit out of character for her at that time in her life. She seemed so restless. I now believe that somehow the forces "that be" were already unknowingly at work in her life. If we had only known what was to come.

A week had passed when Mother called me on the telephone. I could tell immediately by the sound of her voice that she had good news. "I got a job!" she exclaimed.

"That's great, Mom!" I replied. "What is it?" Her next words hit me in a weird sort of way. Looking back on it, I can't really explain my reaction. I just felt there was something wrong with her decision.

"I got a part-time job at a convenience store," she said.

The next words out of my mouth would haunt me the rest of my life. Did I indeed experience some sort of evil premonition, or is this a now-documented case surrounding the innate power of the spoken word?

"Mom, you're going to get yourself killed!" I scolded. Maybe these words came to mind, due in part, to the everyday scenario that played out on the evening news in Dallas—that of yet, another helpless convenience store clerk killed in the middle of the night for nothing more than chump change and a pack of cigarettes!

For whatever reason, these words came out of my mouth automatically as if I was not the one speaking them or as if they were forced upon my conscious, spilling quickly to the tip of my tongue.

"Oh no," she replied. "Don't worry! I already told them I didn't want to work nights. The manager has promised me a day shift."

I couldn't help the sudden and overwhelming feeling of concern I had for her. "Mother, that store is on a main highway to Dallas. Regardless of what shift you work, it's still a dangerous job!" I said.

I could tell by now that my discouraging words were upsetting her hopeful spirit. She had been in need of something—almost anything for quite a while now—and this little job meant more to her at the time than the thought of her own safety.

My attitude then changed slightly on her behalf. "Okay, Mom, if you think you'll be safe, then I guess you have to do what you think is right. But wouldn't you rather just come back here to my house and let me try to help you again?" I asked.

"No, Don, I really want to live in my house. I appreciate what you've done to help me, but I'm only planning on doing this until my disability kicks in," she said.

It was obvious that I wasn't getting anywhere in changing her mind, and I felt the best thing I could do at this point was support her decision. "Please be careful, Mom," I cautioned.

"Don't worry," she said. "I'll be okay!"

With that, we exchanged our I love you's and good-byes, and I hung up. Still, there was something unsettling about the conversation that I couldn't get off my mind.

A couple of weeks went by. It was Thanksgiving Day, and I had promised Mother we'd spend the day with her. So I loaded up the family—the wife and daughter—and drove the seventy-five miles south to her home in Malakoff.

Mother ran out the front door as I pulled into the driveway. She was so excited to see us! I could smell that familiar odor blowing through the front door, reminding me of Thanksgiving past. In predictable fashion, she had prepared her famous turkey and dressing, mashed potatoes and gravy, green bean casserole, homemade rolls, and chocolate pie! I have never known any other cook but Mom who could produce the same taste consistently over and over, year after year. Cooking had always been her strong point! From my first remembrance till now, every fellowship dinner we ever attended brought about the predictable question to each of us kids, "Which dishes did your mother make?" Her food was always such a huge hit that we would rarely get to eat it. The dishes were nearly always wiped clean by the time we would get through the line. Often, Mom would set a few helpings aside for each of us so that we could savor our favorite chef's delights.

As usual, the table was set with her finest china, nameplates at each setting, in spite of the fact there were only four of us at a table built to seat eight. We held hands, and I said grace over what would unknowingly be my last meal with my mother.

The day was a delight as Mother played with Kara, laughing back and forth—all day long, capped off by the traditional setting on the porch that evening. It was getting late, and we had a pretty good drive back to Dallas. So I said my good-byes to Mom and walked toward the car.

"Don Aubrey!" she yelled.

I turned back, thinking maybe I had forgotten a baby bottle or something (a normal routine).

"Would you guys please come back for Christmas dinner? I'll make you a homemade Christmas meal!" she said. I could tell it meant a lot to her, and of course, it would mean a lot to me as well.

"Sure!" I replied. "We will see you then!"

I really hadn't planned to go back till Christmas. It was only a little less than four weeks away, and money was tight; hence, gas was a big-ticket item for us. Nonetheless, I had the following weekend off and, once again, decided that Mom might enjoy the company.

As I pulled into her driveway, she was just coming out of the house, all dressed up, purse in hand. She smiled and waved at me. I parked the car and stepped out. "I didn't expect to see you!" she said excitedly.

"Well, I had the weekend off and thought you might like some company," I replied.

"Oh, baby, I'm so sorry! But the boss changed my schedule, and I am on my way to work right now. I won't get off till later this evening," she told me.

"Man, that's a bummer!" I said. "I really wanted to spend some time with you."

She came over to me and hugged my neck. "I'm sorry, Don, but I have to go to work. But I'm still looking forward to seeing you Christmas!" she exclaimed.

"Okay," I said, "I guess that will have to do!"

With that, she kissed my daughter, hugged my wife, then came over and gave me a hug and a kiss on the cheek. "I love you!" she said.

"I love you too, Mom!" I returned. I got in the car, backed out of the driveway, and watched her pull out and drive away. Little did I know that this was the last time I would ever talk to my mother or see her alive.

A couple of days passed. It was 2:00 a.m., December 6, 1988. We were fast asleep in our Dallas apartment when the phone rang. I rolled over and answered it in a fog.

"Hello?" I said.

A deep, serious-toned voice came back over the line. "Mr. Willingham?" the voice inquired.

"Yes," I replied.

"Is this Betty Willingham's son?" the voice asked in clarification.

"Yes, it is. Who's this?"

"This is Sergeant Brown of the Malakoff Sheriff's office," he said.

I will never forget the chill that ran over me! I knew immediately that Mother was dead. I knew not yet how it had happened, but I somehow sensed this would be his news to me.

I immediately sat up in bed.

"Mr. Willingham," he continued, "I found your name and number in your mother's purse. I am sorry to inform you that your mother, Betty, is deceased."

There was a silent pause... Then I broke down into tears. My suspicion was confirmed in one harsh blow! I struggled through the tears to speak. The officer tried his best to calm me. Finally, I asked the obvious question that I know *he knew* was coming. "How did it happen?"

His next sentence caught me completely off guard. My vivid imagination was already at work in high gear, painting the grim scene of her demise, veering off the road in her car, late at night, and hitting a tree. Or maybe she just skidded off the road, and the car rolled over. But he had chosen his next few words carefully in a blatant attempt to shield me from the horror of the truth. "I really don't want to discuss this on the phone with you. If you would come to my office this morning, I will go over all the details at that time with you," he said.

"No!" I shouted. "I want to know how she died!"

Again, he said insistently, "Sir, I really don't think it's a good idea to tell you this information over the phone! I would rather you come in to see me."

"I don't care!" I said persistently. "I want to know *now*! I have a right to know!" But in my haste and insistence, I didn't know what I was asking. Unknowingly, I was setting myself up for the shock of a lifetime. Nothing could have prepared me for the next words that would come through my phone: "Mr. Willingham, your mother was murdered!"

I immediately felt the blood running out of my head like a fast-flowing river. I felt lightheaded, as if I was about to faint. I fell back on the bed, phone still in hand, and gave one gigantic shout of agony at the top of my lungs. "*No!*" I yelled. "*No!* That can't be!"

My wife finally woke up enough to come to my side. I told her what had happened, and she began to cry too. How was this happening? How could it be that my original premonition and nightmare were playing out before me in an unimaginable and horrifying reality?

I finally turned my attention back to the phone, poised myself as best I could, and brought myself to interrogate the officer for more detail. By now, he had given in to my demanding demeanor.

"Well, sir," he replied, "the manager where she was working at the convenience store called in drunk for his shift last night, and your mother agreed to cover it. About one o'clock, a school bus driver came to the store to fill his bus with fuel upon returning from a trip. When he went in to pay, no one was at the counter. He began to yell but got no response. There were signs of a struggle behind the counter. Suspecting something was wrong, he went to the back stock room, and there discovered your mother's deceased body on the floor."

I didn't feel as if I could cry or moan any harder, but with each shocking word, my grief swelled that much more. As if I hadn't had enough, I asked him to continue to describe what they had discovered.

"Have you caught the murderer?" I demanded.

"No, sir, not yet," he replied.

"Do you have any leads?" I asked.

"Yes sir, we do. We just need a little more time to process the crime scene, and then we plan to pursue her killer," he said. He then went on to inform me that they believed there were two suspects. Upon my insistence, he painted the gruesome picture that was the last minutes of my precious mother's life.

"It appears that the crime lasted in the neighborhood of thirty minutes. Your mother put up quite a fight, considering her small size. She had skin under her nails. It appears that they beat her severely, breaking her neck at some point with a blow to the face. By the bruises on her wrists, we can tell that one of them held her down. The other one...raped her! Finally, they stabbed her several times. We won't know the cause of death until we get the coroner's report later today. I'm sorry, Mr. Willingham. I will be waiting on you at my office. Come when you're ready. If there's anything I can do, please let me know."

By this point, I was numb. I had no words in response to the brutal account of my dear mother's suffering and death. But all of the sudden, a new emotion surfaced.

"Sheriff," I said through tears, "get them for me!" I yelled.

"I will, Mr. Willingham" he assured. "I promise I will!" With that, I thanked him for his candidness with me and hung up.

I sobbed for a good thirty minutes before realizing I had the first of many unpleasant tasks to fulfill. I would have to call my brother, sister, and father, to relay the tragic news. One by one, I had to relive the story and suffer their hysteria on top of mine all over again. The last call to my father was made shortly before dawn. Of course, everyone took the news very hard.

Although Mom and Dad had been separated for some time at this point, there was absolutely no ill will between them. Sherry's death and the scars of many years in the ministry had left their marriage in shambles. But I know from talking to them both that they still loved each other. Dad's first words to me over the phone were, "You know this isn't what I wanted for her, right?"

If I knew anything at this point, it was that no one in our family would have wanted this outcome, and it wouldn't have mattered to whom it happened. The feeling would have been the same.

Later that morning, with little sleep, I called into work and began that familiar drive down Highway 175 south out of Dallas that I had taken so many times before on much happier occasions. It was the same drive I had made just a couple of days before while on my surprise visit to see mother. I kept recalling our last words to each other. "I love you!" Then, there was the embrace of maternal love she shared with me shortly before disappearing in that old yellow Cadillac for the last time.

I met up with her mother (my grandmother), her brothers (my uncles) at the sheriff's office in Malakoff. The sheriff once again went over the details and advised us that they had one of the suspects in custody. He was a fifteen-year-old black man (if man was appropriate) and was linked to several other robberies and assaults in the area. In fact, he had allegedly raped a seventy-plus-year-old woman in her mobile home just a few weeks before. He also had another convenience store holdup to his credit just down the road. They would never catch the second suspect as there was a lack of forensic evidence, and the defendant would not cooperate in the investigation.

We were told that "should any harm come to this man, whether before or after his incarceration, the men in our family would be the number one suspects." He also said, "I know how difficult it must be for you to hear this, but I need all of you to step back and let the law handle it! Don't mess up your lives any further or the lives of your family members by doing something that will send you to prison too!"

He was right, of course. But it was all any of us could do to restrain our emotions! I already had a hatred for this young man beyond anything I can describe—a rage so deep and so strong that I would not have hesitated for one second to blow him away had he been in my presence!

And please let me clarify why I mentioned the killer's color. Before anyone insults me or my mother's memory with a cry of discrimination, let me assure you that I have never been prejudice in any manner. I am married to a Mexican woman and have three daughters that are of mixed descent. I had a good friend and roommate in college that was black and have had numerous black friends and coworkers throughout my life. At this moment, it wouldn't have mattered if the murderer had been purple! It just so happened that he was black. To this day, I harbor no prejudice toward his race.

The reason I mentioned he was black was to make this point. Wouldn't it stand to reason that if *anyone* had a right to be prejudiced, it would be me? But those that harbor animosity toward others based on the actions of one person, or one small group of people, are seriously twisted in their thinking.

As a whole, the rest of the black race is no more responsible for my mother's death than I am! Can an entire race of people be held responsible for the actions of just a few individuals? If that were the case, then would they not also be responsible as a whole for what happened to my mother? I don't believe so. I have never handed down any hatred to my children either. I don't wear a chip on my shoulder in regard to the wrong doings of a small group of individuals in spite of the fact that it was later determined that the killer came from a family of criminals. His father and brother were already in prison. Obviously, this family was full of misdirection, hate, and cruelty. If anyone was prejudiced, it was this family! In spite of what happened, I have taught my daughters to love and respect *everyone* equally.

The rest of the African American race is no more responsible for my mother's death than I am responsible for slavery or the mistreatment of their people today. I wasn't there and do not, in any fashion, condone their actions. There are good and bad people of *every* color! I wish we could all get that on straight. All that I cared about was that some Godless, heartless, idiot, monster killed my mother! This hatred would eat me up for years to come, as well as eat up the other members of my immediate family. I really believed my uncle was going to kill this man the day he got out of prison.

The coroner's report would unfortunately find that the cause of death was not the broken neck. To me, this sounded like a quicker, less painful way to go, if you could say that *any* of what she suffered was better. It was instead the multiple stab wounds that ultimately took her life, each one hitting a vital organ. The report painted the gruesome picture of mother's painful and horrifying final minutes of life. DNA testing would convict the rapist to prison for first-degree murder.

Adding insult to injury, the court found that because this guy was a minor, he could not be tried as an adult. Therefore, he was only given a twenty-year sentence. That might seem like a long time, but it's a drop in the bucket to what my mother suffered, not to mention what we, the family members, are still suffering to this day! And by the way, he would eventually serve only thirteen years of that sentence. In my eyes, he was not a child. He stopped being a child the moment he made the choice to commit an adult crime!

If you are an advocate *against* the death penalty, then I am certain you have never had your mother raped, beaten, and stabbed to death! (And I pray you never do!) Like it or not, it will change your way of thinking very quickly. We don't ask for these attitudes, and it is only by God's love, mercy, and grace should we ever have a chance of overcoming them.

My brother and sister drove straight through from Rapid City, South Dakota. Upon arrival, we all had a long, hard, weep together. We then got to do what inevitably had to be done; we went to the local funeral home to make arrangements. Coincidentally, the company mother worked for refused to help in any fashion or to any credible degree. Eventually, the offer was made in the total sum of $2,000 from some executive secretary that worked for the convenience store chain.

Unbelievably, I never did get a call of condolence from the firm she worked for. I made repeated phone calls over a two-day period. In fact, when I first called, the woman on the other end seemed surprised. "A murder?" she asked. "In one of our stores? Where? When?"

It was plain to see that no one, including the drunken store manager, had reported to the main office in regard to the murder. One might imagine that this would be standard procedure. I considered their offer of $2,000 nothing less than an insult! "That won't even cover her casket," I told them.

I originally had no intention of suing the company. I did not believe at the time it was necessarily their fault. However, in view of the rotten funeral expense offer and upon discovery that there had been two other murders in convenience stores associated with this company, I had a change of heart.

One of the murders was another female about my mother's age. Five years earlier, she had been abducted from one of their stores and killed. Her family was still in a legal battle at the time of my mother's death. This proved that they were not strangers to this deadly pattern that had developed within their company, but instead of taking it seriously, they continued to digress over the years in preventative techniques that might have kept it from happening again.

Our attorney would eventually discover that the CEO had hired a relative as chief of security. He had no experience and had only loaded boxcars up to this time. When asked in deposition what experience he had in the security industry, he said, "I subscribe to a security magazine."

We would also discover that this man had removed the security alarms, cameras, etc., from every store, stating that they were too expensive to monitor. He then had the phones removed from the cashier's counters due to employee's abuse of privilege.

I would eventually spend over two and a half years battling with this company. One of the stipulations of the suit was that the chief of security must be fired. To their credit, they did have second thoughts shortly before the funeral and, in hindsight, offered to cover all of the funeral expenses. We accepted.

Mother's funeral was a two-fold ceremony of her life. The first half took place in Mabank at the Church of Christ where she attended. The second half took place back in that little Missouri town I mentioned earlier. When Mom and Dad purchased my sister Sherry's cemetery plot, they bought three, believing that one day they would be buried next to her. This had been Mom's lifelong request of us, to be buried next to her daughter in Missouri.

The final ceremony was a closed casket event due to the violent injuries her body had suffered during the assault. Old friends and church members came to the graveside service as we finally laid Mom to rest.

To this day, when I go back to that small town of 3,700 people, I now have two precious souls to visit. For there, in that beautiful, peaceful, little cemetery, buried side by side in the dark Missouri sod lies two of my favorite people: my blessed mother and Sherry Ann.

And there they shall be, resting for now, till Jesus comes again. I wish that I could be there on the day when their graves will open, and once again, they will rise, come forth, and live for all eternity! Thank you both for what you've meant to my life! Until *that* day, my loved ones, enjoy each other's company and rest in peace!

By the way, Walmart finally paid Mom's disability claim. They sent a check to her estate several months after her death. Too little… too late!

## Dad

Dad's death was normal I suspect, if you can call prostate cancer *normal*. The c-word is an all too familiar part of our world's vocabulary, easily recognized in any language, and touching every continent to some degree.

The thing I would like to stress most about my father was that he and I were extremely close and very much alike. I cannot count the numerous times throughout my life that someone has said, "You remind me of your father." To me, there could be no greater compliment! For Dad was not just my earthly father of forty-one years, but also my lifelong idol, my counselor, problem solver, and the most dependable best friend a person could ever have.

I grew up mimicking him. From my earliest memories (somewhere around five years of age), I remember utilizing an old cardboard box turned upside down as a pulpit. I would then initiate my very own private church service in which I would lead the singing, preach a hell, fire, and brimstone sermon, offer the invitation, partake of communion, and baptize my baby brother (over and over again).

While other kids played cops and robbers or cowboys and Indians, I found myself most content with simply playing church. And I'd play it every day, whether I could get my sisters and brother to sit in the makeshift pews or not!

I was a little boy that greatly admired his father. I wanted to be just like him in every way. To me, I could see no flaws, only the gruff exterior of his 6' 2" frame and broad shoulders. When he preached, I observed how he commanded the audience's attention, moving them to laugh one minute and cry the next. It was as if he could control their every emotion at will, taking them on a roller-coaster ride to eternity and back. When his sermons were over, you would always feel as if you were out of breath, leaving a heavy taste in your mouth of what life with God was like, as well as the terrifying reality of what life *without* God would be like. He just had a God-given gift to *move* people!

Preaching his first sermon at the age of eleven years and holding his first gospel meeting at the age of fourteen, Dad was a prodigy beyond his years. As I grew up into a young preacher myself, I would often read my father's old sermon books from the 1950s. In the front of each book, he had inscribed the dates he had preached each sermon, the location, and the number of responses. I could see by the results that this was no *ordinary* little boy.

And so, I too made it a point to start young, giving my first talk to a church at the age of seven years and preaching my first sermon to a large crowd at the age of twelve. Dad would continue to give me opportunities to preach throughout my childhood, pushing me to get in the pulpit, to follow the legacy he had started.

By name alone, I was often invited to preach through my teen years. I routinely made money through the summer months preaching around the area in Missouri where we lived. A full-time job at my age would only net about $100 a week. I was regularly paid that much for a single sermon. So preaching presented a two-fold opportunity for me (i.e., do something I loved and make money at the same time)!

I would eventually be asked to fill in at a congregation where my great uncle had once preached. He had served as a minister in this small, western Oklahoma town, for many years.

From the first Sunday I arrived, it was as if I had always preached there. They were a warm and loving group, and it only took a couple of visits before I was offered the job full time. I would like to say that this took me by surprise, but I was accustomed to these types of opportunities just dropping in my lap, and it would eventually be to my detriment that I took them for granted.

I was only nineteen at the time, with one year of college under my belt. This would cause a faux pas or two along the way, but in predictable fashion, the good brethren were always poised to strike, more than willing to jump on any mistake the young minister might make. I began to learn the hard way that not everyone believed the Bible the way I did, and they were very quick to tell me so! But I was pretty much shock proof as I had seen just about every scenario a preacher could go through in my nineteen years as a PK (preacher's kid).

My lack of a degree did not deter me from pursuing God's will for my life. I have never believed that a degree, plaque, or title makes a good preacher. In fact, some of the driest sermons I've sat through were preached by some of the smartest men I've known, by name, reputation, or title.

From the New Testament description of the gifts of the Spirit, Christians should understand the spiritual gifts to be enablements or capacities that are divinely bestowed upon individuals. Because they are freely given by God, these *cannot* be earned or merited.

Therefore, you cannot *make* a preacher nor *force* one to be. You either have it, or you don't! This doesn't mean that someone who has the desire to preach cannot do so; it simply means that those that possess that particular gift will be easy to spot. "By their fruit you shall know them." Reading the word of God and simply relaying it to others would be more the description of a teacher. But to read the word of God and move people with it, now that's a preacher! There are many preachers that teach every Sunday morning, yet rarely succeed to *move* anyone!

So upon receiving the offer to preach in Oklahoma, I went straight to Dad for input and counseling. It was late one night when the elders called, and Dad and Mom were already in bed. "Dad," I said softly, "One of the elders is on the phone, and they are offering me a full time preaching job. What should I do?"

Dad turned his head toward me, opened his eyes, and asked, "What do you want to do, Don?"

"Serve the Lord, Dad," I replied.

"Then do it!" he told me positively.

"But what about college?" I inquired.

"Seems to me," Dad continued, "that the apostles didn't have a formal education when they were called to preach either! I would say, follow your heart, and above all, Don, do what you believe God is calling you to do!" Then he smiled, reached out, hugged my neck, and said, "I'm very proud of you, Don, and I love you, and I'm behind you no matter what you decide to do!"

As I went back to the phone, I knew in my heart what I had to do! I reasoned that I had years of personal mentoring on my resume with one of America's leading church figures at the time. It was because of Dad that I was even in this promising situation. I had also known for some time that God was calling me to preach, and that it was no accident that I had been born to this one of a kind servant of His.

My father's name was so well-known at the time throughout the brotherhood that when need be, he could pick up the phone, make a few calls, and have a full-time preaching job in less than twenty-four hours. I'm not exaggerating! I've seen it happen on multiple occasions. I felt it a privilege to be called his son!

For these and other reasons, I felt this job offer was just natural for a guy like me. I had been a member of the Preacher's Club while attending a Christian university in Tennessee (Dad's alma mater) and had continual invitations to preach around the area and to as far away as Orlando, Florida, during spring break.

So this was to be my path as well in life, at least for a few years till I, like my father, began to experience the not so pretty side of church work. I had witnessed firsthand the grief and sorrow my father and mother endured over the years, moving all over the place, getting fired without warning, with no place to move overnight with their family of six. This was the less than admirable side of religion, the *ugly* and often *secret* actions of Christians, our brothers and sisters in Christ.

Don't get me wrong, I love 'em… God knows I do! The thing I realize now that I didn't realize then is that Christians are just everyday people, doing their best to get to heaven. They're not perfect, sinless, flawless, or often times, even a good example in what they teach and preach. Without a doubt, they are very much like preachers! If only they understood this concept in reverse, what a different place church would be!

I have actually developed a homemade "Don-ism" regarding the church, and I feel more than qualified to share it with you. It goes like this (and I have quoted this from the pulpit more than once): "The Church would be a great place, if there weren't people in it!" Then I always follow up with "Oh, that's right, the people *are* the Church!" I usually get a laugh or two as anyone who is honest knows there's a lot of truth in these words!

You see, the church, in itself, is perfect! After all, it's the body of Christ! What could be more perfect than that? No matter how great the church is doing, no matter how many souls they are reaching for Christ, it is *people* that muck up the work every single time! They just can't seem to help themselves!

I've seen unwarranted words and actions at every level, from the elders down. I've seen elders installed who could not even lead a public prayer (I'm serious!). I've also seen (on many occasions) elders installed who have virtually *no* biblical knowledge to speak of that are unable to teach, which is a basic commandment of the same. Then there are the elders with bizarre Scripture interpretation, no self-control, and even a genuine lack of compassion for those in need. Many cannot even control their own household. The list goes on. Seems we are good at stretching the word of God to fit pretty much any good old boy. This, in itself, proves that the church is far from perfect due completely to human error and a flippant, lackadaisical attitude toward adherence to divine Scripture.

I've had church members yell at me in the middle of the sanctuary, veins standing out on their neck, I've had members stare me down in the middle of a sermon in an attempt to intimidate me, and I've even been chewed out in my Church office by so-called Christians for everything from preaching *for* baptism to preaching *against* homosexuality! (No kidding!) In each case, they threatened to leave if I continued to preach the truth about these biblical principles. Unbelievable, right? I've even seen hair-pulling, cursing, and out and out brawls at church!

I have witnessed firsthand visitors shunned on multiple occasions, disallowed from fitting into any number of cliques, which have become an all too familiar part of our religion, often disguised under the covert name of "small Groups," an ever-increasing fad in today's modern Church.

I have listened over and over (at numerous congregations) to the leadership rant on about the absolute necessity of becoming a part of one of these small groups. "You just can't get involved or get to the heart of the church unless you join one of these groups," they say. Funny, I believed all my life that all one had to do to become a part of the church was to first be baptized and second to place membership. Seems that the church is no longer one large group but rather dozens of "small groups," each with their own separate theme, meeting place, and activities. Even much of the Bible study has been shifted from the inconvenient Bible class scene to the individual small groups.

Biblically speaking, I cannot necessarily find anything unscriptural with this concept, but I do see many dangerous side effects.

For one, newcomers or those that come along months or years after the original groups have been formed are often thrust into a group to themselves. It seems the *more popular folks* are most often in groups that are conveniently full. My wife and I have even had people in our group move to another more popular group. On the other hand, *we* have also been moved from one group to another group, comprised mainly of the new members.

The very idea that one group can become any more popular than another group reveals the inherently problematic tendencies of such a system. "So we, being many, are *one body* in Christ, and *every one* members one of another" (Romans 12:5, KJV).

This biblical description alone of being *one* presents an interesting argument to the validity of many groups. In the least, it is dangerous to divide the church into separate fellowship groups as it tends to exclude countless individuals that do not feel comfortable in this setting. It also predictably herds the less popular members together, away from the mainstream leadership figures or the more affluent. Though there are likely exceptions to this rule, I have examined this closely on many occasions, in numerous congregations, and I challenge anyone to dispute my findings. You will rarely find the elders or the minister in a group comprised mainly of new members or those deemed to be less popular.

If there is a case *against* such a practice (though I'm not certain that there is), it would be that of making many bodies out of the one body. It's a thin line, to say the least, and as I've stated, my wife and I have been a part of such a group on more than one occasion, but I'm not a fan.

It goes without saying that some of the least friendly people I have met in my life were in church! It's enough to make any preacher want to throw in the towel, if not for the fact that they too are often guilty of many of these ungodly traits as well. It is a fact that Christians are not perfect! I have never professed to be so and have even eluded many times from the pulpit that I, of all people, have little or no right to preach! For those that say, "Christians are hypocrites," I wholeheartedly agree! "For all have sinned and fall short of the glory of God" (Romans 3:23, New American Standard Bible).

I suppose that one excuse for not attending church is as good as another. However, I'd far rather be in the church as a hypocrite than out of the church as a finger-pointer! Those that win the game must first participate in it. Whether they are any good at the game, well, that's another matter altogether, and only the God of heaven is qualified to make that judgment.

But thanks be to God, I have never been deterred from preaching the truth. Regardless of the threats or the ultimate price to self, I (like my father) would always try to reason with them. And when it would finally become evident that all was lost, I would simply look them in the eye and say in a kind, respectful, but serious voice, "Well, we're going to miss you!" I mean, I can't change what God said! It is what it is! It is ours, so take it or leave it. There is nothing in between! Just because someone does not agree with the word of God does not negate my responsibility to proclaim it. I pray that one day I will once again find a Church that is interested in hearing "the truth…the whole truth…and *nothing* but the truth!"

We need to put our "big boy" pants on when it comes to God's will for man and the evident work of the Church associated with those truths. It's time to stop the pretty little *sermonettes* that paint Christ as a meek and lowly weakling! He was by all accounts a man's man!

This is the man that we see driving the moneychangers out of the temple with cords, turning the tables over, and yelling, "You have turned my Father's House into a den of thieves!" And guess what? The crowd left!

This is also the same man that endured unthinkable suffering at the hands of the Roman soldiers, was forced to bear his own cross up Calvary's hill, and was then nailed to that very same cross to die the worst death known to man to this day! That doesn't really paint a picture like the ones we often see.

I am proud to say before God that I have never graced a pulpit and failed preached the truth in its entirety! For this reason, I am both popular and unpopular. Those that like it straight seem to love me; those that can't handle the truth can't stand me! Oh well, even Christ couldn't win them all. In fact, they nailed him to a tree for his beliefs. Guess I've gotten off pretty easy! The world does not need one feel-good sermon after another! God is *balanced*. He has a stormy side, equal and evenhanded to his loving side. People need to know that *now* more than ever! The world needs men and women of God who are willing to tell it like it is, whether it's popular or not, whether it builds a giant church or not!

I owe my faith to my beloved father and mother. Without them, I would have never come to know Christ. But even more I owe to my father alone. For his example, his steadfastness, his willingness to shake the dust from his feet time and time again and simply move on, and yet never quit, I owe everything I am that is worth anything. And if I owe such a great debt to my earthly father, then there is no way to tally the balance due to my Father in heaven. If there be any good in me at all, it is due to these two rich father influences in my life! But as we know, *everything* and *everyone* in *this* life has a beginning and an end.

I will never forget the day Dad first called me to tell me he had been diagnosed with prostate cancer. He was sixty years old at the time and had been in pretty good health the majority of his life. He was told that he had a large tumor, which could not be operated on without great risk. Even with the operation and chemotherapy, his chance of living was less than 10 percent.

Not surprising, Dad chose to opt out of any treatment and simply live out whatever time he had left in as healthy a state as he could maintain. However, God once again had other plans. Through the aid of a good friend and musician he was given the book *The Cure for All Cancers* by Hulda Regehr Clark. He followed it faithfully for several months, and at his next doctor visit was pronounced cancer free!

Of course, we were all thrilled at the news, giving thanks to God for sparing his life. And so, this made it possible for Dad to go back in the ministry once again, preaching first in the northern Texas Panhandle, and eventually settling back down in his childhood town of Amarillo, Texas.

It was at this time that our two lives would cross paths one last time. It had always been a dream of ours to co-minister at the same church. But for one reason or another, we had never been able to pull it off. Finally, that opportunity came home, as I took over the youth minister position at the same church where my father headed the ministry to seniors.

This very special time had to have been a gift from God as neither of us could have known what the near future would hold. After only two years there together, Dad was once again diagnosed with prostate cancer. This time, it had crept into his spine and surrounding organs. The outlook was not good.

I visited the oncologist with my father. We weren't yet sure how far the cancer had spread, and this was the moment of truth for all of us. Dad sat calmly on the table as the doctor read over his chart.

"Mr. Willingham," the doctor said, "I'm afraid your cancer has already moved to the final stage, and there's not anything we can do to completely stop it. At best, we can slow it down a bit with chemotherapy, but you still won't increase your chances of survival by a substantial measure."

I watched my father respond to this news in the same style and dignity that he had displayed throughout his entire life—that of grace and serenity. He never broke his facial expression. No wrinkled forehead, no frown, and not one single tear.

But no one had yet asked the obvious question. I didn't feel it was my place to do so, but I had to know.

"Doctor, how much time does he have left?" I asked. The words that came next were far more than I had bargained for.

The doctor bowed his head slightly, staring at the floor. "Six months…or less," he said quietly.

I was in shock! Dad stood up silently, picked up his coat, and shook the doctor's hand. "Thank you, Doc," he said. "I appreciate your honesty. I know you've done all you could do for me." The doctor smiled back at us hesitantly as we walked out the door.

On the way to the car, Dad said nothing. Finally, I burst into tears. "Dad, he can't be right! You should get a second opinion!" I exclaimed. I was certain there had to be something wrong with this prognosis as at this time, Dad was experiencing little pain and was walking around as well as I was.

"No, Don," Dad said. "He *is* right. That doctor has been doing this a long time. He knows what it looks like at this stage. If he says I'm going to die, then I'm going to die."

It wasn't that I was not impressed with my father's typical demeanor when it came to sorrow. It was like an old friend to him. This man had lost his daughter, his wife, and countless other family members and friends over the years. He himself had preached literally hundreds of funerals as he watched one loved one after another lowered in the ground in his presence. It was as if he had suddenly become aware that his time had come, and there was no reason to draw it out from a hospital bed. He knew firsthand the trauma and suffering associated with cancer treatment. Many people he had seen in this same situation would take the treatment, become terribly ill in their last months, and die anyway. In true "dad" fashion, he would just live it out and take what was coming to him with peace.

If nothing else, Dad was known for his eloquent speech and razor-sharp wit. I'll never forget his next words. They were very familiar to me as I had heard them countless times throughout my life. It was his famous "This Is the Program" speech.

"Well, Don," he said, "this is the program. You live and you die, and it's *my* turn to die."

"But, Dad, " I cried, "I'm not ready for you to die!"

His response was a classic: "I didn't say I was *ready* to die. I said it was my turn!" And with that, we both busted out in laughter! He always had a way of soothing my heart, even in the darkest hours of life.

Turns out, the doctor was right. From the day we left his office, Dad only lived three short months. I would have never believed it. It hit me particularly hard as I lost not one but two people dear to me that day—my loving father of forty-one years and my very best friend in the whole world.

Today my father lies just down the road from me in a cemetery outside Canyon, Texas. I have gone to visit his grave many times. Often I will just pull up next to his grave and park for a while, talking with him as if he's still there. Somehow, it makes me feel better. I never leave without telling him I love him. Coincidentally, those were my last words to him in hospice the night before he died. It does my heart good to know that these three words, the most meaningful pairing of words in *any* language that one person can speak to another, are the very same words I have parted ways with, in each of the three deaths—my sister, my mother, and my beloved father.

> "Precious memories… how they linger. How… they ever flood my soul! In the stillness, of the midnight, precious, sacred scenes unfold!"[25]

In the last two years, I've lost my preaching job (again), taken a fifteen-foot fall off a high line at work, breaking my lower back, fracturing my pelvic bone, and breaking my shoulder. During the same time period, my wife was diagnosed with Parkinson's disease at the age of forty-two. She has also suffered from Grave's disease for the past sixteen years. Once again, I only share my *temporary* miseries with you to make a final point.

When you think life is too heavy, consider this: someone else's life is heavier still. I'm not saying that my life has been harder than yours. I'm saying that we all are having a tough time of it, and we all have plenty of reasons to just throw in the towel and quit!

Although it might not soothe your pain, loss, or suffering to have the knowledge that everybody else is hurting too, maybe it will bring some comfort to your soul to know that you are *not* alone in your grief.

Don't we often identify best with those that have experienced similar suffering as ourselves? That's why there are countless support groups around the world that bring people of like circumstance together in order to relate and comfort one another.

Whether you suffer from the death of a loved one, a devastating divorce, loneliness, or even alcohol and drug abuse, there's someone out there that has been unfortunate enough to suffer in like manner.

Galatians 6:2 (KJV) says, "Bear ye one another's burdens; and so fulfill the law of Christ."

In no more efficient manner do we demonstrate the love and compassion of Christ than by helping each other to swallow the bitterest pills of life. I have taken my medicine on more than one occasion and have swallowed more than my share of pills.

I have since forgiven the now thirty-five-year-old man that killed my mother. It has been, without a doubt, the greatest challenge of my Christian life! And to the one that got away, "No, and I tell you again that unless you repent, you too will all perish." (Luke 13:5, New Living Translation).

But in spite of this God-given heart transplant, I am riddled to this day with a sense of guilt in regard to mother's death. Had my spoken words cursed her life in some way? I was the one to initially say to her, "Mom, you're going to get yourself killed!" I have even preached that there is tremendous power in words and that we must be careful what we speak out loud so as not to bring it to fruition. Is this what I have done? Have I failed to practice the very words that I preach?

And there is yet another guilt I have forever struggled with—that of not being there for Mom in her darkest hour. There I lay in bed asleep, just seventy-five miles down the road while my poor, defenseless mother fought for her very life! Why could I have not had been there for her? Had I known she was going to work all night, I could have simply checked in on her and likely fended off her assailants!

Or maybe I should have been more insistent that fateful day on the phone when she told me where she had gotten a job. But I was not. When the ballots were tallied, I was not there for her. That thought alone will haunt me for the rest of my life. In this matter, I live in constant, never-ending regret!

Then there's the matter of Dad. What kind of a son was I really overall? Was I there for him as well? Despite the bond that only he and I shared, I feel a sense of inadequacy on his account as well. While I lacked the power to cure his cancer, is there something I might have done to comfort him more in his last hours?

I must now face the remaining years, repeatedly asking my heart the agonizing question: "Could I have been a better son?" I beat myself up regularly over my string of inept attempts to care for my parents. When life has ultimately passed, we must all face the resounding question that tallies the sum of our being: "Was I *all* that I could be?"

In spite of all the painful sorrow, the barrels of tears I've cried and the countless spiritual, emotional, and physical setbacks in my life, I have given my all to keeping the faith. Call me stubborn or just plain ignorant, but I have started over more times than I can count and have made it my life's motto to *never give up*! After all, what do I have to lose but yet another loss? But by the same token, I have *everything* to gain!

Remember my father's words? "Life is a cemetery, not a cesspool! We bury the past, not wallow in it!"

Each and every day of your existence on earth, life will present to you both good and not so good events. In many cases, we will be forced to take both. We don't always have a choice. But in the cases where we may choose, we should obviously take the higher ground as this is the only one of the two roads that leads to success, happiness, and ultimately, eternal life.

When the inevitable trauma of life does strike, we must always reflect on the positive as well. It is highly unlikely that your life is void of any happiness. Sometimes, we really have to take a hard look to find it, but it's there just the same.

It is easy to only dwell on the negative. In fact, that seems to be what we are best at. We habitually seek daily that which is wrong with our life rather than ignoring, overlooking, or forgetting it. And it's often not enough to just think about it now and then. Instead, we insist to meditate on it day and night. It then becomes such a dominating force in our life that we can no longer see the future being worth much either.

Take it from me, you *can* overcome! "Death, [pain and suffering] entered the world by one man through sin, and so now, we all sin." (Romans 5:12 NIV). That "one man" was Adam, and "all" is "you and me!" From the very first sin forward, the world would no longer be a pain-free environment. Things got kind of ugly after that.

But regardless of how bad life sometimes hurts, God is faithful in blessing those who remain on the "narrow path that leads to life." Through "Him," and Him alone, you and I can get past every sorrow, overcome every obstacle, and rise from every fall!

From this day forward, use the negative circumstances of life, as well as the often *hidden* happiness that is inevitably present, to propel you toward your fondest dreams and desires. "I can do all things through Christ who strengthens me" (Philippians 4:13, KJV).

- Set for yourself a goal of excellence… today!
- Put first things first… today!
- Go the extra mile… today!

You are *never* too old, *never* too young, and *never* too dumb! Get up and get with it!

- Love yourself!
- Believe in yourself!
- Trust in God!
- Never give up!

I pray that when you finally reach your goal, it will be everything you imagined (dreamed) it would be! You already know all too well what it feels like to fail. It's time to put the negative experiences from your past, as well as the negative input from the world, behind you! Start dreaming! Develop a burning desire for what you want out of life!

Stop finding reasons why you cannot reach your goal! *You* are the only reason why you haven't made it up to now. If you're not where you want to be, it's no one's fault but your own! Procrastinate no longer! The man or woman that gains total control of their three concrete elements "will ascend the mountaintop and tickle the angel's feet!"

> But they that wait on the Lord shall renew their strength; they shall mount up with wings as eagles, they shall run, and not be weary; they shall walk, and not faint. (Isaiah 40:31, kjv)

May God bless you, as you begin right now to get the best out of yourself—body, mind, and soul!

## The New Testament Steps of Salvation

Hear—Romans 10:17, John 8:32
Believe—Hebrews 11:6, Mark 16:16
Repent—Luke 13:3, Acts 17:30, Acts 2:38
Confess—Matthew 10:32-33, Romans 10:10, Philippians 2:11, Acts 22:14–16
Baptism—Matthew 28:18–20, Mark 16:15–16, Acts 2:38, Acts 8:38–39 Acts 22:16, Romans 6:3–5, 1 Peter 3:20–22

## Chapter Eight

# Teaching an Old Dog New Tricks! Diet and Exercise for the Body, Mind, and Soul

You are never too old or never too young to learn. While the older we get, the wiser we should become, we never want to get to the point where we are not teachable. Every bit of knowledge gained is useful, whether it be of a particular interest to you or not. The failure to leave yourself open to new knowledge is a definitive step toward impending doom. Even if you've been successful in the past at whatever it is you are currently attempting to accomplish, always leave your soul and mind open to new or more creative ways of doing the same. No one owns the patent on any given area of success. A genuine willingness to learn is a basic staple of nearly every successful individual and is in reality nothing more than another discipline to which we must adhere.

Having said that, let me begin by reiterating that I believe with all my heart in good, old-fashioned discipline. Whether it's the gentle discipline enacted through the loving hand of a father or mother or that of my own personal self-discipline of the three concrete elements of our existence—the body, mind, and soul. You will *never* find success to its fullest potential until you have become the master of your whole being.

Although this word is not traditionally popular, discipline is an ever-present parameter in every recorded success. It matters not if we look at the lives of successful businessmen and women, a great athlete, or the everyday Christian. Whether they are aware of it or not, discipline is a part of every one of their lives in one form or another.

When you get right down to it, discipline is nothing more than self-control, which happens to be one of the foremost biblical "Fruits of the Spirit" (Galatians 5:22–23). I find it extremely intriguing that the God of heaven included discipline as a part of his directives to his children. It then goes without saying that parents should include this all-important parameter as a part of every child's rearing as it is an important, lifelong attribute that God himself endorses. "Train up a child in the way he should go: and when he is old, he will not depart from it" (Proverbs 22:6, KJV).

Never does this verse ring more loudly than in the area of discipline.

It doesn't take a genius to see the devastating effects on a child that has been raised with little or no discipline. Not only does it cause a general disrespect for everyone they come in contact with, but also, they often fail to complete their education or else never learn to take care of themselves. As a youth minister, I saw this ever increasing but disturbing similarity in countless young people.

Nowadays, parents are increasingly adamant about overprotecting their children from the *real* world. The result is one generation after another failing to launch, unable to support themselves, leaning on Dad and Mom late into their twenties, thirties, and beyond.

I have always told my children that home is always a constant, no matter how old they are. Everyone needs a safety net of some kind. I had that net in the form of my mother and father's home. I even fell back on my siblings a couple of times early in life when I ran into unexpected difficulties. It's nice to have a place to go and people you can count on to help and understand. But the modern-day method of parenting has taken this concept to new and unnecessary lengths, allowing children to move back in permanently with Mom and Dad as a means of escaping *real* responsibility in life.

I have personally witnessed an epidemic of elderly parents who are raising a second family due to the irresponsible and often nonchalant choices of their own children. Their children have babies they don't want (irresponsible act number 1) and simply *give them away* to whomever will take them (irresponsible act number 2) so as not to face the reality of their choices.

Mom and Dad seem to be the people most often abused under these circumstances, both physically and financially. My wife and I are continually amazed at the number of women now days that get pregnant unexpectedly. Come on now, ladies and guys, this is the modern age! Pregnancy prevention is available in multiple forms, (abstinence being the God-preferred method) and extremely easy to administer. I am *not* condoning fornication here! I'm just wondering why those who seem to be the most promiscuous also often seem to be the least prepared, as well as the least thoughtful of what their immediate choices will do to their life and the lives of others.

Making a baby comes with tremendous responsibility that presumes a lifetime of commitment. A lack of forethought or planning is a flippant and selfish attitude in comparison to the actual reality that naturally comes with a child. You're not just making a choice for yourself but for your child and your family as well as there are others to consider in the long-term scheme of things. There has always been a rash of "split-second" children in the world. But having an unexpected baby between two married individuals that have already agreed and are open to the idea of children is a completely different concept from the that of the popular "come what may" attitude of many young adults now days. This persistent attitude seems to stem from the fact that Mom, Dad, and our modern society has made an out for these poor choices, the most disturbing and ungodly being the incessant insistence of our government to allow the murder of millions of unwanted babies a year. The sin of abortion alone has condemned us before the almighty God. The miracle of life is his most precious gift to us save that of his own son, Jesus Christ, yet we treat these little angels as if they are an unimportant option.

Creating unwanted babies is not the only disturbing characteristic of today's *modern* child. Children also turn to Mom and Dad every time they run out of money, have a car break down, need money for something they can't afford, and so on. Don't get me wrong. I have helped my children on multiple occasions when they *needed* a hand. But *need* is the key word here. For some reason, we have migrated our parenting from that of preparing our children for the inevitable downturns in life toward that of trying to shield our children altogether from the same struggles we and everyone else before us has had. We believe that they're not going to survive life if we're not there to cover every need, solve every dilemma, or cover every bill. That's simply not true, and in fact, that will eventually enable a child to the point that they become mentally and emotionally handicapped in life, unable to do much of anything on their own.

Home should always be available to your children. However, think of it less as a safety net and more like a trampoline. What I mean to say is your children should be able to count on you and your resources from time to time but only in a temporary fashion. Instead of continually *catching* your children every time they fall, allowing them to get swallowed up in the net back home, they should momentarily hit the homestead like a trampoline and then bounce back into the world on their own.

This nanny mentality of raising children has also caused a dip in the economy as more and more young people are coming to rely on government entitlements. It's not as much their fault as it is the fault of their parents who failed to teach their children the basic disciplines of work, independence, self-reliance, and respect. As parents, we must stop this ceaseless nonsense of running ahead of our children in every matter, lead-blocking every opponent that attempts to tackle them! Children need to understand the cold, hard fact that life is comprised of more failures…than successes! Failure isn't a sign that they did something wrong, but instead, they attempted to do something right and didn't succeed. These hard lessons are a necessary step for us all; they serve to weed out all the methods that *do not* work so that we might get onward and upward to that which does work!

In my grandparents' day, children got married in their early teens, and immediately went to work to support themselves. That standard has steadily decreased over the years as today we find numerous adults still sponging off of their parents! While we never want to harm our children, too little discipline does just that, creating the false impression that they can do pretty much whatever they want and get by with it, and that someone will always be there to take care of your needs if you simply put your hand out. A lack of discipline only serves to enable your child to continually fail. The *best* education you can give your child is that of the reality of the real world they are about to live in. Better they learn it under your protective guidance than the hard way! Either way, it's inevitable they will find out one way or the other.

Look at the word "disciple," a very familiar term used throughout the New Testament, which refers to one becoming a "devotee" or ardent "follower" of someone, or a particular type of movement. Thus, we read examples of many people becoming

Disciples of Christ, calling themselves by this title, first at Antioch. You see, the term "Christian" mentioned here in Acts 11:26, refers to one who seeks to be "Christ-like" or in essence "more like Christ"—that is a "disciple" of Christ (disciplined to act like him).

Though the left has ignorantly misconstrued this term, it *does not* refer to "one that is perfect" or one that is exactly like Christ himself. Instead, it refers to the original term "disciple" translated as someone who is a "supporter," "follower," and even "learner" of Christ. Since "discipline" comes from the root word "disciple," it is unquestionably a challenging walk, like any other worthwhile ambition in life. If we criticized everyone that is striving to better his or her self, yet falls occasionally along the way, no one would ever achieve any worthwhile purpose!

Personally, I have never understood the position of bashing people who are striving to live morally. After all, morality is the central theme of our own constitution, and was at one time the basis for every imposed law. Though that parameter has obviously changed drastically in the last century, it doesn't preclude the concept that being good is a bad thing! Shouldn't that be the basic target for *every* citizen? I submit that if we intend to lower crime, then the moral foundation of the average person becomes a matter of utmost importance.

Like it or not, morality lies at the nucleus of every crime, regardless of what the particular wrongdoing or original motive might have been. Stretching the definition of morality to fit everyone is equal to condoning lawlessness as one regularly causes the other. So we should not be in the practice of condemning those that seek to live by a higher standard, even when they sometimes fail to do so. Once again, the concept of morality starts in the home at an early age, as well as the reality that to err is *human*. There's no way to get around that one, seeing that's what we all are!

To this extent, *none* among us is perfect or even close to perfect! We are merely "disciplining" ourselves to do our very best to mimic the flawless character of Christ.

I mention this to bring to light an elementary deduction: being disciplined does not make you perfect! It only means you are daily giving your utmost attention toward taking the higher road. You may not be there yet, but you are one step closer to reaching the pinnacle of that which you long to one-day mirror.

So don't believe that if you become disciplined, you can never fall from grace. As in the case with Christianity, we as the apostle Paul must "buffet our bodies daily" (1 Corinthians 9:27 KJV), that is, cleanse it abrasively, discipline it by hardships. "Working out our own salvation with fear and trembling" (Philippians 2:12, KJV).

We are only human, and thus, mistakes are going to happen. *No one* is above them or beyond them. There is only one in the entire history of the world that was perfect in all three: body, mind, and soul. He is sitting now at the right hand of God. Expect mistakes! But always discipline yourself to both avoid them and/or learn from them so as not to repeat your folly. The *only* dumb aspect of our mistakes is the failure to learn from them! "Those who cannot remember the past are condemned to repeat it."[26]

Despite our habitual insistence of blaming everyone else for our problems, situations, and predicaments in life, the very fact that what happened is personal links an inference to self and therefore points a finger directly back at me. I am the sole proprietor of my actions and, by association alone, directly responsible for wherever I find myself in life. While outside influences might push me in one direction or another, it is indeed how I react and the choices that I make that will ultimately determine the outcome.

No one need lecture me on the pain associated with this often ignored, "don't like to hear it," highly unpopular word. But it's an absolute that you and I must cope with and include, if we truly intend to reach any goal or aspiration.

It is for this reason that I have included this final chapter, a sort of bonus, as a part of this book. I never have liked someone simply telling me that I need to change my life, without at least giving me a few examples of how I might actually get it done.

Since we have pretty much covered the how-tos of the soul and mind in previous chapters, the following instruction manual will mainly focus on discipline of the body. I have included, however, a daily guide to success that merely suggests what a typical day in your newfound life might look like. Use it or not, or just make up your own schedule. This is meant only as a means to give you a general idea of where to start, as well as what is possible.

Having said that, be ever so diligent to apply the techniques for exercise covered thoroughly in chapter 4 "The Body." By initializing and personalizing the directives of that chapter in harmony with the suggested exercises and diets in this chapter, you can become better acquainted with your body, and you will be surprised at the tremendous results that will come as a result of your disciplined efforts.

Throughout the rest of your life, *never* forget that if you manage only to discipline one parameter of the trio of concrete elements, you will still not be entirely successful. The *total* person, as God fully intended, is one that strives to keep each and every one of the three in check every day.

May God bless and keep you safe as you endeavor from this day forward to be the best you can possibly be in your life for him!

## Getting Started

Every significant life change requires a starting point. When it comes to the human body, little has as much effect on the way we look and feel as what we eat! So let's begin by putting the most efficient substances in our mouths in order to enact the desired outcome, whether it be just feeling better or looking better. It will take no time at all to recognize that there is as much discipline involved in eating correctly as in spiritual and physical exercise.

There are as many guides to proper nutrition out there as there are choices in deodorant! For this reason, you may use your own, but my wife and I would like to share an effective program that has worked many times for us in the past. Keep in mind that everyone is different, and you may have to adjust your personal diet according to your desired results.

Let's begin with a brief discussion about the word "calorie." Often misunderstood, a "calorie" is nothing more than a unit of "energy" that is derived mainly from the food we eat. It makes since that every machine demands an energy source. Your body is no different. But just like you wouldn't overfill your gasoline tank on your car, you too need only a specific amount of fuel each time you fuel up in order to produce the impending demand. Unlike your car, your body does not get full and then simply burn whatever gas is in the tank. The body redundantly stores all excess fuel, hoarding it for possible future use, instead of flushing away whatever it does not need. This is where the majority of well-intentioned dieters slip up as the body has no maximum storage limit. So the question would then be, "How much fuel do I actually need?" ("Need" and "want" are not the same thing!)

This question can only be answered accurately by first determining what you expect the demand to be on any given day. If you plan on initializing the complete body fitness program as described in this chapter, it might be wise to take in a few additional calories. However, where you get those calories from is a key component and influence in the actual outcome.

The US Government nutritional guide recommends that the average daily caloric intake should not exceed two thousand calories. Keep in mind, however, that this applies *only* to those that do not wish to gain any additional weight. It does not necessarily mean that this is a low enough intake to spur weight loss.

If your desire is to shed some unwanted pounds, you will likely have to go quite a bit lower. You obviously can't starve yourself, but you have to get your body in the fat-burning mode before you can expect any weight to actually come off. It can take anywhere from several days to a few weeks to get your body's metabolism in high gear, depending on the individual and the habits you have formed previously. Your body is a creature of habit and will act according to that which it has previously been accustomed to, not to that which you have suddenly changed overnight. So in the beginning of your program, it will initially react in much the same manner as before—that is, business as usual—until the change becomes more the rule than the exception.

In order to get your body kick started, you're going to have to get well below what you are accustomed to taking in each day, which breaks down to what you take in with each meal and even each snack.

I am fortunate to have married a certified fitness instructor who has aided hundreds of students over the years in both weight loss and physical fitness. By her recommendation, it is crucial that you get your total caloric intake below two thousand calories a day.

But on that same note, you don't want to go *too low*. In fact, she recommends no lower than 1,200 calories per day due to the fact that your body demands a certain amount of protein, fat, and other nutrients just to sustain its basic functions (i.e., heart pumping, healthy muscle tissue, digestion, and immune system, just to name a few).

Without this minimum daily caloric intake, these systems can eventually malfunction or fail all together, thereby making you feel ill or possibly even creating permanent damage. This would obviously defeat your original goal of looking and feeling better—what you started out to do in the first place. There will always be those who believe they can shift their daily calorie intake around to justify a single meal or binge. There is some truth in this, but *only* if it is done properly and in a well-disciplined manner.

Think of your metabolism as a stop watch. The button on top obviously starts and stops the second hand. Notice how quickly the second hand moves once you push the button. Notice also how quickly it stops moving when you push the button again.

This is a wonderful example of what you do, each and every time you mess around with your caloric intake. As I mentioned above, your body, like the other two of your concrete elements, is a creature of habit. In fact, it might be driven more by habit than by any other means.

Once you get your body on any daily routine, it will fight you to stay on that same routine. This includes both good and bad routines. But always remember that the body will cry at the first sign of pain or discomfort. The stomach will be as big a baby as any other member. The second it feels like it's not getting what it's used to, it will send a signal to the brain, and the brain (who is sympathetic to the body), in turn, will force the quickest action to remedy the discomfort.

In order to get your body into the fat-burning mode, you're going to have to make some gradual adjustments to your caloric intake. People that simply jump in with both feet, slashing the habitual caloric intake drastically, will usually fail within a few days or less. It's just too big of a shock to the system.

But just like the stopwatch, your metabolic rate can be stopped quickly, depending on the habits that you form. For instance, if you get in the habit of starving yourself through breakfast, your button never gets pushed to begin with. Your metabolism will simply sit idle all morning, burning no additional calories beyond the basic necessities.

If there be any difference between the stop watch and the human body, it would be that your body cannot start burning calories in a split-second, if it is in the habit of burning very little. However, the reverse is true. A sudden change in eating habits can push your metabolism button, bringing your calorie burn to an immediate halt. This is most often done by a sporadic change from eating regularly to not eating at all.

No food is a signal to your body that there is a famine on the horizon. Although this may not be factual, keep in mind that your body is blindly commanded by the mind, with no real knowledge of its own. Its automated features are all initiated by the control center—your mind.

Just because your mind knows you're going to eat lunch does not presume that the body has that same knowledge. In fact, it knows nothing of the lunch to come, and you have already sent it a signal that there is no more food when you denied it breakfast. In this regard, the stop watch example is extremely accurate. The moment your body goes beyond a reasonable time to eat (generally within the first hour after you get up), it pushes the Stop button, and your metabolism comes to an immediate halt!

Of course, there is always some calorie burn, or else, you would collapse. But when it comes to burning *significant* amounts of calories, it just won't happen unless you are willing to eat regularly!

This is where most people get into trouble. They believe that they are the way they are because of the way they eat. Okay, this *is* true to some extent! However, it's not because they eat that they are overweight. It's what they eat, how much they eat, as well as when they eat that causes the problem. Eating is *never* the real symptom. In fact, eating is a basic necessity for us all! It's all about timing and portion. So let's discuss those one at a time.

Let's say that you are allowing yourself a total of 1,200 calories a day. It only takes a few minutes reading labels at the grocery store to realize that this is going to be a strict diet. However, there are some foods that are low enough in calories that would thereby allow a bigger portion. The whole point is to diet—that is, lose weight—while feeling somewhat full or satisfied. This is where timing comes in.

First, the actual time of day you eat is of the utmost importance. The idea of "three square meals a day" is correct, but you also have to figure in a small (well chosen) snack in between each meal as well. The overall idea here is to keep your metabolism running at the optimum rate. Again, there are only two ways to make this happen: increase your activity level and/or time your eating appropriately. A combination of the two is the most efficient method and will yield the greatest results.

So begin immediately to time your meals out consistently each day, starting with breakfast. Try to get your body on a regimen it can count on routinely. Remember, your body loves habit!

Next, it's imperative to keep your motor racing by ensuring your tank *never* runs dry. In order to accomplish this, you absolutely *must* have a single snack between each meal. You may or may not be hungry. That's not the point. You don't ever want to allow your body to sense hunger.

By keeping fuel in your tank, you are sending the continual positive message to your body stating "there's plenty of food!" Once your body gets adjusted to this sensation, it will turn up the calorie burn regularly. In other words, you will burn more calories than you have in the past by eating more often, whether in motion or not.

It's sort of like having lots of money in your bank account or just a little. One prods you to be a shopaholic, while the other makes you a spend thrift. You tend to burn less money if you don't have much or when you aren't certain when more money will arrive.

This is where the greatest misconception in dieting normally occurs. Most believe that they will lose more if they eat less. That's only true in regard to your total daily caloric allowance. As long as you stay within the allotted total number of calories, the timing in how you consume those calories then becomes the *most important* aspect. *Not* whether you will eat or not eat.

A portion of anything that looks small does not necessarily mean that its low calorie. Don't be fooled by the size of a particular food or snack. That has absolutely nothing to do with how many calories might be in it. Granted, you can eat some foods by merely cutting down the portion, but it's dangerous to guess at the calorie count, judged only by size alone.

For instance, a small snack might appear in your cabinet in the form of candy-covered almonds. After all, they are tiny. What harm could two or three of them possibly cause? But a closer examination on the back panel reveals that 3.5 of these almonds equal 220 calories. That's far too many calories for a snack. So what about snacking on a single cup of Maruchan Instant Soup? It will be more filling, and after all, it's only soup. Most people automatically think low calorie when they think of soup. But once again, the back panel proclaims a single serving to be the whole cup at 290 calories. Again, this is far too many calories to be considered as a snack.

What you're looking for here, in regard to a reasonable snack, is somewhere between 100–150 calories. This isn't always found in foods that appear to be smaller. Four slices of honey ham is only 60 calories, along with two slices of light wheat bread at 90 calories, equaling only 150 calories total. So in this case, more is less! Not only are you going to stay within your allotted calories for this particular snack, but you will likely get far fuller on the larger portion of the sandwich than you would have with the three tiny almonds or the cup of soup. Think *calories*, not *size*!

While the majority of diets stress the total number of calories you should eat in a day, many of them fail to stress the when you eat factor as well. So back to the binge. You're extremely hungry, and you haven't eaten all day. The reasonable logic would be to assume that since you still have two thousand calories at your disposal, you can simply eat every one of them right now and just not eat another morsel the rest of the day. Right? Wrong! You couldn't do anything more harmful. In fact, you might as well not diet at all.

Each time you starve your body, you once again enter the starvation mode by sending a message that there's not going to be enough food. You may remember in a previous chapter that we discussed your body's built-in safety mechanism geared toward survival. It does not apply only toward immediate life or death situations. It also works over the long haul.

Your body realizes that a steady intake of calories translates into an abundant supply of food. However, when mealtime comes around and nothing comes down the pipe, your energy furnace, better known as your metabolism, simmers down immensely, causing you to go into the calorie-reserve mode, which is the last thing you want to do if you are on a diet! The whole idea is to burn more calories, not less! The less you burn, the more you store. Storing excessive amounts of calories only adds to weight gain and causes you to continually slide backward on your diet.

This is why you have found yourself dieting and exercising faithfully, only to step on the scale at the end of the month to discover you have made little or no progress. Turning your metabolism off in the middle of an otherwise successful program only delays your progress and often becomes the determining factor as to whether or not you will continue.

It might also be important at this time to touch on which particular counting method you choose. My wife and daughter completely follow the calorie counting method, while I have always had great success counting fat grams. In reality, fat grams actually convert to calories anyway with one gram of fat equaling approximately nine calories. Either way, you need to do some serious label reading and just assure that whichever method you begin with is the one you consistently stick to. (Remember, habit.)

Now, let's talk about the preferred food sources from which you get your daily calorie allowance. Which food you eat is just as important as how many calories it contains. There are empty food calories versus nutrient dense calories.

Nutrient density is the amount of nutrients per unit of energy or calorie. Two food choices can have the exact same number of calories but vary greatly in the amount of vitamins and nutrients.

It should be obvious that drinking a low-cal protein shake would be a far better choice for an occasional beverage than a diet soda. On the same note, eating a regular size bowl of chili would be a far better choice over a chocolate bar. While the chili might sound fattening as well, an average-sized portion contains about 270 calories (the same as the chocolate bar) but also includes a good serving of protein from the beans and meat.

Get in the habit of looking deeper into the foods you select for each meal *before* you make them your final choice. When you get caught in a situation, such as at a fast food restaurant, where there are few low-fat selections, always take the nutrient healthy choice first. Just be sure to continue to count the calories by controlling the portions.

The point here is that calories are not always equal in value simply because they are equal in number. In order to sustain a high-enough energy level to both diet and exercise, you have to insist on trading your daily-allotted calories for the highest nutrient rich content possible.

All this diet talk might sound a bit depressing. It's never enjoyable to force your body to eat less than it desires. But there is something you can do that might curtail your anxiety and assure your success that much more.

I have always believed the old adage "All work and no play makes Jack a dull boy!" We are all naturally geared toward having a good time once in a while. This is normal as long as we *balance* the recreational time in a logical proportion to the serious, or work time. This applies to eating and exercise as well.

If you diet and exercise 24-7, it is likely that you will eventually burn out. This is where most people either binge or quit altogether. Again, the important factor to remember is that this is a rewards program, not an all-out free for all! In order to understand the rewards program, let's first take a look at why people eat and/or exercise in the first place.

Who benefits from a diet and exercise program? I certainly gain little for all the effort my wife puts forth, save the one big plus of being seen in public with this slim little buffed-up beauty on my arm. While I'll take that any day of the week over the alternative, what my wife looks like does not affect how I treat her, how I see her, or how much I love her. When you get right down to it, the person that benefits the most is my wife!

I mention this for good reason as we are all often guilty of dieting and exercising for the wrong *person*, not just for the wrong reason. Let me elaborate.

There's no denying that emotions play a huge role in both diet and exercise. When we are feeling up or good, we have very little trouble sticking to our regimen as compared to when we are feeling down or not so good. I will refer you to chapter 3, "The Mind," as to some of the reasons behind a lack of self-control. As we have established, the soul controls the mind, and the mind controls the body. It then goes without saying that if your mind gets out of control, then so will your body.

We all begin a routine for different reasons although they are often similar (i.e., "I don't feel good," "I'm overweight," or "I just feel uncomfortable in my skin"). But if you look at each of these individually, there's a common denominator within each one. That common denominator is *you*!

We would rarely go through the time, pain, and effort required to change the way we look, simply to please everyone else. As I've stated before, most people couldn't care less what we look like and hardly even notice us. In fact, we are all noticed far less than we would like to admit. We each like to believe that we are the center of attention wherever we go. But that isn't reality. Even though we ourselves may take momentary notice of a particular person in public, it is just that—momentary at best. An hour later, you have already forgotten that person for good!

So the real, deep-seated reason for changing yourself—whether it is physical, emotional, or spiritual—is because *you* solely desire to see a difference. Recognizing this reality is of the utmost importance as it has very much to do with whether or not you succeed.

A good example of this would be a couple that is married. One of the two decides to diet and exercise for the obvious benefit to self. However, one day their spouse does something that hacks them off, so in some weird act of retaliation, they gorge themselves for a day or two, believing all the while that they are somehow "getting back" at their mate.

But the reality of this situation is that they are only hurting themselves! If I truly love my wife unconditionally, then she could eat all day every day till she pops, and it would not hurt me in the slightest. I have, in real life, loved my wife equally at her heaviest weight, as well as at her lightest weight. I was unaffected either way. True love cannot be measured in pounds. If it is, then it's not true love!

Once again, this is a lack of mind control in that your soul (the original pursuer of your goal) is allowing the mind to determine your success based on inaccurate information. It's inaccurate in that you are *never* going to impair your significant other in any way by harming yourself, except by the apparent exception of maiming or, God forbid, killing yourself. The measurable difference between the damage we inflict upon ourselves, versus that to others, is night and day.

So let us now readdress the matter of the reward program. Again, it is an ever so crucial fundamental in your diet-exercise strategy that there be some type of reward system for a job well done. But even this must be done in a highly disciplined fashion, or else, this too will become a weak link and might even initiate an opportunity to go overboard. It's a reward, not a change of lifestyle!

First, we need to look at the wrong kind of reward program. This would be a situation where someone has remained disciplined for a day or two and then uses the logic that since they have done so well, they can now cheat in a big way. In this scenario, there hasn't been a significant enough amount of progress to merit the reward. Also, the reward itself is usually overdone. Keeping the following thought in mind best summarizes the correct method of reward: "Large amount of progress, little reward." Of course, it's up to you to determine logically the definition of large in your case. Just use common sense as your guide. If you've only lost one pound, you wouldn't want to reward yourself with food. That's illogical. You would likely wind up gaining the one pound right back.

A more sensible approach might be to reward yourself to a movie, a knick-knack you've been wanting, or maybe a good book. But at this rather small level of success, you need to match the reward in a balanced fashion to the progress.

But even without weight loss, you are going to need an occasional reward as long as you are truthfully sticking with the program. Again, my wife recommends no more than two delicious treats per week. Still, these too must remain within a reasonable and controlled portion. Let's say, one chocolate bar cut in half would serve as your reward for the week. In the case where you feel you can't stick to just one, eat the other half three days later. Just do not ever eat the whole thing at one time! Again, discipline and common sense is the key here!

Another way of rewarding your success is to take a day off from the gym. It just can't be every day or more than two days in a row. You need to work out a minimum of three days a week, preferably four to five days a week. And don't stack your workouts on one end of the week but rather spread them out so that you never go more than two days off. There will always be those busy weeks when something unexpected comes up and disrupts your routine. In this case, just do the best you can to do *all* you can! Make sure you get right back in the routine at the start of the following week.

Set reasonable rewards for yourself, keeping in mind that every time you cheat, you stand the chance of messing up your progress or denying yourself your ultimate goal or dream.

While we are at it, I'd like to talk about secret snacking. There are a lot of things in life that we should keep in secret, but snacking is not one of them! In reality, the more open you are with your diet, the more likely you are to succeed. Sneaking food behind close doors has a two-fold effect. First, it will very much interfere with your weight control, and second, it causes you to be dishonest to others about how well you are actually doing. The latter in turn creates a state of guilt/depression, which, in turn, makes you eat that much more.

Also, do not fall into the trap of becoming an instigator due to your own lack of discipline. It's not uncommon to find several people embarking on the same diet/exercise routine. We often find strength in numbers as well as a sense of security in knowing we're not alone in our struggles.

The main problem that usually comes out of this convenient relationship stems from a weak team member that continually slips up. No harm done if it's only them that slips. But all too often, these weak links require a partner in crime in order to make themselves feel better or to justify their sinful actions.

These well-meaning individuals will sometimes discourage others in the group to cheat with them, eating an outrageous meal or snack, or continually making excuses to not work out. They reason thusly, "We've all been doing well, so we deserve to cheat!"

Or there's the scenario where everybody is making progress. Then all of the sudden, someone brings a box of donuts to work. Granted, no one has to eat them. But the mere act of subjecting the rest of the group to such torment shows a genuine lack of devotion or concern for everyone else. If you want to backslide, kindly do it on your own. Just don't be guilty of dragging everybody else backward with you.

Now that we have discussed the basic ins and outs of eating, let's talk about what your daily routine should look like.

I would recommend starting *every* day with your meditation time. Again, this doesn't have to be more than ten minutes, focusing mainly on reconfirming your ISP, and beginning or ending each session with prayer in regard to your pursuits. This time is in addition to any regularly scheduled devotion you might engage in. Do not take time away from God!

Once you enter your meditation area (see chapter 3), sit quietly, clearing your mind of *everything* that has nothing to do with your ISP. It may sound meaningless, but try to always sit in the same place, facing the same direction. (Your three elements love habit!)

Remember also, this is not the time to decide what your ISP should ultimately be. That needs to be accomplished through thoughtful consideration and prayer in advance of beginning your actual trek toward your goal.

At this moment in time, you're only focusing on what it is you wish so desperately to achieve. It is possible however to do a total makeover in which you pursue multiple qualities. This is not only admirable but preferred as well! There's no rule prohibiting the improvement of several delinquent aspects of your life at the same time. If you like very little about yourself, then remake yourself from top to bottom!

*See* yourself reaching your goal or acquiring your dream. Picture what it will look like. Go ahead… *imagine greatly*! Don't be afraid to talk to yourself either. If others can hear you, you might want to talk it out in your head. But when possible, verbally speak your intentions as often as possible. Just hearing yourself reconfirm your goal makes it more believable.

Again, if you have a favorite Bible verse or motivational reading, now is the time to go over it. In time, strive to memorize these words, and repeat them to yourself through the day.

Before closing, renew your agreement of cooperation (see chapter 3) between your soul, mind, and body. Make sure to reaffirm each of their individual responsibilities for today in making your goal one step closer to reality. Make each party shake hands mentally, rising to their expected duties for the next twenty-four-hour period. Take no excuses from either of the three, insisting and encouraging each other toward an overall positive attitude.

Also, *never* relinquish the power of the soul to either of the other two entities! In other words, whatever the soul demands, the soul gets! Any disputes will be left to the judgment of the soul to settle. The soul steers the mind, and in turn, the mind steers the body. It absolutely has to remain this way! *Everyone* must agree that the *soul reigns supreme*!

I recommend closing in prayer, asking God to bless your efforts with success. Once your meditation time has ended, do your best to focus only on the next several hours, cutting it up into increments if necessary. *Never* look too far ahead as this can become discouraging. You're only interested in the next twelve hours or so. Success is not one giant leap but rather the result of several smaller steps. Take it easy… Take it slowly! Rome wasn't built in a day, but a significant part of it was.

One of the dirtiest words in modern society has to be exercise! I know several people that have no trouble proclaiming their hate of it and flat-out refuse to participate in any program that even slightly resembles physical fitness! We actually know a couple that humorously brag about their refusal to lift a finger toward athletic activity.

In view of the fact that our bodies were designed to move, it is scientifically proven that they operate most efficiently when kept in motion consistently. The sedentary lifestyle has claimed its millions of lives over the ages and has only gotten worse in the industrial age in which we now live.

I would ask that you quickly review chapter 4, "The Body," for specifics dealing with control of the same. The following guidelines are based on the fact that you have thoroughly read this book up to this point and have thereby familiarized yourself with the driver's manual in *your* personal vehicle.

Whether your workout period is best suited to your schedule in the morning, or at night, is a preference that only you can decide. I have found great benefit in years gone by getting my workout out of the way in the wee morning hours, but my job of the past twelve years does not allow for that luxury, so I now workout in the evenings *after* eight to ten hours on the job. Yes, I am tired before I workout. But take it from me, it *can* be done!

The important thing here is to set a consistent time of day, *every* day, and then go through with it, whether you are tired or not. In time, you will develop a greater resistance to fatigue, simply by getting healthier and stronger. The key is to get past the first six to eight weeks of your program. By then, your routine is established as a habit and, in turn, becomes a natural part of your life.

In most instances, I have found that getting to the gym is half the battle. For this reason, I recommend the avoidance of sitting too long after you come home, so as not to slow your heart rate and metabolism too much. Once you wind down, it's far more difficult to wind up again.

As discussed earlier, you might want to consider working out at home initially before committing to an expensive gym membership or investing in workout clothing, gear, etc. Again, if you cannot consistently complete the most basic floor exercises at home, then you're never going to stick to a program that includes traveling to another location, changing clothes, and so on. Better you find out right up front if you are fully armed for what you are about to undertake *before* you spend any money.

Once you arrive to your workout destination, do not hesitate to begin! We often spend more time dreading an exercise than actually performing it! Situate whatever beverage you take along in such a manner that you don't have to continually walk a long distance to retrieve it as this only serves in a negative fashion to cool you down. You want to keep your heart rate and calorie burn up as much as possible so as to net the greatest result.

Begin your first exercise as quickly as possible, using the counting method discussed in chapter 4, "The Body." Focus only on the very next rep, the very next set, etc. Just as in the case with your ISP, never look any further down the road than necessary. By focusing on how much workout you still have to complete, you're reverberating negative messages that can eventually become overwhelming, leading you to quit altogether.

Each rep is as important as any other rep you will ever do. Just because you're not presently where you want to be does not diminish the intrinsic value of each and every repetition. Your ultimate physique will be the accumulated results of many thousands of individual efforts.

Also, to avoid the inevitable cries from your all-too-predictable body, try focusing during each exercise on a particular spot in the room, whether on the floor or the wall. Use the same spot every time you move to that particular area of the room. Find a different spot for each area. Since the body and mind are creatures of habit, do your best to always perform each exercise in the same spot, facing the same direction. The only exception to this rule is in the case where you might eventually peak, unable to make any further progress. This will inevitably happen to everyone.

Remember that the mind and the body will adapt no further than the required demand. Once your body acquires the strength and agility to do a particular weight or exercise with ease, it will peak in growth and performance, and your forward progress will come to a standstill. Not to worry, you simply have to either up the demand (i.e., more weight, more reps, etc.) or shock your body forward by starting a completely new and different routine.

If you have already taken the responsible step in getting a thorough physical *before* you begin your program, you now have a green light to push yourself a bit. Don't overdo it, but on the other hand, don't be ridiculously susceptible to the endless whining of your mind and body. Expect it in advance, and be prepared to deal with it! Keep your soul in charge, continually driving the mind and body toward what you demand! Take no less that what you want and deserve! This is why you came to workout in the first place, so you might as well get the biggest bang for your buck! Don't waste time walking around, visiting or resting. Try to keep moving at all times, so as to squeeze as much exercise as possible into each and every session. You will also find that this will help to shorten the actual length of your workout, making it less grueling and giving you more time for things you'd rather be doing.

It is appropriate to rest for two to three minutes between each set, but don't use this as a time to sit around, visit, or get off track. You're on a mission here, so stick to the plan! If someone tries to start up a conversation, be polite, but excuse yourself as soon as possible. Just explain that you have to keep moving.

I like to group my exercises according to body parts while others might prefer circuit training. I've experienced great results with either method. Circuit training is defined as working several body parts at once. You begin with an exercise that targets, say, the biceps and then next do an exercise that targets the quadriceps (the big muscles on your thighs.) Then go back to the upper body, maybe working your chest, then back down to your calves on the following exercise. Regardless of what method you use, I would always do no less than three sets, (preferably four) on every exercise, and at least eight to twelve repetitions per set. This will give you a total of thirty-two to forty-eight reps per exercise. Some methods require that you burn out the muscle by working it to failure. This simply means that you keep doing repetitions until the muscle cannot do any more.

You can also pyramid either up or down on weight. This is accomplished by starting as heavy on weight as you can stand and still finish the set, then immediately removing an increment of weight, say 5 lbs. at a time, doing the same number of reps again, and then repeat the process till you're down to the last weight left. You will be shocked as to how weak you will become toward the end. This is a good thing as it puts so much demand on the muscle, causing it to eventually tear and rebuild. It is also a natural process and is in fact the physiological means by which a muscle grows larger. It's the body's natural response to a continually increased demand. You may also choose to burn out the muscle on each set using the pyramid method as well—that is, adding weight to each set, doing as many reps as possible with each new weight increase. Test both techniques to see which one yields the greatest gain for you personally.

If you aspire to workout like I do, concentrating on different muscle groups for each workout, pick the theme of the day, say, arms, and then do at least four exercises that target the same. Again, do at least eight to twelve reps per set and three to four sets per exercise.

Along with every workout, I recommend exercising your abs as they can handle the daily load without injury and take a lot of work to tame. Just throw in four sets of some kind of abdominal work somewhere along the way each time you work out. Actually, a recent study has proven that planks are the very best abdominal routine and will save you several hours of exercise in the long run, as well as a sore back down the road. I highly recommend them!

They have also found that doing your abdominal routine at the beginning of your workout seems to have a greater benefit in regard to getting your blood flowing more efficiently throughout your body. The proper form and technique for planks is illustrated in the latter part of this chapter.

And another thing, don't forget to breathe! I know this sounds like common sense, but this natural and automatic act of survival often goes neglected when we are exercising, lifting, or straining. The tendency seems to be to hold one's breath at the height of physical demand. If you look around the gym, you will observe what I am saying in numerous individuals.

# Getting the Best Out of Yourself: Body, Mind, and Soul

In order to get proper blood circulation, as well as to avoid passing out, it's vitally important to inhale a large quantity of air on the negative side of the exercise, and always exhale, or push the air out on the positive side. To give you an idea what this would look like, imagine for just a moment that you're doing bicep curls. It doesn't matter if you are standing or sitting, the breathing would be the same in either case. Grab the curl bar firmly with both hands. Before you begin the first repetition, take a deep breath, so that your lungs are fully charged, and all of your muscles are full of fresh, oxygenated blood. As you start the upward movement of the bar toward your chest, exhale continually until the positive motion is complete. As you start the bar back downward toward the ground, breathe in, then repeat the process on the second rep and so on.

Most people are conscious of nearly everything in the workout except their breathing. Surprisingly, the natural tendency of the body is to breathe just the opposite of what I've just described, inhaling on the upward or positive motion, and exhaling on the way back down. This method actually works detrimentally toward your progress as it does not allow for your muscles to have a fresh oxygenated blood supply at the peak of greatest demand. Since muscles need oxygenated blood to grow, it makes sense that old blood, or blood that is oxygen depleted, *would not* be the best source for optimum growth.

Just remember this rule: out with the old is positive, and in with the new is negative. And above all, *never* hold your breath while exercising! That's a pretty sure way to get lightheaded and pass out!

Another area of controversy seems to be the length of each workout session overall. With the countless number of infomercials now days proclaiming workouts from twenty minutes all the way down to ten minutes a day, it's sometimes difficult for the well-intentioned newcomer to establish the difference between hype and what really works.

It's medically proven that in order to burn the maximum amount of calories per aerobic workout session, you must establish and maintain your heart rate at a minimum of 75 percent of your max, for a sustained period of at least twenty minutes. On the other end of the spectrum, too much aerobic exercise can be detrimental as well. For this reason it is not advisable to go more than one hour as your muscles will actually begin to atrophy, and your body will become cannibalistic, eventually feeding on the very muscle you're attempting to build.

We recommend that you never take off cold from a dead start but rather warm up gradually for about five minutes on your way toward your target heart rate.

The key to remember is that everybody's heart rate is different. In fact, there's a simple formula you can follow in order to determine your target heart rate, which is also known as your range or zone.

Always begin by taking your pulse while at rest. You can accomplish this from your wrist or neck. If you're not sure how to take your pulse, I would suggest you Google it. It's not difficult.

Take your pulse for ten seconds, and multiply the number of beats you get times six. This is your heart rate per minute at rest. You can repeat this process every few minutes while you're working out in order to determine if you need to increase or decrease your activity to stay within your zone.

Take the mathematical constant of 220 minus your current age. The resulting figure will be your individual maximum heart rate. This is the rate you should *never* allow yourself to exceed.

Next, take the number you got above and multiply it by .55, then by .85. The reason you have to multiply by two different numbers is to allow you to find the low side and the high side of your target or zone. This is known as your range. Now that you have a range, just make sure that you always keep your heart rate somewhere in the middle.

You can always adjust your heart up or down by simply speeding up or slowing down the exercise, increasing or decreasing movement or increasing or decreasing resistance.

If you don't have a pulse monitor on the machine you're using or if you are working out freestyle, it will be necessary to take your pulse from time to time as described above in order to stay in your range. I've have included below a sample of this formula applied to my own situation.

220 (always standard)

-50 (my age)

170 (maximum heart rate)

Low side of Target range = 170 × .55 = 93.5 or 94 beats per minute

High side of target range = 170 ×.85= 144.5 or 145 beats per minute

Divide by six to find the ten-second pulse rate = 16 to 24 BPM.

Understand that this target range must be maintained in an uninterrupted fashion for at least twenty minutes. Starting and stopping doesn't count toward the twenty-minute interval. All you're doing is speeding up and slowing down your heart rate and, in turn, failing to reach your optimum calorie burn. You're wasting your time! It must be constant if you wish to succeed.

In the beginning, you may not be able to maintain the pace. If this is the case, then slow down, decrease the resistance, and gradually work your way toward your target range after a few workouts. But whatever you do, do it for at least twenty minutes! You're already working out, so you might as well get the maximum result for your efforts while you're at it. There's a proven science behind this method. Don't try to reinvent the wheel!

I told you how to do all that to say this: "If you don't exercise within your personal target range for at least twenty minutes, it's unlikely you will lose much, if any, weight. It doesn't necessarily have to be accomplished through aerobic exercise. It is possible to attain this rate from lifting weights alone as I have personally done it on many occasions although there is obviously some cardio advantage using the aerobic approach. But a recent university study proved that if a person keeps their rest time between sets to a minimal (2-3 minutes), they could actually burn more calories lifting weights correctly than through aerobic exercise. Once again, the method you use is the determining factor.

The idea is to keep moving, resting as little as possible between sets. We still recommend consistent pulse monitoring if you start to feel winded. Just play it smart and safe. Know where you are at internally at all times!

We also suggest a moderate cool down period after an extensive workout in your target range. This keeps your blood from pooling in your extremities, allowing the blood to return in significant amounts to your heart and brain, preventing lightheadedness or fainting, most often caused by stopping too abruptly. The first time you do this the wrong way, you will recognize it immediately!

I'll never forget my first experience with this awkward sensation. My mother decided several years ago to begin a workout regimen in an effort to tone up a bit and shed a few unwanted pounds. She asked if I would teach her a few basic floor exercises she could do every morning at home.

I arrived at her home on the first morning of her newfound program. We began with the basics, consisting of stretches, crunches, pushups, etc. Finally, I pulled a Bullworker out of my bag. For those of you that aren't familiar with this old-time exercise apparatus, it consisted of four metal springs, strung between two plastic handles. You could add or remove the springs in order to get the ideal resistance. This mechanism was designed as a means of mainly building your chest. You just grabbed a handle in each hand and began pulling them apart as far as your arms could reach. Then you slowly brought the springs back together and started the process over again. Primitive maybe, but it actually worked pretty well as long as you didn't get your chest pinched in between the springs! Ouch!

I was in the middle of demonstrating the Bullworker to Mom, when after eight or ten reps, everything went black. The next thing I remembered was coming to, slouched down in the couch. As Mother's face came slowly into focus, she had a puzzled look on her face and asked, "What do you call that?"

I thought for a second. "Passing out!" I replied. Truth of the matter is that I simply forgot to breathe! It will get you every time! Thank God there was a couch behind me! You might not be so lucky! Proper breathing technique is as important as any other dimension of a successful workout routine.

Finally, I'd like to fulfill a promise I made to you a couple of chapters back. There's no doubt that millions of unfortunate people suffer from thyroid disorders, ranging from a mild defect to no active thyroid at all. Over the years, my wife and I have heard numerous friends, family members, and even perfect strangers relate their thyroid woes to us. They speak of impossible mountains to climb, uncontrollable weight gain, and an overall attitude of helplessness. We are sympathetic to their individual situations, and now, even empathetic as well.

I have been quite blessed in my lifetime up till now with a healthy thyroid. Like most men, I put weight on quickly but can lose it just as fast when I set my mind to it. I realize that women in general don't share that blessing. In fact, my wife, Corrina, is one of the very unfortunate women to deal not only with all the extenuating circumstances of just being a female but with the horrific reality associated with the total loss of her thyroid. I asked her to share her story with you as I believe it will inspire great hope in regard to the tremendous amount of misinformation surrounding thyroid disorders. Since she is the one that has lived this scenario out for over fifteen years now, I want you to hear the account directly from the source. The following story comes directly from her hand and from her heart. I hope it brings a sense of hope to many of you who have felt trapped up till now.

## Corrina's Thyroid Story

I will never forget that special revelation one Sunday in 1996. No, we weren't studying the book of Revelation, but rather it is about what God revealed to me on that day that likely saved my life.

We were living in a small town in the Texas panhandle. I took the children to their separate classes, baby in the nursery, etc., and was headed back toward the sanctuary for worship service. I was walking through the lobby when a stranger approached me. Reaching out, she shook my hand and introduced herself. She said, "You don't know me, but I'm a nurse. Do you know that your thyroid is enlarged?"

I didn't know what a thyroid was or where it was located on the body, but I was extremely embarrassed that mine was hanging out for everyone to see! I shyly asked her to clarify what she was referring to. She gently touched the front of my neck where there was a large lump. I was already aware of the lump but thought it was nothing more than a fatty deposit. I had been exercising, trying my best to get it to decrease in size. It had been less than a year since the birth of my last child, and I was working diligently to get the last of the "baby fat" off.

By the grimaced look on her face, as well as the urgency in her voice, this was no laughing matter. In fact, she told me it was a serious matter and "you shouldn't waste any time getting it evaluated!" I thanked her kindly and then turned away, regrettably residing to do nothing at all about it. I just thought that it would somehow go away on its own. After all, I hadn't done anything to cause it. I just woke up one day, and there it was, swollen up on my neck like a golf ball under my skin.

Not having any knowledge of what a thyroid was, let alone its many vital functions to everyday life, led me to believe it was just another lump along life's road that I could overcome on my own if I became determined enough to get it done.

A few more weeks went by, and the goiter grew larger. Worst of all, it grew at an accelerated rate. It was *very* noticeable now. My husband kidded me about "growing an Adam's apple." We both began to notice that my heart was beating far beyond its normal rhythm. My hands started trembling uncontrollably. My eyes were protruding out of their sockets. When I swallowed, I felt like I was choking. I could not ignore my declining health any longer. I secured an appointment with one of the leading endocrinologists in the Texas panhandle.

After several tests, he diagnosed me with Grave's disease. As if that weren't bad enough, he advised me that I was in the latter stages, and at this point, the only treatment was to "completely destroy my thyroid with radioactive iodine." I was advised that the side effects would be minimal, a small amount of weight gain, etc., and that after a short while on medication, my life would be normal. I should have asked him to elaborate more clearly his definition of normal!

I went on to have the treatment in early February 1997. Little did I know that I was about to embark on the roller coaster ride of my life! Within five days after the treatment, I had already gained over five pounds, and I felt very ill! My moods changed from moment to moment. My hair started falling out in huge globs! My sensitivity to temperature was ridiculous. My memory retention was poor at best. I was lethargic. When I forced myself to exercise, I would predictably seize up in a temporary paralysis. The muscle contractions became excruciating! The list goes on.

I started on the medication, Propylthiouraciland Inderal from March to April of 1997. At that time I was switched to Synthroid. I have to admit that in time, I would gradually overcome many of the symptoms associated with thyroid loss. But the weight gain was a far different story and would continue to be a growing issue in my life for many years to come.

I had always been interested in physical fitness and had earned my first fitness instructor certification in 1992. However, I didn't really pursue this option until 1997. I became both the student and the instructor. I would exercise till I dropped, at least five days a week, and I tried every diet I could get my hands on. Though I remained toned, nothing seemed to change my constant weight-gain crisis. My body composition was changing more toward muscle, but in spite of my successes, I simply could not deny the fat gain as well.

From 1997 to 2009, I gained forty-one pounds. That may not seem like a lot, but for a girl that was used to wearing size 5 jeans, this was devastating! I constantly complained to my endocrinologist. In desperation, I finally wrote him a lengthy letter of disappointment, disgust, and anger over my thyroid condition, as well as the shortcomings of my medication. This was not the normal lifestyle picture he had painted earlier.

It was at his point that our doctor-patient relationship changed dramatically. He read my sincere letter and took it to heart. He went from just talking *to* me as a patient to talking *with* me as a person. He then began to steadily increase my Synthroid and monitor me closely.

Against his advice, I would not allow him to decrease the dose. It had once again elevated my heart rate, and I often felt like I was going to explode. My husband was not happy with this decision either, but it was the only thing that would keep my metabolism at a high enough rate and, in turn, prevent me from gaining more weight. I didn't lose any… I just didn't gain as much.

To say the least, I was desperate to lose weight! At this point, I would have done just about anything! After a long argument on the matter, I told my husband, "I'd rather die thin than live fat!" Maybe this was a bit excessive, but my soul had this picture of what I wanted to look like and feel like, and it just seemed that I had no way to get there, outside of something drastic! Yes, I have some personal weight loss issues!

In August of 2009, I noticed a slight tremor in my left hand. It was nothing serious, just a minor twinge at the time. I thought I might have strained a muscle working out, so once again, I didn't get it checked immediately. By now, I had gotten my fill of doctors and didn't want to deal with anything else. The trembling increased. There was a lot of pressure in my life during this time (i.e., my children, my marriage, my job, my husband's ministry, my dogs, and oh yes, *my weight*).

Finally, I had had enough! Due to so many overwhelming events occurring in my life simultaneously, I made up my mind to do something about it! I really believed that I had already done this to the best of my ability before. I was wrong! Struggling with an issue is not the same as resolving an issue. Sometimes we get confused about real effort toward changing our life and the daily suffering that leads us to believe we are doing all we can. We rationalize our current state somewhere between passive and proactive. We somehow become satisfied with the knowledge that at least we are doing something, regardless if it is working or not.

I knew all the myths. I had heard *every* story of failure and defeat! In spite of it all, I made up my mind to *take my life back*, no matter the emotional or physical cost to myself! It's amazing what "renewing your mind" can do! If what you are doing hasn't worked, you simply need to look at the situation differently.

By this time in 2009, I had earned many different physical fitness certifications. I taught yoga, Pilates, kickboxing, body ball, high and low impact aerobics, body conditioning, and spinning classes. I was a personal trainer. I had just recently taught a twelve-week weight loss class. (I often taught the classes *I* needed most!) I was the exercise coordinator for the Continuing Education Department at Amarillo College. I took my knowledge and put it into practice!

I set my goal. I made my plan. I focused. I followed through. When my students asked me what my weight loss goal was, I said, "One pound!" They laughed and told me that one pound wouldn't make a difference. But what they didn't understand was that up till now, I couldn't even lose one pound. I just needed to lose the first pound to prove to myself that I could do it! Besides, one pound is significant as it leads to one more pound, then another, and so on. I was a living testimony to what one pound gone unchecked can eventually do! All the "one pounds" had caused me to wake up one day at 162 pounds. That was pretty excessive for my height.

I kept my daily calorie intake between 1,200 to 1,500 calories. I continued to exercise five days a week, in addition to the numerous classes I was already teaching. I always participated in every class. I alternated between the upper and lower body, did at least twenty-five minutes of cardio, and worked my abs every session. When I didn't feel like working out, I *made myself* work out! When I was running short on time, I *made time* for my workout! When I was stressed and wanted to eat comfort food, I *made myself* stick to my diet! When I was hungry, I *made myself* control my food intake! Before I did *anything*, I would ask myself, "Is this going to bring me closer to my goal or further away?"

I finally lost… one pound! I was so excited! I knew that if I could lose one pound, then I could lose another. And so I did! And another and another and so on. It was slow, but it was so fulfilling to watch my steady progress. I began to feel better about myself, more confident, more in control. Everything seemed to be going my way. Well, almost everything.

The trembling on my left side was getting worse. I finally had to submit to a neurologist. It was a Wednesday evening. Don wanted to go to the doctor with me for support, but I didn't believe it was anything serious, so I insisted on going alone. I was convinced that the diagnosis would be something less than life changing. I had been around the block a few times by now, and wasn't afraid to hear whatever the doctor had to tell me. But nothing could have prepared me for what he would say. "Mrs. Willingham, I'm afraid you have Parkinson's disease."

I was floored! How could this be? Isn't that an old people disease? I was only forty-two years old! This couldn't be right! Unfortunately, within a short period of time, three other doctors concurred with his diagnosis. So, I now have Grave's disease and Parkinson's disease (just to name of few of my ailments)! I tell people, "I'm collecting diseases!" Some people collect shot glasses, but me? Not so much!

It's been quite a blow. Although there have been many advances in the treatment of this debilitating disease, the medication has only helped slightly. I still have tremors but less pronounced than before. I also have a long list of additional annoying symptoms with which to deal daily. The medication makes me nauseous; the lack of medication makes me tremble. Catch-22.

All I know to do is to stick with the program I've always followed, and of course, pray! Now days, I do a lot of that! Regardless of the load I've been handed, I am still very blessed! Today, I look in the mirror and find myself fifty-two pounds lighter! The exercise keeps me strong and mobile! One day at a time, one step at a time, one workout at a time. You can overcome *anything*! God is great, and he is living within you! I know from personal experience that there's *nothing* the two of you cannot overcome or achieve! Set for yourself a goal of excellence! "I can do all things through Christ who strengthens me!" Believe it! Live by it!

---

I think anyone would acknowledge my wife's account to be nothing short of extraordinary! She must daily overcome many obstacles in order to not only accomplish new goals, but also to simply "maintain" her current status. Even common, everyday tasks are often more difficult for her than for other individuals. I wanted you to hear her inspiring story to make you aware of an all-important truth in life: "Everyday people overcome everyday hardships, every day!" And the way they do that is the same way we all overcome adversity; our *soul* sets the goal and in turn informs the *mind* who, in turn, informs the body.

Stop taking less than you want out of your life. You can have *anything* you set your heart on! No excuses! Stop looking for reasons why you can't accomplish your dreams and goals! Don't procrastinate another second! Stop talking about it and just do it! Get the *best* out of yourself—body, mind, and soul!

God be with you in your newfound direction in life!

Don and Corrina Willingham

Note: The following page is a guide to be used in planning your daily meditation and ISP confirmation. We've also included an exercise illustration guide to help you get started toward a healthier lifestyle. For best results, use it in conjunction with a balanced daily diet program. The trick is not so much in what you do as it is in sticking consistently with whatever program you choose. You can do it! May God bless you and bring you peace and happiness in your new life!

## Daily Meditation Guide

| | |
|---|---|
| Wake Up: | Whatever time you normally get up, rise fifteen minutes earlier. |
| Kitchen Stop: | Grab your favorite morning drink, preferably low fat. |
| Meditation & ISP: | Move quickly to your prearranged meditation area. |
| Prayer: | Begin with prayer. Ask God to bless your ISP. |
| Affirmation: | Reaffirm your ISP—that is, your overall dream or goal. Say it out loud several times with conviction! |

| | |
|---|---|
| Inspiration: | Read a favorite Bible verse, poem, or quote. Focus on surrounding pictures or stimulus relating to your goal. |
| Close: | Close with a prayer. Tell God you have once again chosen to use this new day he has given you to better yourself so as to become a better husband, wife, child, etc. Foremost, you promise to use his blessings in your endeavor to better serve him, whenever and wherever possible. |
| Routine: | This concludes your morning meditation. Move now to your normal morning routine. |
| Note: | Remember that your entire meditation time must be held to no more than ten minutes. This time is solely for the purpose of reaffirming your ISP. All other devotional and prayer time is separate. (*Do not* take away from or replace your regular Bible study or prayer time!) |

## Physical Exercises for the Body

Apply a balanced variety of the following exercises three to five days a week, rotating between body parts, and including at least twenty minutes of some type of cardio and abdominal routine as a part of each session. Keeping the body in shape is not only an important key to feeling more enthusiastic about accomplishing your ISP, but it is also a great way to improve mental acuity and always makes for a more positive attitude overall.

The following are merely examples of a few key exercises one can do for each of the major muscle groups. There are countless others available to the more dedicated individuals. Perform a simple Internet search for the particular muscles or body part you wish to improve. There are thousands of free workout routines available online. Just pick one and get with it! In every case, *consistency* is the key to success.

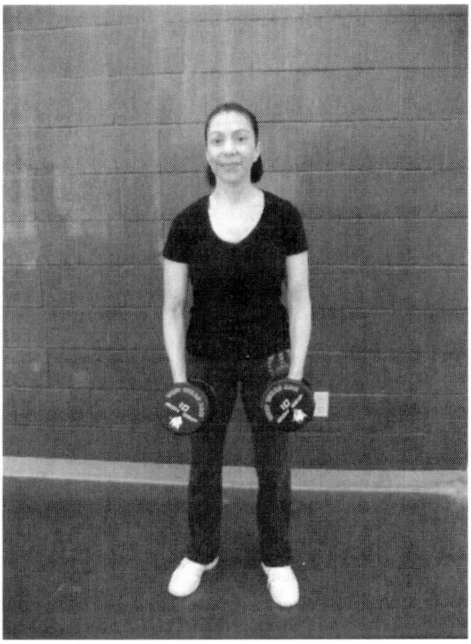

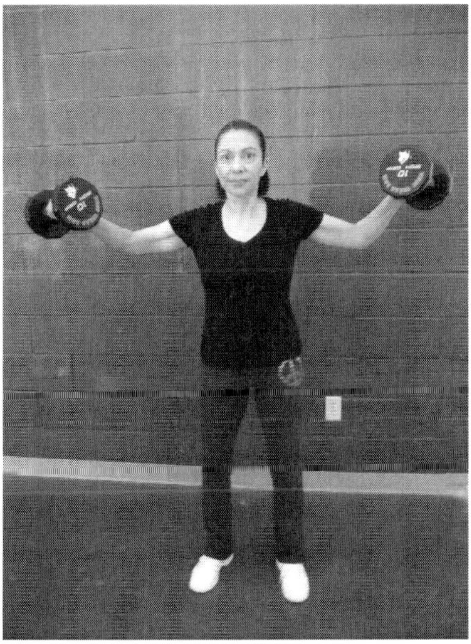

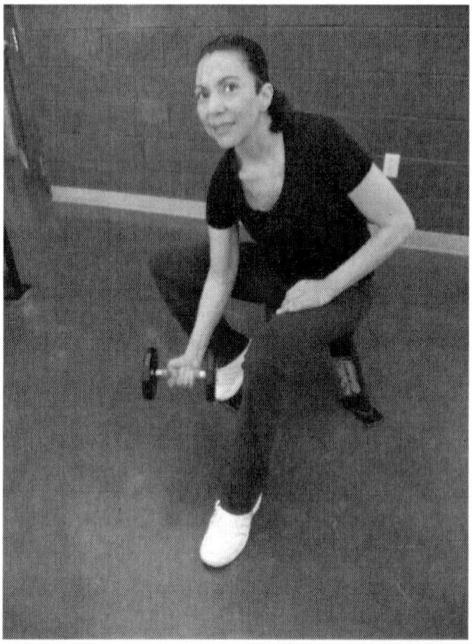

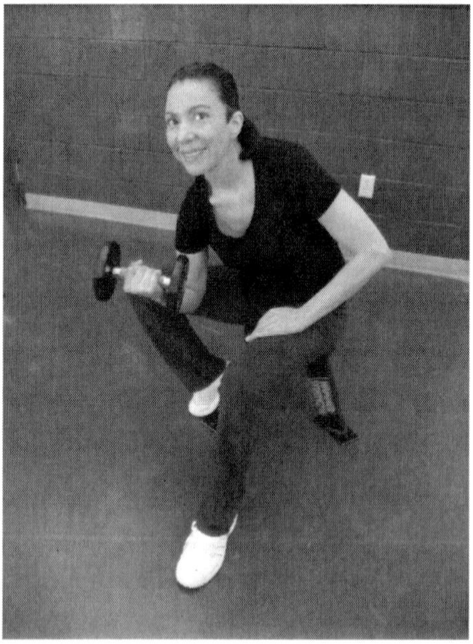

GETTING THE BEST OUT OF YOURSELF: BODY, MIND, AND SOUL

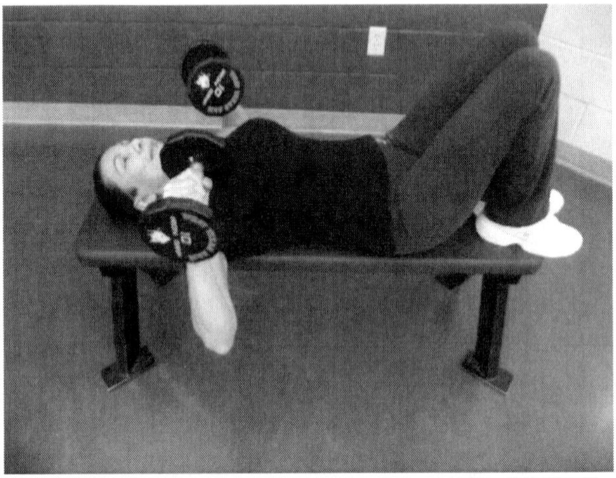

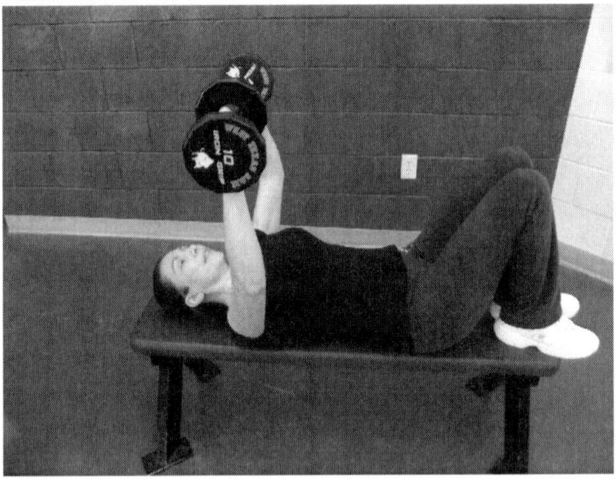

GETTING THE BEST OUT OF YOURSELF: BODY, MIND, AND SOUL

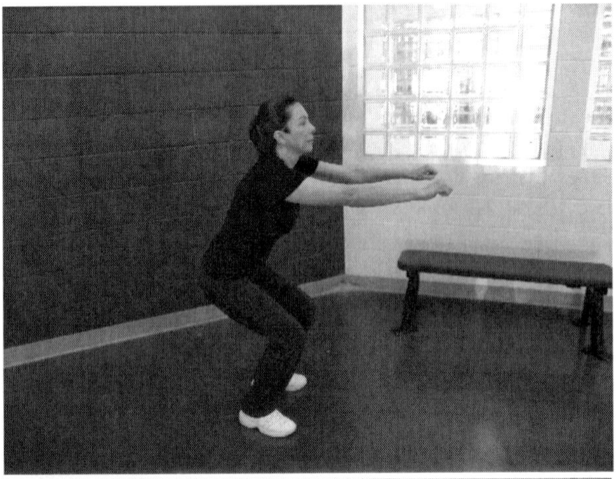

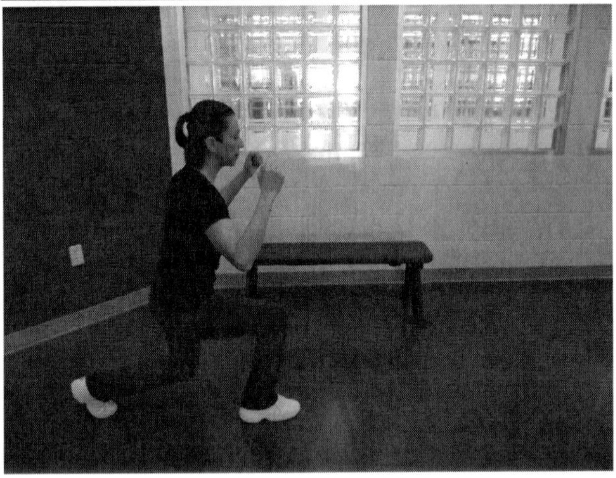

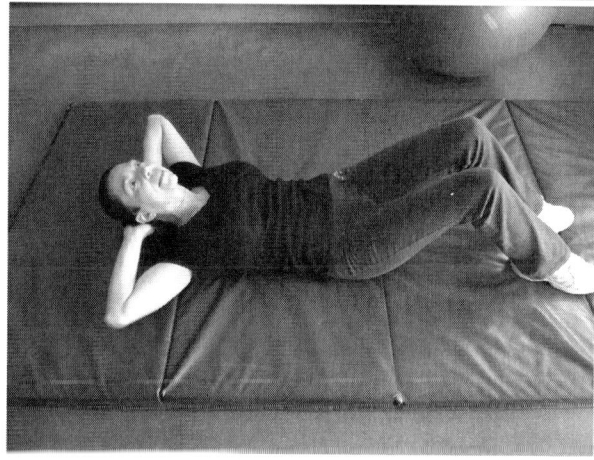

GETTING THE BEST OUT OF YOURSELF: BODY, MIND, AND SOUL

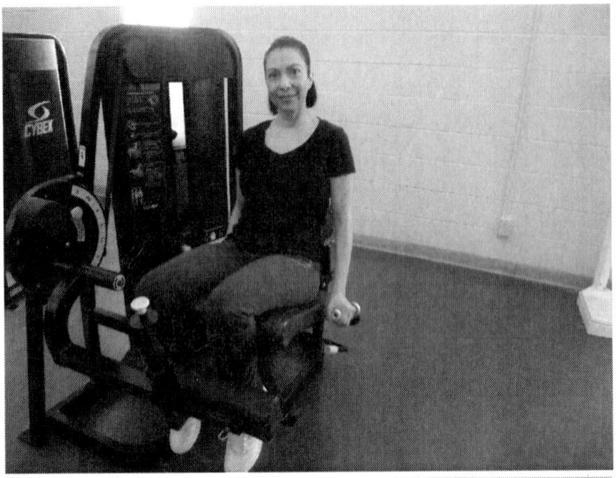

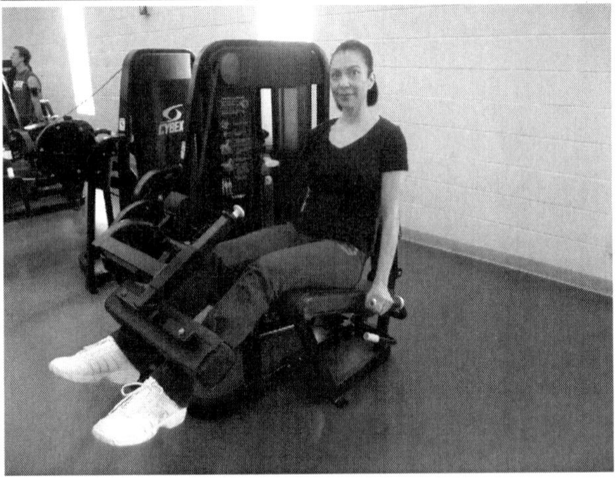

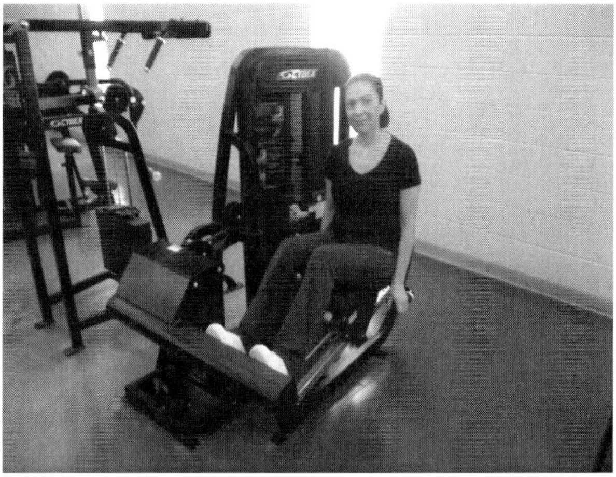

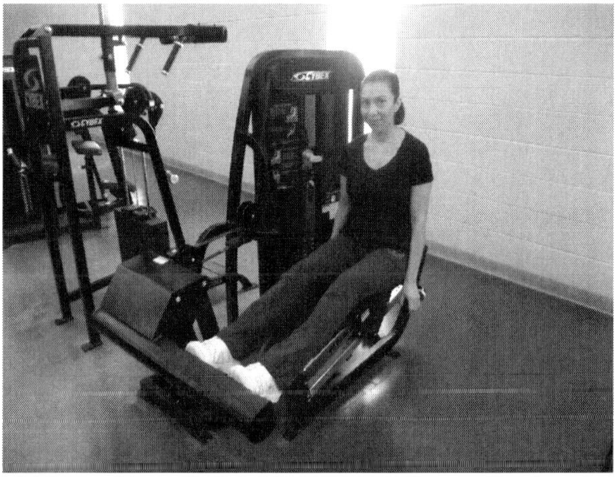

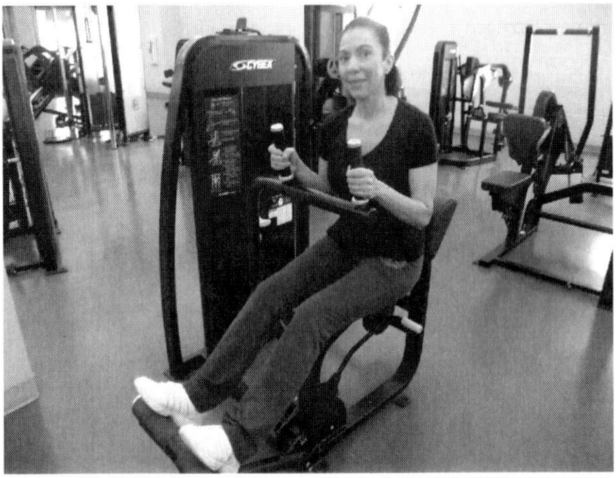

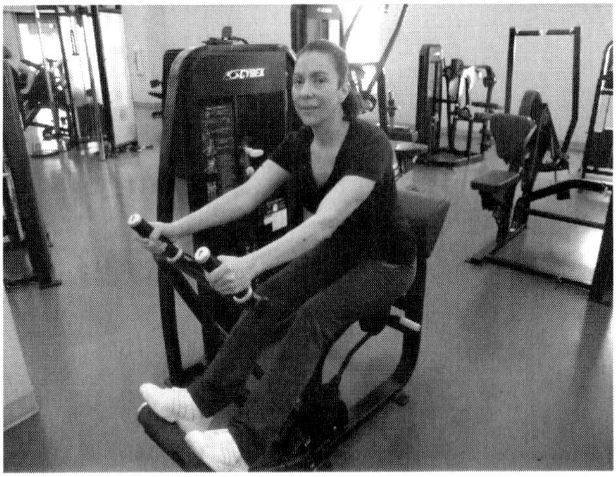

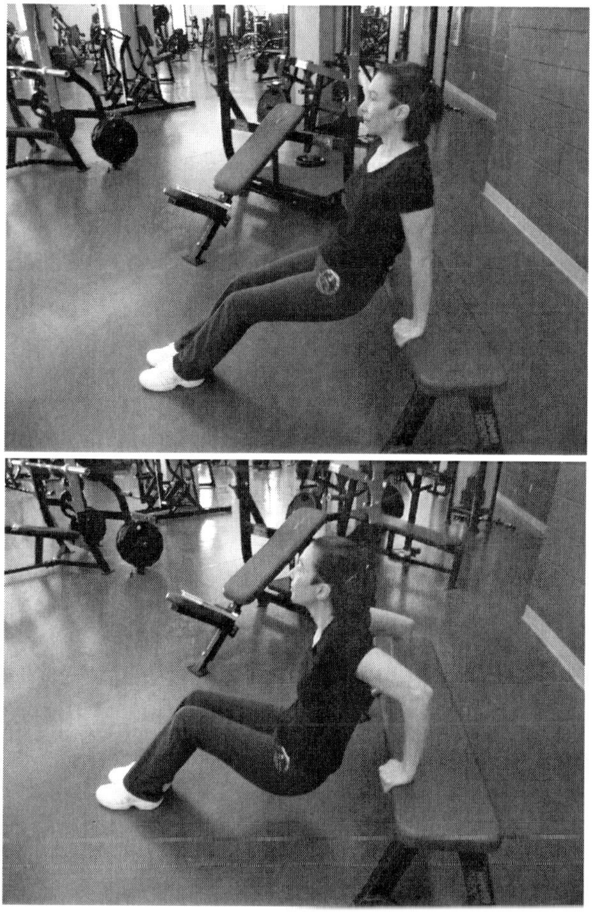

# End Notes

1. http://en.wikipedia.org/wiki/Men's_pole_vault_world_record_progression
2. http://en.wikipedia.org/wiki/Men's_pole_vault_world_record_progression
3. http://en.wikipedia.org/wiki/Men's_pole_vault_world_record_progression
4. http://en.wikipedia.org/wiki/Men's_pole_vault_world_record_progression
5. Wikipedia, as derived from: Bertolote JM, Fleischmann A (October 2002). "Suicide and psychiatric diagnosis: a worldwide perspective". World Psychiatry 1 (3): 181–5. PMC 1489848. PMID 16946849
6. http://en.wikipedia.org/wiki/The_Six_Million_Dollar_Man
7. www.folgers.com
8. www.cowboylyrics.com/lyrics/haggard-merle/mama-tried-507.html

| | |
|---|---|
| 9 | www.ushistory.org/declaration/document/ |
| 10 | www.directlyrics.com › Lyrics › Zac Brown Band |
| 11 | en.wikipedia.org/wiki/As_a_Man_Thinketh |
| 12 | en.wikipedia.org/wiki/Cosmetics |
| 13 | www.hauteliving.com/.../numbers-don't-lie-a-look-at-cosmetic-surge |
| 14 | edhelper.com/poetry/Opportunity_by_Walter_Malone.htm |
| 15 | goodreads.com/quotes/show/351861 |
| 16 | hourofpower.org |
| 17 | http://showcase.netins.net/web/creative/lincoln/education/failures.htm |
| 18 | www.quoteland.com/topic/Imagination-Quotes/81/ |
| 19 | "Secrets of Closing the Sale" by Zig Ziggler |
| 20 | www.quotationsbook.com |
| 21 | Merriam-Webster Dictionary |
| 22 | www.poetry-archive.com/w/maud_muller.html |
| 23 | www.notable-quotes.com/f/fortune_quotes.html |
| 24 | www.christianity.co.nz/life_death2.htm |
| 25 | JBF Wright 1925 |
| 26 | en.wikiquote.org/wiki/George_Santayana |